The Moral Compass of Public Relations

T0298401

The civic and moral responsibilities of public relations are hotly contested topics. While many researchers call for focusing on ethics in public relations, they concentrate on ethics in relation to how people do their jobs. In actuality, emphasis should move beyond professional codes of ethics to include general morality and citizenship. Currently, as the profession receives greater scrutiny, it is important to be aware of the value of public relations in the community. This book centers on four areas of public relations' conscience in order to examine its role in morality and citizenship: civic professionalism, corporate social responsibility, ethics, and public communication. This approach will help to answer the question of what is public relations' responsibility to the public good.

Brigitta R. Brunner, Ph.D., is Professor in the School of Communication and Journalism at Auburn University, Alabama. Her first edited volume, *Creating Citizens: Liberal Arts and Community and Civic Engagement in the Land-grant Tradition,* was published in May 2016.

Routledge Research in Public Relations

The Moral Compass of Public Relations

Edited by Brigitta R. Brunner

LONDON AND NEW YORK

First published 2017 by Routledge

2 Park Square, Milton Park, Abingdon, Oxfordshire OX14 4RN
52 Vanderbilt Avenue, New York, NY 10017

Routledge is an imprint of the Taylor & Francis Group, an informa business

First issued in paperback 2019

Library of Congress Cataloging-in-Publication Data

Names: Brunner, Brigitta R., 1971– editor.
Title: The moral compass of public relations / edited by Brigitta R. Brunner.
Description: New York: Routledge, 2016. | Series: Routledge research in
public relations; 8 | Includes bibliographical references and index.
Identifiers: LCCN 2016023186
Subjects: LCSH: Public relations—Moral and ethical aspects.
Classification: LCC HM1221 .M67 2016 | DDC 659.2—dc23
LC record available at https://lccn.loc.gov/2016023186

ISBN: 978-1-138-12154-6 (hbk)
ISBN: 978-0-367-87624-1 (pbk)

Typeset in Sabon
by codeMantra

Contents

PART III
Moral and Civic Responsibility in the Digital Age

Introduction

Brigitta R. Brunner

The civic and moral responsibilities of public relations are hotly contested topics. Some questions with which thought leaders grapple include the following: What does it mean to go beyond the moral minimum?; What are the costs?; What obligations do publics owe organizations and society?; and Are there reciprocal duties between an organization and its public? (Bowie, 1991). While many researchers call for focusing on ethics in public relations, they concentrate on ethics in relationship to how people do their jobs. However, the ethics and values of individual practitioners are not enough to serve the public interest in a responsible way; the field of public relations must support idealistic values such as contributing to informed debate, developing mutual understanding, and using collaboration to work for societal good (J. E. Grunig, 2000). Public relations must then revitalize the importance of the common good by focusing not only on professional ethics, but also on "moral life as a whole" (Christians, 2008, p. 3). This manuscript will attempt to resolve the uncertainty over public relations' moral and civic obligations to society.

Some may say it is impossible, pie-in-the-sky thinking to suggest public relations (PR) could work for the public good. After all, organizations aren't people, and practitioners are often in the role of advocate. Also causing cognitive dissonance are the field's roots, founders, and definitions. For example, Ivy Lee defended and explained away the Ludlow Massacre and Edward Bernays took on clients such as Lucky Strikes—two public relations campaigns that bring ethical practice into question to this day. As Wright (1979) suggests, the field has suffered from a poor reputation and image, in part, because many of its earliest practitioners had little regard for ethics or social responsibility. However, the field and its practitioners should not abandon the idea just because it is difficult. Times have changed and practices have evolved, thereby making this move of moral conscience possible. Although American public relations, at one time, focused nearly exclusively on persuasion (Kruckeberg & Stark, 1988), by the 2000s, the oversight of relationship building and maintenance came to the forefront of definitions for the field, thus helping to bring ethics in public relations to the forefront. Furthering this role change of public relations' function, Yang and Taylor (2013) have argued that it is through relationships and dialogue that public relations supports the democratic elements of society. Even Bernays in his later years wrote, "Public relations is the practice of social responsibility" (as quoted in Clark, 2000), thus speaking directly to public relations' values and morals in respect to society.

Although the issues with which public relations practitioners work may not have changed, the ways in which practitioners manage issues has (Holtzhausen & Voto, 2002). Therefore, this book traces public relations' moral development in the 21st century to record how it responds to issues such as technology, crisis, health, social media, and globalism. This manuscript will focus on four areas of public relations' conscience—civic professionalism, corporate social responsibility, ethics, and public communication—examining the opportunities and challenges brought forth by each approach. Although these concepts intersect, they all contain unique perspectives regarding responsibilities of the field to society and build a framework for how public relations practitioners can work to better define the tipping point between public interest and self-preservation in public relations' social context. Ultimately, the goal of this manuscript is to delineate public relations' responsibility to the public good. To better understand this quandary within which public relations finds itself, I next provide context and definition to explain why it is important to remind society of the value of public relations in society.

Corporations, Organizations, and Society

Bellah, Madsen, Sullivan, Swidler, and Tipton (1991) argue that societal problems, especially those in America, are tied to corporate power and can be solved not by helping individual organizations to do better ethically and morally, but by reforming all corporations to do so. However, can a corporation be held accountable if it is an organization and not a human? Can it be expected to be ethical and moral? Should it be responsible to society in some way? Theorists and researchers argue, yes, corporations can be held ethically responsible for their actions because they control their actions and can make rational decisions (Elfstrom, 1991). Other researchers (see J. E. Grunig & L. A. Grunig, 1996; Heath & Ryan, 1989; Manheim & Pratt, 1986) further suggest that corporations exist because of society and are, therefore, responsible to it. Since organizations have freedom and rationality, both required for moral action, it is reasonable to suggest that corporations are responsible to society beyond profit because corporations are citizens (Bowie, 1991; Buchholz, 1991). And it is into this difficult role of corporate conscience that public relations is often thrust.

To their credit, corporations are doing more to enhance ethics by creating omsbudsman and ethics officer positions, creating guidelines for ethical behavior, encouraging employees to attend ethics seminars, and other actions to engrain ethics within corporate culture (Pratt, Im, & Montague, 1994). However, corporations have responsibilities outside their own walls.

These responsibilities include solving societal problems (especially if the corporation helped to create said problem), thinking of publics beyond stockholders, and serving human values because organizations serve at the discretion of society (Bowie, 1991; Buchholz, 1991). However, these responsibilities are not specific to corporations. They also apply to agencies, nonprofits, educational institutions, government agencies, and every other organization in existence.

Managing communication is one role of public relations (Roper, 2005), and it is through this function that public relations becomes involved in the discussion. Since the ethical and moral center of many organizations is often reflected in the communication process, public relations practitioners are crucial to the moral position and actions organizations take (Pratt et al., 1994). Some even suggest the moral and ethical conscience of an organization rests within public relations' domain. Others claim such a mandate puts far too much pressure on the field, stating it is impossible for one organizational function to speak for all. Therefore, while helping an organization be accountable for its behaviors should be a primary contribution of public relations (Bowen, 2008), the public relations practitioner should be thought of as one of many organizational consciences rather than the singular conscience of the organization as a whole (Holtzhausen & Voto, 2002).

Another ethical and moral dilemma that faces corporations and other organizations alike is the prioritization of individual rights and social good (David, 2004). Public relations practitioners face the difficulty of trying to respond to questions of how one can advocate for a client or cause while still serving society (Bivins, 1993), because the two can often seem mutually exclusive. Some scholars worry that practitioners lack the ability to serve the public interest due to undeveloped morality and the obligation to serve clients and employers (Bivins, 1993; Martinson, 1995). In truth, public relations, much like every other profession, can be used for purposes that only serve the individual, and do nothing to further the public good (Bernays, 1971). However, to define public relations in such a way is ethical hedonism (Martinson, 1995); public relations can rise above such definitions. For example, when public relations is used to build conversations and dialogue between an organization and its publics, thus allowing for a free flow of information and feedback, it is working to fulfill both individualistic and societal demands.

Working for the public interest, however, creates dilemmas for practitioners, because, at times, individual interests may differ from common ones (Stoker & Stoker, 2012). All individuals and organizations face the challenge of doing well while not doing harm to others (Watson, 1991). After all, "the first obligation of responsible living is to care for oneself in ways without being a nuisance or causing harm" (Watson, 1991, p. 99). Bernays supported this concept when he said public relations would gain value in society when it allowed the public to evaluate the merits of ideas and messages, thereby allowing for a free exchange of ideas, even those ideas tied to individual profit (cited in Stoker & Stoker, 2012). While he cautioned public relations practitioners to never advocate for harmful ideas or causes because with influence so came responsibility, he also stated it is possible to simultaneously pursue the interests of society and those of a client (1971). He further explains how such a conceptualization of the field works for societal good by claiming, "Public relations as a profession is an art applied to a science, in which the public interest and not pecuniary motivation is the primary consideration" (Bernays, 1971, p. 299), thus demonstrating even one of public relations' founders believed the field could and should serve the public good despite being in an advocacy role. Furthermore, J. E. Grunig and Hunt (1984) remind us that true professionals "believe serving others is more important than their own economic gain" (p. 66).

Ethics, Morals, and Values

Ethics and morals can and are used interchangeably (Fawkes, 2012; J. E. Grunig, 2000), because ethical questions typically ask what is morally right or wrong and what should be valued. However, to be precise, ethics are the rules one uses to solve problems when morals and/or values are uncertain (J. E. Grunig, 2000). Appiah (2008) says ethics is more about how one lives well, while morality speaks to how one should and should not treat others. The ethical grounding of public relations has been, and is still being, researched by many scholars. While there is not room to explain the various perspectives of public relations ethics (see Bowen, 2007, 2008; Fawkes, 2012; Holtzhausen, 2012, for more information), it is fair to say that traditional, Western, and normative views of ethics are often at odds with feminist, postmodern, and Jungian ones, further obfuscating the matter. However, the intent of this book is not to decide that one perspective is better than another, but rather to discuss how each can, and does, add to the discussion (Fawkes, 2012).

Moral development encompasses how people's thoughts about ethical issues change over time and in response to the environment (Coleman & Wilkins, 2009). Related to morals are values, which "are assessments of worth" (L. A. Grunig, Toth, & Hon, 2000, p. 64). Public relations practitioners' values are the reasoning behind the decisions made for the profession (Toth & Pavlik, 2000). For example, one might consider the Flint, Michigan, water case. While at first it was obvious that ethics were violated because people in that town were not informed about the potential health dangers of lead in their water system, the situation has grown to be much more. Flint has now become a case study in the lack of morality shown by government officials. Ironically, those people who were elected to protect citizens and the public interest not only did not value the citizens of Flint and their concerns, but their actions caused further harm to the public good. J. E. Grunig (2000) states that morality is part of public relations because the values and problems of publics become part of public relations' strategic function as can be seen in the previous example. Someone needed to listen to the citizens of Flint. Someone needed to allow the free flow of information so that the people of Flint knew about lead levels in their water and the potential health risks. Someone needed to act as a moral agent with the public interest at heart. However, it is often hard for that one voice to rise above the others. That difficult position is why the field must move beyond individual and organizational ethics to define morals and values of public relations as a profession and practice (J. E. Grunig, 2000), for behaving without regard to morals not only harms the reputation of the individual, but also that of the field of public relations as a whole (Heath, 2000). "One of the many challenges that faces public relations is to define the values by which it operates: the ethical perspectives that it affirms by the manner in which it operates, the value perspectives it adopts and creates that influence society, and the values it adds to the efficient operation of the marketplace and the public policy arena" (Heath, 2000, p. 69). Therefore, if public relations is able to define its values so as to find a moral compass, it can also help clarify its purpose in society by working for the public interest.

One tangible way in which public relations uses ethics, morals, and values, and by which others can see these concepts at work, is through codes. Codes of ethics are guidelines for how practitioners should conduct and practice public relations. We all individually have our personal codes of ethics. Most organizations also typically have them as well. Even professional organizations such as the Public Relations Society of America (PRSA) and the International Public Relations Association have codes. However, the effectiveness of codes is often debated. Some believe codes are, at best, idealistic and hypothetical (Fawkes, 2012). Others do not think codes do enough. For example, Stoker and Stoker (2012) argue the PRSA code of ethics does not explain what working in the public interest entails or the moral function of public relations. Perhaps what leads to codes' shortcomings is that although essential, codes are merely lists that define what is and what is not acceptable at only the tactical level; they do not further strategy or strategic thinking (Kruckeberg, 2000). Therefore, conversations about ethics and public relations need to move beyond discussions of professional codes of ethics to include talking about general morality and citizenship. By thinking with ethics and morals in mind, the field of public relations can gain respect while taking on a new level of responsible conduct (Coleman & Wilkins, 2009).

Public Interest and Civic Responsibility

The field has long held that to be a professional, a public relations practitioner must serve the public interest (Stoker & Stoker, 2012). But what does that mean? What is the public interest? The public interest is the welfare or well-being of the general public, or society. Lippmann (1955) suggests that "the public interest may be presumed to be what men would choose if they saw clearly, thought rationally, acted disinterestedly and benevolently" (p. 42). Similarly, Held (1970) explains:

> A decision is said to serve special interests if it furthers the ends of some part of the public at the expense of the ends of the larger public. It is said to be in the public interest if it serves the ends of the whole public rather than those of some sector of the public. (p. 213)

At best, the public interest is an abstract ideal, yet it is still "an ideal by which public relations must be guided" because the public interest is of "paramount importance" to all public relations activities and strategies (Martinson, 1995, p. 221).

In order to better understand the concept, Martinson suggests operationalizing the term *public interest* using two concepts important to ethical decision making—reversibility and universalizability (see Jaksa & Pritchard, 1994). Reversibility asks one to think through a decision or action by looking at the situation from the other's perspective. Therefore, when making a decision, a practitioner concerned with the public interest would think through what it would be like if he/she were on the receiving end of the action and the positions were thus reversed; doing so would help him/her to transcend a self-interested position (Martinson, 1995). Martinson also states that practitioners should learn more about a concept called "original position," which asks individuals to forget the inside knowledge they have about a situation because that information might bias and cloud their judgment (see Rawls, 1971). Using the original position can help practitioners to be guided by morals and ethics because it excludes specialized knowledge (Martinson, 1995). Finally, practitioners need to not only ask if they would accept the decision or action taken by the other party if roles were reversed, but they must also ask whether or not the action or decision is universalizable, meaning it is impartial to all involved (Martinson, 1995). When all of these conditions are satisfied, public relations will be acting in the public interest.

Therefore, working in the public interest in the realm of public relations entails communication and discussion. When public relations helps publics to trust one another through the free flow of information and debate, it serves the public interest, community, and society through dialogue (Heath, 2000). When public relations helps society in such ways it is acting as a moral agent and with civic responsibility because it is allowing publics the freedom to determine their destiny while strengthening interconnectivity discussion and inquiry (Stoker & Stoker, 2012). "The point becomes not *whose* interest is being served, but rather that *all* interests have an opportunity to be served" (Bivins, 1993, p. 121). Furthermore, public relations practitioners should remember that "doing the 'right thing' is not something one does if it is convenient or because it returns benefits. It is done because someone believes it should be done—because he believes higher concerns call for it" (Watson, 1991, p. 103). At all times, public relations should choose the public good because it is committed to it, not because it helps the bottom-line (Bowie, 1991). When public relations works in the public interest it demonstrates its moral integrity, professionalism, and commitment to civic responsibility.

The chapters included in this volume work to make more accessible what we as public relations scholars and practitioners create as guidelines for the moral beliefs and civic responsibilities of the practice of PR. The first part of the book looks at moral and civic responsibility and strategy. In Chapter 1, Park and Dodd examine corporate social responsibility (CSR) as a strategic function of public relations by detailing how CSR evolved from its roots in business ethics to become a goal-oriented function of public relations. Synthesizing existing literature and identifying gaps, the authors discuss what it means to engage (or not engage) in strategic CSR activities for public relations. Woo, Gulotta, and Gulotta investigate Penn State's Sandusky crisis and discuss how PRSA's professional values are reflected in publics' responses to the situation. Further, their work helps to determine how ethical and professional communication can help a community rebuild and protect its social capital.

Nonprofit organizations are the subject of Waters' and Ott's work. The results presented in their chapter paint an interesting picture for the discussion of social responsibility communication and public relations as the organizational conscience. It seems that the more credible and believable channels are, the more they detract from the information publics want about nonprofit organizations' programs and services. The practical implications of these findings are also discussed. In "*A Rising Tide Lifts All Boats? The Constitutive Reality of CSR in Public Relations,*" Stokes draws from constitutive rhetorical scholarship to develop a useful framework through which to analyze how corporations communicate their CSR initiatives. In order to design effective CSR messages, she suggests it is necessary for companies to find the tipping point between acting in the public interest and inviting public criticism by shouldering responsibility for problems their business cannot realistically address.

Part II explores public relations' moral and civic responsibility in theory and in practice. Kleinmann's chapter considers four approaches, or postures, sports organizations assume toward social responsibility and the role of the PR professional in the process. The author delineates how internal and external factors influence the postures that organizations assume, as well as considers the role of the public relations professional in identifying and managing the postures of social responsibility. Gallicano and Matthews make use of online discussion groups to study the ethical dilemmas Millennial agency practitioners confront, as well as ideas for the profession to improve ethical decision making in their chapter. The results of their work have implications for students, Millennial agency practitioners, senior agency executives, clients, and professional associations. In "Public

Relations and Development: Ethical Perspectives on Communication for Societal Effectiveness," Kennedy, Xu, and Sommerfeldt state an area in which public relations arguably exists in practice but yet is underrepresented in scholarship is development communication. The chapter adds to this underdeveloped body of knowledge by assessing the ethical implications of public relations in development communication using the lens of traditional ethical theories such as deontology and consequentialism, as well as newer models such as the feminist ethic of care to develop "glocalized" public relations efforts that are culturally concerned.

Kim, Hwang, and Zhang also focus on ethics in their chapter. Their work investigates the effects of an organization's ethical approaches such as ethics-of-justice and ethics-of-care strategies in different crisis situations. Employing an experimental design of 2 (crisis type: victim versus preventable) × 2 (crisis severity: high versus low) × 2 (ethical approaches: ethics-of-justice versus ethics-of-care), this study identifies effective ethical approaches by different crises in terms of reducing negative public responses. The next chapter, written by Vujnovic and Kruckeberg, critically examines the most recent literature establishing public relations as practice in the service of public good focusing on the discrepancies between the theory and practice of public relations. The authors argue that contemporary public relations theory and practice must be situated within the context of neoliberalism and neoliberal global economy to uncover the gaps existing between aspirational theorizing and actual public relations practice.

Since the September 11th attacks, Hurricane Katrina, and other environmental and man-made disasters in the early 2000s, the state of community disaster preparedness and infrastructure resilience has become an exigency for local, state, and federal governments; public health agencies; and the third sector (e.g., nonprofits), say Tindall, Uhrick, and Vardeman-Winter, noting the important party missing is the private sector. The authors explore civic professionalism and responsibility in relation to disaster preparedness, public health, and corporate social responsibility through a review of programs incentivizing private businesses to participate in community preparedness to map out the extant programs and prescribe requirements for future programs in their chapter. Using a case study analysis of the 2014–2015 Disneyland measles outbreak, Auger considers, through a critical/cultural lens interwoven with ethical theory, the concept of public interest communication and the greater "good," in her chapter, "Public Interest Communication and Polarized Issues: More Than a Case of Measles."

The last part of the book questions what Moral and Civic Responsibility in the Digital Age entails. Kent and Taylor observe most professional communicators have embraced the wonders of new technology, especially in the realm of social media, which many argue gives public relations the capacity to bypass mainstream media gatekeepers and take messages directly to key stakeholders and publics. However, the authors caution that technology has altered the practice of public relations, leading to a swing back toward the one-way, amoral, journalist-in-residence practices that characterized early public relations. Their essay takes up the ethical issues embodied in our new technologies by focusing on two areas of ethical practice: dialogue and communitarianism, thus encouraging professionals to think about the relationships and well-being of all stakeholders and publics. In "Interplay in the Digital Media Environment: Putting Focus on the Blurring Line Between Advertising and Public Relations in South Korea," Jo considers how journalistic values are being encroached upon by information subsidies created by multinational corporations in South Korea. The author examines how this situation compromises the essence of public relations by turning it into a function much more like advertising, as more and more media space and content are bought. In sum, the chapter assesses a fundamental question, "What is public relations' ethical value in digital media environment?"

Hon's chapter explores how digital technologies provide unprecedented opportunities for individuals and citizen groups to mobilize and pressure for social change. This chapter extends Hon's (2015) model of public relations and social digital advocacy by examining how one organization, Million Hoodies for Justice, illustrates how grassroots public relations unfolds in the digital realm. Ending the compilation is Tilson's study that examines the nature and extent of public relations practice using a broader interpretation than traditional views. He challenges Western public relations constructs narrowly defining "publics" solely as people (and only those who are alive) and stretches societal obligations and public relations practice to include a wider range of "community" embracing diversity in all its forms. This chapter concludes with a review of futuristic "entities"—from automata with artificial intelligence and human emotions to animal-human and other hybrids—that not only will challenge the concept of "publics" but also that of humankind.

In closing, I hope this book brings about discussion, debate, dialogue, thought, and future research so that these important ideas and concepts can ultimately better inform our body of knowledge and practice. While working for the public interest and with moral and civic responsibility perfectly will always remain an unattainable ideal, it is still "something for which we can imperfectly strive" because the ideal represents not only what public relations can be, but also what it should be (Martinson, 1995, p. 219).

References

Appiah, A. (2008). *Experiments in ethics.* Cambridge, MA: Harvard University Press.

Bellah, R. N., Madsen, R., Sullivan, W. M., Swidler, A., & Tipton, S. M. (1991). *The good society.* New York, NY: Vintage Books.

Bernays, E. L. (1971). Emergence of the public relations counsel: Principles and recollections. *Business History Review*, 45, 296–316.

Bivins, T. H. (1993). Public relations, professionalism, and the public interest. *Journal of Business Ethics*, 12, 117–126.

Bowen, S. A. (2007). The extent of ethics. In E. L. Toth (Ed.), *The future of excellence in public relations and communication management* (pp. 275–297). Mahwah, NJ: Lawrence Erlbaum.

Bowen, S. A. (2008). A state of neglect: Public relations as "corporate conscience" or ethics counsel. *Journal of Public Relations Research*, 20, 271–296.

Bowie, N. (1991). New directions in corporate social responsibility. *Business Horizons*, 34, 56–65.

Buchholz, R. A. (1991). Corporate responsibility and the good society: From economics to ecology. *Business Horizons*, 34, 19–31.

Christians, C. G. (2008). Media ethics on a higher order of magnitude. *Journal of Mass Media Ethics*, 23, 3–14.

Clark, C. E. (2000). Differences between public relations and corporate social responsibility: An analysis. *Public Relations Review*, 26, 363–380.

Coleman, R., & Wilkins, L. (2009). The moral development of public relations practitioners: A comparison with other professions and influences on higher quality ethical reasoning. *Journal of Public Relations Research*, 21, 318–340.

David, P. (2004). Extending symmetry: Toward a convergence of professionalism, practice, and pragmatics in public relations. *Journal of Public Relations Research*, 16, 185–211.

Elfstrom, G. (1991). *Moral issues and multinational corporations*. New York, NY: St. Martin's Press.

Fawkes, J. (2012). Saints and sinner: Competing identities in public relations ethics. *Public Relations Reviews*, 38, 865–872.

Grunig, J. E. (2000). Collectivism, collaboration, and societal corporatism as core professional values in public relations. *Journal of Public Relations Research*, 12, 23–48.

Grunig, J. E., & Grunig, L. A. (1996, May). Implications of symmetry for a theory of ethics and social responsibility in public relations. Paper presented at the meeting of the International Communication Association, Chicago, IL.

Grunig, J. E., & Hunt, T. (1984). *Managing public relations*. New York, NY: Holt, Rinehart, & Winston.

Grunig, L. A., Toth, E. L., & Hon, L. C. (2000). Feminist values in public relations. *Journal of Public Relations Research*, 12, 49–68.

Heath, R. L. (2000). A rhetorical perspective on the values of public relations: Crossroads and pathways toward concurrence. *Journal of Public Relations Research*, 12, 69–91.

Heath, R. L., & Ryan, M. (1989). Public relations' role in defining corporate social responsibility. *Journal of Mass Media Ethics*, 4, 21–38.

Held, V. (1970). *The public interest and individual interest*. New York, NY: Basic Books.

Holtzhausen, D. (2012). *Public relation as activism: Postmodern approaches to theory and practice*. New York, NY: Routledge.

Holtzhausen, D. R., & Voto, R. (2002). Resistance from the margins: The postmodern public relations practitioner as organizational activist. *Journal of Public Relations Research*, 14, 57–84.

Jaksa, J., & Pritchard, M. (1994). *Communication ethics: Methods of analysis*. Belmont, CA:Wadsworth.

Kruckeberg, D. (2000). The public relations practitioner's role in practicing strategic ethics.*Public Relations Quarterly*, 45, 35–39.

Kruckeberg, D., & Starck, K. (1988). *Public relations and community: A reconstructed theory*. New York, NY: Praeger.

Lippmann, W. (1955). *The public philosophy*. Boston, MA: Little, Brown.

Manheim, J. B., & Pratt, C. B. (1986). Communicating corporate social responsibility. *Public Relations Review*, *12*, 9–18.

Martinson, D. L. (1995). Difficult as it is to define, ethical public relations practitioners must not ignore the "public interest." *Journal of Mass Media Ethics*, *10*, 210–223.

Pratt, C. B., Im, S., & Montague, S. N. (1994). Investigating the application of deontology among U.S. public relations practitioners. *Journal of Public Relations Research*, *6*, 241–266.

Rawls, J. (1971). *A theory of justice*. Cambridge, MA: Harvard University Press.

Roper, J. (2005). Symmetrical communication: Excellent public relations or a strategy for hegemony? *Journal of Public Relations Research*, *17*, 69–86.

Stoker, K., & Stoker, M. (2012). The paradox of public interest: How serving individual superior interests fulfill public relations' obligation to the public interest. *Journal of Mass Media Ethics*, *27*, 31–45.

Toth, E. L., & Pavlik, J. H. (2000). Public relations values in the new millennium. *Journal of Public Relations Research*, *12*, 1–2.

Watson, C. E. (1991). Managing with integrity: Social responsibilities of business as seen by America's CEOs. *Business Horizons*, *34*, 99–109.

Wright, D. K. (1979). Professionalism and social responsibility in public relations. *Public Relations Review*, *5*, 20–33.

Yang, A., & Taylor, M. (2013). The relationship between the professionalism of public relations, societal social capital and democracy: Evidence from a cross-national study. *Public Relations Review*, *39*, 257–270.

Part I

Moral and Civic Responsibility and Strategy

1 The Historical Development of Corporate Social Responsibility as a Strategic Function of Public Relations

Young Eun Park and Melissa D. Dodd

The concept and definition of corporate social responsibility (CSR) represent a sizable body of academic and professional literature. CSR is generally understood as voluntary organizational actions that serve to benefit society, often in the form of economic, ethical, legal, and philanthropic activities (Caroll, 1999). Historically, CSR has evolved directly alongside the public relations discipline. Scholars have suggested that CSR *is* public relations, and in practice, CSR initiatives are commonly recommended and implemented by public relations professionals.

Traditionally, the public relations discipline, and CSR as a function of it, has suffered from corporate misuse as a reactive communication tactic, employed by management for short-term gains or merely as a defense mechanism. For example, the terms "greenwashing" and "pinkwashing" arose in response to illegitimate corporate involvement in environmental and breast cancer campaigns, respectively. Avon's "Kiss Goodbye to Breast Cancer" campaign launched in 2001 with six new shades of lipstick aimed at fundraising for breast cancer. It was later discovered that the lipsticks may have contained carcinogens linked to cancer (Lubitow & Davis, 2011). Campaigns such as these purport to cause real change and position the organization as a good corporate citizen, yet ultimately diminish corporate reputation and violate stakeholders' expectations of companies.

Modern public relations practice emphasizes ethics, morality, and good corporate citizenship as central to CSR as a strategic function of public relations. Strategic public relations is goal directed and outcome oriented. Corporations seek legitimacy in the eyes of their stakeholders; that is, corporations seek to achieve objectives while conducting themselves in ways that are perceived as appropriate among their stakeholder groups. Sethi (1977) explained that a legitimacy gap occurs when there is a difference between how companies are perceived to be operating and how stakeholders believe they *should* be operating. The result of legitimacy gaps is the withholding of stakes by organizational stakeholders. It is in this way that public relations, and CSR as a function of it, negotiate expectations and contribute to society.

Public relations professionals are the primary internal and external communicators in organizations, which allows them to represent the publics' opinions, interests, and values to the organization (and vice versa). Public relations professionals may therefore act as the corporate conscience for an organization. "Public relations practitioners can be instrumental in fostering an organizational culture that is sensitive to ethical concerns. Shaping the organizational values and culture to include ethically conscientious behavior and regular consideration of the moral implications of decisions can result in more responsible organizational behavior" (Bowen & Rawlins, 2013, p. 204).

When public relations professionals forward organizational CSR standards grounded in ethical, morally appropriate behavior, they contribute to society in a meaningful way and may simultaneously achieve organizational objectives. The challenge, however, is in determining what CSR standards can be met to satisfy which corporate stakeholders and under what circumstances. In other words, CSR initiatives are goal driven and outcome oriented, yet may differ across multiple contexts (e.g., crisis communication) and channels (e.g., social media). Thus, CSR is a dynamic process that may require more macro-level theoretical examinations.

This chapter paints a broad picture of the historical development of corporate social responsibility into a strategic function of public relations. It is important to address the historical context and modern literature surrounding the interrelated areas of public relations and CSR in order to identify the contributing environmental and social factors that have led to modern thought on the topic. Multiple contexts, channels, and outcomes are addressed in this review of the literature. The chapter concludes with a discussion of future directions for CSR research in public relations. Ultimately, this review of research finds that at a tactical level, CSR may vary greatly, but is generally positive in outcome. The conceptual development of CSR (and the public relations discipline) should move beyond justifying itself via evidence of positive outcomes and "into the fog" (Heath, 2006) toward an examination of societal-level implications aimed at ethics, morality, and community.

Early Beginnings

The concept of CSR can be traced to the early 1950s, reaching widespread recognition among communication scholars and practitioners by the mid-1970s. Notably, CSR evolved alongside modern conceptualizations of public relations. Early scholars and practitioners often addressed the two interchangeably. "Bernays (1980) said, 'Public relations is the practice of social responsibility.' And, J. E. Grunig and Hunt (1984) said, 'public, or social, responsibility has become a major reason for an organization to have a public relations function' (p. 48)" (cited in Clark, 2000, p. 368). The term "stakeholder" and the notion of strategically managing relationships with constituent groups who had a claim to the organization, whether explicit or implicit, was similarly introduced around this time (Freeman, 1984). Duhé (2009) used stakeholder theory to demonstrate that an organization's reputation for social responsibility has important implications for both stakeholders and stockholders.

One particularly noteworthy timeframe in the development of both CSR and public relations was the 1960s when anti-corporate sentiment was at an all-time high. During this era of activism, the organization-public relationship evolved greatly. Companies were forced to acknowledge public attitudes and claims toward the organization in order to maintain legitimacy (Heath & Palenchar, 2009). Clark (2000) explains, "The much-publicized era of activism began to change the way in which corporations interacted with society, and thus how they communicated with society. [...] Nuclear power, civil rights abuses, regulation of business' activities, the consumer rights movement, and the women's movement were just a few key developments that contributed to the tension between business and society" (p. 365). This historical perspective is consistent with a systems theory approach (L. A. Grunig, J. E. Grunig, & Dozier, 2002) that suggests corporations and publics are interrelated parts, interacting in an environment where they must adapt and accommodate to achieve homeostasis. Likewise, fully functioning society theory poses that in order for organizations to be effective, they must contribute to society. Heath (2006) positions CSR as central to the achievement of organizational effectiveness in this regard.

Tracing the early roots of CSR finds it was a matter of personal managerial ethics; that is, it addressed the question of "what responsibilities, if any, do corporations have toward society?" Early thought leaders argued that the only responsibility of business to society was profit maximization, and anything else may take the form of socialism (Friedman, 1970). Yet, ethical implications aside, even capitalists argued that if engaging in CSR initiatives worked for the company's economic self-interest, then it was justifiable. Modern thought on CSR generally suggests that companies do have a responsibility to society, and that responsibility is to act as a good corporate citizen. Today, acting ethically and morally appropriate are societal expectations, as opposed to some feel-good initiatives.

In the 1980s, scholars focused on *how* CSR should be practiced, as opposed to *if* it should be practiced (Clark, 2000). This change symbolized the move from reactive corporate stances toward proactive initiatives. Proactive CSR initiatives acknowledged the interdependence of companies and society, giving way to an emphasis on the strategic management function of public relations. The move from reactive to proactive CSR coincided with widespread corporate recognition of the public relations function as more than "mere" media relations or crisis communication. It was also at this time that J. E. Grunig and Hunt's (1984) seminal work prompted a discussion about two-way symmetrical communication with stakeholders. Two-way symmetrical models of communication were held up as the ideal, suggesting that organizations should engage in ethical, open, and honest communication with stakeholders. The model suggests that organizations should negotiate meanings, compromise, and adapt to public expectations, to include expectations about what constitutes socially responsible behaviors.

As it evolved, it became clear that CSR may provide both tangible—namely, financial—and intangible benefits for organizations. Likewise, the role of public relations professionals as coordinators of CSR programs became more pronounced and important to corporate managers. Kim and Reber (2008) identified five distinct roles for public relations professionals' function in CSR, finding that the largest number of participants indicated that they played a significant management role. This advisory role is defined by counsel to clients and management about strategic planning and leadership in the execution of CSR programs. Heath and Ni (2008) stated, "Both as a 'listener' and communicator, public relations can aid organizations' ability to foster mutually beneficial interests proactively as a problem solver rather than reactively as lessons learned." The CSR literature today has slowed at this point. Scholarship surrounding public relations and CSR continues to focus largely on the management of CSR programs and campaigns, and the outcomes they give rise to across multiple contexts and channels.

The outcomes of CSR on business objectives have generally been viewed in one of three ways. CSR is viewed as providing a return-on-investment that demonstrates a positive, negative, or offsetting impact on corporate outcomes. For example, CSR may increase consumer purchase intentions, demonstrating a positive return. On the flipside, CSR may not provide an adequate return on organizational resources, ultimately resulting in a loss of investment. Last, some argue that the cost of investment in CSR is offset by the return in tangible and intangible organizational resources. For example, the financial cost of engagement in an environmental CSR campaign may be offset by reduced stakeholder demands, activist attention, and potential governmental oversight.

Outcomes of CSR

Generally, the outcomes of CSR that have been studied to date may be categorized as financial or nonfinancial. Financial outcome measures have ranged from stock returns to manufacturing costs (see Margolis & Walsh, 2003 for a full review); whereas, nonfinancial outcomes may be further subdivided into attitudes (e.g., perceptions of the organization) and behaviors (e.g., purchase intention). Business and advertising disciplines have primarily concerned themselves with the financial, while marketing and public relations research has focused more on nonfinancial outcome measures. However, the line between disciplines is increasingly blurred, and "turf wars serve only to obstruct the productive discussion of new trends and the application of strategic approaches" (Kim, 2001, p. 90). If the public relations discipline is to maintain its authority on CSR, then it is dependent upon scholars and professionals to address both traditional business outcomes, as well as emergent trends.

Financial

In order to successfully execute CSR initiatives, financial resources are required. Thus, whether CSR is an investment (and not a cost) that generates positive returns on financial outcomes for the company has been a major concern for public relations scholars and practitioners. Specifically, the categorization of CSR as a public relations function—a discipline that faces its own issues with demonstrating return-on-investment—results in a necessary need for rationalization to corporate management. Indeed, managers typically conceptualize CSR as a financial initiative (Beauchamp & O'Connor, 2012). Relatedly, Kim and Reber (2008) found that several public relations professionals identified the organizational bottom line as their primary CSR function. However, some professionals noted that their contribution was limited by a lack of influence and authority within the organization. Studies have focused on whether or not CSR positively influences a company's financial outcomes. Although there are mixed results based on different measures and definitions of CSR (Griffin & Mahon, 1997), in general CSR is believed to result in a small, but positive impact on corporate financial performance (Cai, Jo, & Pan, 2012; Dodd & Supa, 2011; Orlitzky, Schmidt, & Rynes, 2003; van Beurden & Gössling, 2008). In other words, engagement in CSR results in a small, but positive financial return-on-investment.

Nonfinancial

Although the business literature has focused primarily on financial outcomes, the relationship between CSR and nonfinancial outcomes is more commonly studied in public relations and related strategic communication literatures. The marketing literature has emphasized cause-related marketing (CRM), a type of CSR practice that targets consumers with partial proceeds from product sales going toward charity causes. The CRM literature has demonstrated that engagement in CRM results in positive attitudes toward corporations' involvement with causes (Webb & Mohr, 1998), positive attitudes toward the company (Nan & Heo, 2007), perceptions as a responsible company (Ross, Patterson, & Strutts, 1992), and increased purchase intentions for the company's products (Smith & Alcorn, 1991).

Similarly, public relations scholars find positive relational outcomes for engagement in CSR programs. CSR could generate positive organization-public relationship outcomes such as higher trust, control mutuality, commitment, and the creation of communal relationships (Hall, 2006) and increased dialogic communication intention and identification with the company (Hong, Yang, & Rim, 2010). Also, CSR information could be helpful for the recruitment of employees. Kim and Park (2009) found that when CSR information (i.e., philanthropy and community contributions) is good, potential employees (i.e., students) indicated high ethical fit with the company and more intention to apply than when poor CSR information was provided.

CSR Contexts: Crises and Poor Reputations

Within certain contexts, such as a crisis, and depending on the industry type, CSR can generate negative outcomes or even backfire, thus harming a company's image and reputation. When companies considered unethical engage in CSR initiatives, stakeholders exhibit doubt regarding the company's motives and perceive CSR activities as the company's illegitimate attempt at image building (Yoon, Gürhan-Canli, & Schwarz, 2006). Factors that could increase stakeholder doubts and generate negative outcomes include high benefit salience, meaning that a company gets more benefit from CSR initiatives than publics do (e.g., a tobacco company supports the lung cancer association); self-generated messages (e.g., CSR advertisements); and a low CSR program/advertising ratio (e.g., a company spends more money on a CSR advertisement than on CSR contribution) (Yoon et al., 2006).

A corporate crisis situation could generate perceptions of high benefit salience. When a company initiates CSR programs during a crisis or immediately following a crisis, it will generally be perceived as an attempt to improve the company's image through CSR programs. In this case, such CSR initiatives are ineffective. Indeed, in order to reduce skepticism and the potential backfiring of CSR efforts, transparency and honesty in communicating CSR motives are important. It is suggested that communication of both self- and society-serving motives is better than communicating society-serving motives alone in terms of reducing skepticism and higher behavioral intentions (i.e., support the company, seek employment, invest, and purchase) (Kim, 2014).

Social responsibility programs are initiated and communicated by companies that need to create profit. It seems unrealistic and irresponsible that the company would care only for the society and not consider strategic outcomes. In fact, scholars suggest one of the most important concerns for a company is its economic responsibility to make a profit and facilitate the economy of our society (Carroll, 1999). Creating a profit is not unethical behavior, because it has positive outcomes (e.g., hiring, creating products, facilitating economy) and publics know about these benefits. Therefore, not providing true motives (e.g., communicating society-serving motives only) means that the practice of hiding or not disclosing the truth generates less positive evaluation of the company than telling both motives of self-serving and society-serving motives.

Companies must devote special attention during communication, and need to exhibit high ethics when revealing their CSR. In particular, companies with poor reputations due to recent crises or those in controversial industry sectors such as tobacco, oil, or alcohol, should not focus excessively on altruistic motives when they communicate CSR. Companies in controversial industries still need to be socially responsible, as they legally engage in business by minimizing harm and maximizing good (Lindorff, Jonson, & McGuire, 2012). Most often, companies in controversial industries are inevitably perceived as harmful and as the course of environmental or social problems. Therefore, highlighting altruistic motives is seen as hypocritical, regardless of the business behavior. Ellen, Webb, and Mohr (2006) suggested that "self-serving motives" (i.e., CSR aimed at the achievement of specific business objectives) can generate positive purchase intentions similar to "other-serving motives" (i.e., CSR driven by corporate values). Therefore, a communication message presenting both self- and other-serving motives could mitigate potential negative outcomes for these companies.

CSR Channels: Publicity to Social Media

Similar to other public relations campaigns, CSR can be communicated through various channels, including publicity (i.e., traditional media), business reports, annual reports, sustainability reports, websites, corporate advertisements, social media, and so on. Here, we highlight the traditional and newest ways of communicating CSR.

Publicity, the Noncorporate Source

Early public relations literature, such as Manheim and Pratt (1986) suggested that in order to achieve public support and the creation of a business-friendly environment, practitioners should impact the publics' perceptions of social responsibility through influencing the media's agenda. Noncorporate sources such as the media are considered less biased in communicating a company's CSR initiatives when compared to corporate sources. Compared to other company information, CSR requires special attention, because it can increase suspicion and skepticism regarding a company's motives and could backfire, resulting in negative outcomes (Skard & Thorbjørnsen, 2014).

Contemporary studies continue to propose noncorporate sources as a strategic communication approach in order to minimize suspicions regarding the self-serving motives of the company (Dawkins, 2005; Du, Bhattacharya, & Sen, 2010; Yoon et al., 2006). Communication outcomes (i.e., attitude toward company) were better when the information source was presented as a nonprofit monitoring entity of an organization or newspaper than as a corporate advertisement (Yoon et al., 2006).

From the media perspective, unfortunately, CSR has been considered as of less news value compared to other corporate news, such as corporate crises (Manheim & Pratt, 1986). Following the negativity bias (Baumeister, Bratslavsky, Finkenauer, & Vohs, 2001), people are usually prone to negative news or events rather than positive ones, especially when it comes to the simplistic and common CSR activity (i.e., monetary donation) with a one-time event that will not have a great impact on readers if at all. Public relations practitioner's role as building close relationships with the media (Manheim & Pratt, 1986), and consistent CSR initiatives of the organization will be helpful to increase coverage in the media. Thus, it has been more likely that we see more negative media coverage with fewer CSR stories. The media coverage of negative corporate news often adds more problems, because it creates contradictory public perceptions of corporate behavior, ultimately resulting in suspicion toward CSR initiatives. In fact, research that examined CSR news stories and readers' comments found that overall about half of the comments about the CSR news stories were negative. Negative comments increased when the articles were released after a company's crisis or when a simple monetary donation was reported (Cho & Hong, 2009).

Modern research indicates that media relations might not be the most effective method of communication about organizational CSR initiatives. Communication scholars have identified the need for effective CSR communication and research (Clark, 2000; Dawkins, 2005; Kim & Ferguson, 2014). For example, Kim and Ferguson argued that scholars needed to study not just the outcomes of CSR activity per se but also the evaluation of CSR communication. Without effective CSR communication, the public will not be fully informed about corporate ethical behaviors and remain unsatisfied (Dawkins, 2005).

Social Media

The development of social media and online platforms has shifted CSR communication from one-way to two-way communication. In social media, anyone can join and create dialogue with organizations and other people. Generating dialog is an aspect of ethical public relations, since "it gives a voice to all… based on principles of honesty, trust, and positive regard for the other rather than simply a conception of the public as means to end" (Kent & Taylor, 2002, p. 33). Public relations should bring the publics' voice into the organization and involve it in the decision-making process in order to establish its position as a strategic management function in the organization (J. E. Grunig, 2006). According to the previous practice of executing and communicating CSR, however, a two-way approach has not been well adopted.

Korschun and Du (2013) posed that companies have begun to engage in "virtual CSR dialogues," which refer to the co-creation of CSR initiatives where customers participate in the production process. The major difference between virtual CSR dialogue compared to traditional CSR communication is that CSR programs and/or the communication of ideas are co-created by the publics and not solely by the company. This practice is a more ethical example of CSR because the company and the publics become more equal. Also, throughout this process, a company could minimize suspicions toward its extrinsic motives (e.g., image or profit making), while creating increased interdependency and long-term relationships with the publics (Sheth & Uslay, 2007). Indeed, dialogue and co-creation in social media can bring better ethical practice of CSR and public relations because they invite and actively incorporate various publics' voices into the programs.

However, not all co-created ideas will be considered as successfully satisfying both the company's and the publics' goals. In ideas that lack an understanding of the company's goal and philosophy, the company may not experience positive outcomes (Kim & Slotegraaf, 2016). Here, communicators' roles are particularly important: ongoing interactions with the participants (e.g., answering questions) and personalized communication (e.g., providing requested information, calling each participants' name) will be helpful for generating constructive ideas that have mutually beneficial outcomes for both the company and its publics (Kim & Slotegraaf, 2016). CSR initiatives throughout the co-creation process generate outcomes that are not corporate centered but are public centered and that improve our society (Andersen & Johansen, 2014).

Furthermore, a company should consider the ownership of the ideas and compensation provided to the participants for their contributions. Participants of the CSR co-creation may not receive direct financial compensation but may receive social recognition or self-fulfillment as one contributes positively to society. Such individuals are basically unpaid idea submitters, and the company might receive greater benefits through engagement in the process. If the company does not carefully consider ownership and compensation, it could be perceived as unethically exploiting its publics. Practitioners should explicitly communicate details about the policy regarding compensation or prizes they are planning. Individuals' moral decisions and actions are part of CSR, because organizations are composed of many individuals, each having the responsibility to behave ethically (Wood, 1991).

Conclusion

Public relations scholars and professionals are those most qualified to engage in the planning and management of organizational CSR initiatives. By describing the historical evolution of public relations alongside CSR, as well as the multiple outcomes—both financial and nonfinancial—that may result from socially responsible corporate practices, this chapter has identified how CSR is best approached as a strategic function of public relations. Business, advertising, and marketing goals should be aligned with public relations–led CSR initiatives, because the outcome literature demonstrates that CSR may be perceived as inauthentic when approached from particular corporate contexts. Emerging channels, such as social media, demonstrate how CSR can be co-created among strategic audiences and communicated in new ways.

In order to run a business in society, companies receive power and legitimacy from society (Davis, 1973; Wood, 1991). They need to act responsibly according to their power. The more power they have, the more responsibility they need to fulfill. If not, the business will not survive in the long term and will lose its power (Davis, 1973).

Ethical practice of a company's public relations involves two-way communication with its publics. In planning and executing CSR using social media, practitioners can co-create CSR initiatives with their publics while the decision-making process is transparent and open. Co-created CSR utilizing social media and the Internet is vastly different from traditional CSR in that the old version was firm-centric, focusing on returns to the company, while the new one is public- and society-centric (Andersen & Johansen, 2014). Through the co-creation process, both companies and society become strongly interrelated helping each other toward a better society (Sheth & Uslay, 2007).

Future research should focus on emergent areas for the study of CSR in a global context (Bortree, 2014); as related to controversial social-political stances (Dodd & Supa, 2014, 2015); as an ethical function (L'Etang, 1994) and a continued emphasis on theory development. Perhaps of most importance for a continued public relations emphasis on CSR research and practice is the emergence of perceptions of CSR as an organizational requirement, not voluntary initiatives. As CSR continues to evolve, strategic approaches by public relations must do so too.

Ultimately, CSR may vary greatly but is generally positive in outcome. Negative outcomes emerge when organizations violate stakeholder expectations of ethical and morally appropriate behavior. The conceptual development of CSR as a strategic function of public relations should move beyond a context- and channel-specific outcome orientation and toward an examination of societal-level implications aimed at ethics, morality, and community. Using various theories reviewed in this literature to underpin these approaches, this research may focus on the ways that the public relations discipline engages in CSR programs on behalf of organizations to impact perceptions of legitimacy (issues management, stakeholder theory), resource exchange (social exchange theory), the functioning of society (fully functioning society theory), public relations roles/corporate conscience (excellence theory), networks and community building (relationship management theory, social capital theory), and so on. These macro-level approaches to CSR continue a history of mutual evolution that suggests public relations can be an ethical practice that seeks to contribute positively to society.

References

Andersen, S. E., & Johansen, T. S. (2014). Cause-related marketing 2.0: Connection, collaboration and commitment. *Journal of Marketing Communications*, 1–20. doi:10.1080/13527266.2014.938684.

Baumeister, R. F., Bratslavsky, E., Finkenauer, C., & Vohs, K. D. (2001). Bad is stronger than good. *Review of General Psychology*, 5(4), 323.

Beauchamp, L. L., & O'Connor, A. (2012). America's most admired companies: A descriptive analysis of CEO corporate social responsibility statements. *Public Relations Review, 38*(3), 494–497.

Bortree, D. S. (2014). The state of CSR communication research: A summary and future direction. *Public Relations Journal, 8*(3). Retrieved from http://www.prsa.org/intelligence/prjournal/documents/2014bortree.pdf.

Bowen, S. A., & Rawlins, B. (2013). Corporate moral conscience. In R. Heath (Ed.), *Encyclopedia of Public Relations II* (pp. 202–206). Thousand Oaks, CA. Sage.

Cai, Y., Jo, H., & Pan, C. (2012). Doing well while doing bad? CSR in controversial industry sectors. *Journal of Business Ethics, 108*(4), 467–480.

Carroll, A. B. (1999). Corporate social responsibility: Evolution of a definitional construct. *Business and Society, 38*(3), 268–295.

Cho, S., & Hong, Y. (2009). Netizens' evaluations of corporate social responsibility: Content analysis of CSR news stories and online readers' comments. *Public Relations Review, 35*, 147–149. doi:10.1016/j.pubrev.2008.09.012.

Clark, C. E. (2000). Differences between public relations and corporate social responsibility: An analysis. *Public Relations Review, 26*(3), 363–380.

Davis, K. (1973). The case for and against business assumption of social responsibilities. *Academy of Management Journal, 16*(2), 312–322.

Dawkins, J. (2005). Corporate responsibility: The communication challenge. *Journal of Communication Management, 9*(2), 108.

Dodd, M. D., & Supa, D. W. (2011). Understanding the effect of corporate social responsibility on consumer purchase intention. *Public Relations Journal, 5*(3). Retrieved from http://www.prsa.org/intelligence/prjournal/documents/2011doddsupa.pdf.

Dodd, M. D., & Supa, D. W. (2014). Conceptualizing and measuring "corporate social advocacy" communication: Examining the impact on corporate financial performance. *Public Relations Journal, 8*(3). Retrieved from http://www.prsa.org/intelligence/prjournal/documents/2014doddsupa.pdf.

Dodd, M. D., & Supa, D. W. (2015). Testing the viability of corporate social advocacy as a predictor of purchase intention. *Communication Research Reports, 32*(4), 287–293.

Du, S., Bhattacharya, C. B., & Sen, S. (2010). Maximizing business returns to corporate social responsibility (CSR): The role of CSR communication. *International Journal of Management Reviews, 12*(1), 8–19. doi:10.1111/j.1468- 2370.2009.00276.x.

Duhé, S. C. (2009). Good management, sound finances, and social responsibility: Two decades of U.S. corporate insider perspectives on reputation and the bottom line. *Public Relations Review, 35*(1), 77–78.

Ellen, P. S., Webb, D. J., & Mohr, L. A. (2006). Building corporate associations: Consumer attributions for corporate socially responsible programs. *Journal of the Academy of Marketing Science, 34*(2), 147–157.

Freeman, R. E. (1984). *Strategic management: A stakeholder approach*. Boston, MA: Pitman.

Friedman, M. (1970, September 13). The social responsibility of business is to increase its profits. *New York Times Magazine, 13*, 122–126.

Griffin, J. J., & Mahon, J. F. (1997). The corporate social performance and corporate financial performance debate twenty-five years of incomparable research. *Business and Society, 36*(1), 5–31.

Grunig, J. E. (2006). Furnishing the edifice: Ongoing research on public relations as a strategic management function. *Journal of Public Relations Research, 18*(2), 151–176.

Grunig, L. A., Grunig, J. E., & Dozier, D. M. (2002). *Excellent public relations and effective organizations: A study of communication management in three countries*. Mahwah, NJ: Lawrence Erlbaum.

Grunig, J. E., & Hunt, T. (1984). *Managing public relations*. New York, NY: Holt, Rinehart and Winston.

Hall, M. R. (2006). Corporate philanthropy and corporate community relations: Measuring relationship-building results. *Journal of Public Relations Research, 18*(1), 1–21.

Heath, R. L. (2006). Onward into more fog: Thoughts on public relations' research directions. *Journal of Public Relations Research, 18*(2), 93–114.

Heath, R. L., & Ni, L. (2008, September 28). Corporate social responsibility. *Institute for Public Relations*. Retrieved from http://www.instituteforpr.org/corporate-social-responsibility/.

Heath, R. L., & Palenchar, M. J. (2009). *Strategic issues management: Organizations and public policy change* (2nd ed.). Thousand Oaks, CA: Sage.

Hong, S. Y., Yang, S. U., & Rim, H. (2010). The influence of corporate social responsibility and customer-company identification on publics' dialogic communication intentions. *Public Relations Review, 36*(2), 196–198.

Kent, M. L., & Taylor, M. (2002). Toward a dialogic theory of public relations. *Public Relations Review, 28*(1), 21–37.

Kim, S., & Ferguson, M. A. T. (2014). Public expectations of CSR communication: What and how to communicate CSR. *Public Relations Journal, 8*(3). Retrieved from http://www.prsa.org/intelligence/prjournal/documents/2014kimferguson.pdf.

Kim, S., & Park, H. (2009). Corporate social responsibility as an organizational attractiveness/relationship building role for prospective public relations practitioners. Paper presented at the 59th Annual International Communication Association Conference, Chicago, IL.

Kim, Y. (2001). The impact of brand equity and the company's reputation on revenues. *Journal of Promotion Management, 6*(1/2), 89–111.

Kim, Y. (2014). Strategic communication of corporate social responsibility (CSR): Effects of stated motives and corporate reputation on stakeholder responses. *Public Relations Review, 40*(5), 838–840.

Kim, Y., & Reber, B. H. (2008). Public relations' place in corporate social responsibility: Practitioners define their role. *Public Relations Review, 34*(4), 337–342.

Kim, Y., & Slotegraaf, R. J. (2016). Brand-embedded interaction: A dynamic and personalized interaction for co-creation. *Marketing Letters, 27*, 183–193.

Korschun, D., & Du, S. (2013). How virtual corporate social responsibility dialogs generate value: A framework and propositions. *Journal of Business Research, 66*(9), 1494–1504.

L'Etang, J. (1994). Public relations and corporate social responsibility: Some issues arising. *Journal of Business Ethics, 13*(2), 111–123.

Lindorff, M., Jonson, E. P., & McGuire, L. (2012). Strategic corporate social responsibility in controversial industry sectors: The social value of harm minimisation. *Journal of Business Ethics, 110*(4), 457–467.

Lubitow, A., & Davis, M. (2011). Pastel injustice: The corporate use of pinkwashing for profit. *Environmental Justice, 4*(2), 139–144.

Manheim, J. B., & Pratt, C. B. (1986). Communicating corporate social responsibility. *Public Relations Review, 12*(2), 9–18.

Margolis, J. D., & Walsh, J. P. (2003). Misery loves companies: Rethinking social initiatives by business. *Administrative Science Quarterly, 48*(2), 268–305.

Nan, X., & Heo, K. (2007). Consumer responses to corporate social responsibility (CSR) initiatives: Examining the role of brand-cause fit in cause-related marketing. *Journal of Advertising, 36*(2), 63–74.

Orlitzky, M., Schmidt, F. L., & Rynes, S. L. (2003). Corporate social and financial performance: A meta-analysis. *Organization Studies, 24*(3), 403–441.

Ross, J. K., Patterson, L. T., & Stutts, M. A. (1992). Consumer perceptions of organizations that use cause-related marketing. *Journal of the Academy of Marketing Science, 20*(1), 93–97.

Sethi, S. P. (1977). *Advocacy advertising and large corporations: Social conflict, big business image, the news media, and public policy.* Lexington, MA: D.C. Heath.

Sheth, J. N., & Uslay, C. (2007). Implications of the revised definition of marketing: From exchange to value creation. *Journal of Public Policy and Marketing, 26*(2), 302–307.

Skard, S., & Thorbjørnsen, H. (2014). Is publicity always better than advertising? The role of brand reputation in communicating corporate social responsibility. *Journal of Business Ethics, 124*(1), 149–160.

Smith, S. M., & Alcorn, D. S. (1991). Cause marketing: A new direction in the marketing of corporate responsibility. *Journal of Consumer Marketing, 8*(3), 19–35.

Van Beurden, P., & Gössling, T. (2008). The worth of values—A literature review on the relation between corporate social and financial performance. *Journal of Business Ethics, 82*(2), 407–424.

Webb, D. J., & Mohr, L. A. (1998). A typology of consumer responses to cause-related marketing: From skeptics to socially concerned. *Journal of Public Policy and Marketing, 17,* 226–238.

Wood, D. J. (1991). Corporate social performance revisited. *Academy of Management Review, 16*(4), 691–718.

Yoon, Y., Gürhan-Canli, Z., & Schwarz, N. (2006). The effect of corporate social responsibility (CSR) activities on companies with bad reputations. *Journal of Consumer Psychology, 16*(4), 377–390.

2 Penn State's After-Sanction Response Strategy

Chang Wan Woo, Michael Gulotta, and April Gulotta

Social capital is one of the principal capitals that Bourdieu (1985) introduced along with economic capital and cultural capital. According to Bourdieu, capital is a resource that enables people to gain profit by participating or competing in a given social area. Economic capital is generated by economic activities, while cultural capital is generated by cultural understanding of who has a higher position. Social capital is generated by a durable network. While Bourdieu developed the idea that social capital creates social inequality, Coleman (1988) insisted that social capital produces trust and trustworthiness, which would bring about reasonable returns to a market along with financial capital and human capital. Putnam (2000) viewed social capital as a way to bring people together in a democratic society because it promotes civic engagement and a sense of belonging in communities, which has been lacking in the United States. According to Putnam, social capital builds networks, norms, and trust among people, which entail more forms of civic engagement, such as reading local newspapers, volunteering, and voting. Meanwhile, community bonding would also arise. This function of promoting civic engagement is closely related to the role of public relations practitioners, who are often forced to closely monitor social issues and be involved with community relations (Dodd, Brummette, & Hazleton, 2015).

In crisis management, public relations practitioners need to understand that they are protecting the reputation of their organization in crisis by facilitating communication between their organizations and various social actors. Choosing appropriate communication strategies needs to be done in a strategic and deliberate way (Coombs, 1999), because one's reputation is not determined by organizations, but by audiences (Benoit, 2000). Very often, the influence of a crisis reaches much further than just the organization itself. Employees, investors, supporters, as well as surrounding communities would lose economic capital and human capital. At the same time, they will lose networks, norms, and trust, which are all forms of social capital. As Luoma-aho (2009) insisted, if public relations is a profession that creates and maintains the social capital of organizations, meaning that practitioners need to gain trust and support, recognizing what aspects of the organization's social capital are damaged and how to fix those aspects by using appropriate image restoration strategies would be the most important role of public relations.

We looked at the 2012 Pennsylvania State University (Penn State) scandal. Jerry Sandusky's sexual abuse scandal is unique considering it hurt not only the university itself but also the community around the university including students, fans, alumni, faculty and staff, and anyone who identified himself or herself with Penn State. Following Sandusky's final sentencing in October 2012, the former president of Penn State, Graham Spanier, was also charged with conspiring to conceal reports of the abuse (Pearson, 2012). The Penn State community still felt pain after 3 years. For example, on March 8, 2014, Al Clemson, an outgoing member of the Penn State Board of Trustees, said he regretted voting to fire Joe Paterno, long-time head coach of Penn State (Schackner & Langley, 2014). New criminal charges are still pending against former Penn State officials (Drape, 2016) The purpose of this study is to investigate how the university as well as the community of Penn State made an effort to protect their social capital. Specifically, we looked at the way that Penn State and its stakeholders tried to restore and protect social capital established by its football team when using image restoration strategies and if this way was ethical and professional.

Sports as a Community Asset and Civic Engagement

Very often, sports build social capital by providing public goods in the form of sports competition, fan networks, culture, and trust between a team and its fan community. The sense of social belonging is one of the effects of sports spectatorship, which creates imagined group membership (Horky, 2013). Once this kind of group identity is created, fans are more than customers; they not only identify themselves with the team they cheer, but also with the community the team represents (Heere & James, 2007). Sport brings about a sense of belonging in a community as well (Palmer & Thompson, 2007). For example, Putnam (2000) noted that sports participation could promote social capital because it is an activity that builds social networks, and trustworthiness would arise from involvement. Clopton and Finch (2010) argued that the role of sport as a builder of social capital has been discussed in sport research even though the term is not explicitly mentioned. For example, Harris (1998) found that sport participation enhances civic engagement, such as coaching a local youth league and organizing a run to raise funds for a local nonprofit organization. Toma (2003) also found that the entire university community, regardless of age, gender, and political view, is engaged together with the university's football team. Putnam, Feldstein, and Cohen (2004) said that creating a sports league would strengthen social capital. Other researchers have supported this notion. Clopton and Finch (2010) found that identifying with a sport team strengthened perceived social capital among college students. Their findings are similar to those of Wann and Polk (2007) that showed a positive correlation between identifying with a team and trust toward the team.

However, Tonts (2005) and Smith and Ingham (2003) found that homogenized sports groups may divide a community. Very often, sports leagues are run by people of the same ethnicity. Also, some sports are associated with certain ethnicity; for example, Tonts found out golf was considered a "White sport" in the Northern Wheatbelt in Australia. All in all, both sports participation and spectatorship build social capital, which also promotes civic engagement; however, it may not be inclusive enough to connect all citizens in a community.

Ethical Perspectives of Social Capital and Civic Morality

The ethical perspective of social capital has been discussed in the literature as well. Trust is a core concept of social capital and the most frequently studied topic in social capital research (Portes, 1998). Trust is a prerequisite of building a strong social capital (Putnam, Leonardi, & Nanetti, 1994), and it can be developed by cooperation and social interaction (Ayios, Jeurissen, Manning, & Spence, 2014). Furthermore, honesty is a core concept of civic morality (Letki, 2006). Letki explained civic morality as "an ethical habit forming the basis of most theories of civic virtue, and it is often linked with trust and reciprocity" (p. 306); therefore, social capital and civic morality can be linked.

During the process of building social capital in an organization, while managers develop social capital of employees in various social interactions, employees also build an organizational moral structure for themselves (Pastoriza, Ariño, & Ricart, 2008). At a societal level, the sense of community built by social interactions and civic engagement would also lead to social networks, norms, and trust, in other words, social capital. Social capital is accumulated through labor and takes time to build (Bourdieu, 1985).

However, Ayios et al. (2014) recognized that social capital has a "dark side"; for example, too much emphasis on having a sense of cohesiveness within a group creates exclusion, which causes a trust deficit between people inside and outside the group. Bourdieu (1985) also warned that social capital is one of the capitals that creates social inequality because it is generated based on who people know instead of what they do. Putnam (2000) recognized a "dark side" of social capital as well in his discussion of "bonding social capital (ties that link individuals or groups with much in common) and bridging social capital (ties that link individuals or groups across a greater social distance)" (p. 279). Very often, when bonding within a group is too strong, homogeneity is emphasized and diversity is lacking.

Social Capital and Public Relations Ethics in Crisis

Sometimes, people tend to exclude outside groups in order to protect the social connectedness within their community (Almedom, 2005). If a role of public relations is to create and maintain social capital on behalf of organizations (Keenan & Hazleton, 2006; Luoma-aho, 2009), crisis communication managed by public relations professionals should be planned and executed in a way to promote and protect social capital of people around the organizations. According to the *2015 Annual Trust Barometer Research*, the trust deficit between organizations and their publics becomes deeper and deeper every year ("Trust around the world," 2015). Trust is a core value of social capital. If a trust deficit becomes even bigger in a crisis, social capital built around an organization and its publics will weaken.

The Public Relations Society of America (PRSA) suggests professional values and ethics to its members: advocacy, honesty, expertise, independence, loyalty, and fairness (PRSA, n.d.). These professional values of public relations are not different from the concept of social capital defined by Putnam (1996), who said that social capital builds trusting social networks and norms of reciprocity by connecting individuals in society. PRSA professional value also represents sanction, one of the elements of social capital (Halpern, 2005), because practitioners are required to provide independent advice to their organization and be fair to both organizations and their publics. Taylor and Kent (2014) explicitly claimed that social capital is a product of relationships and that public relations is a profession of promoting engagement; therefore, it should generate social capital. Therefore, any crisis communication executed by public relations professionals should strengthen social capital.

In terms of crisis communication, a crisis harms the reputation of an organization because it gives people the chance to think badly about a wide array of features of the organization (Coombs, 2007) and subsequently lose their trust in the organization. To regain trust, organizations need to appropriately respond to their publics. One crisis communication strategy was developed by Benoit (1995) based on two assumptions. The first is that communication is a goal-directed activity. The second is that maintaining a favorable reputation is a key goal of communication. Benoit stated that "when people have goals or desires, they present the messages that they think will be instrumental in obtaining their goals" (p. 67) and will offer multiple messages if they believe it will assist in accomplishing their goal.

Benoit (1997) developed five types of image restoration strategies: denial, evading responsibility, reducing offensiveness, corrective action, and mortification. The strategy of denial has two variants: simple denial and shift the blame. Simple denial occurs when the entity in question states that they did not do the act in question. Shifting the blame occurs when the entity in question states that another person or corporation is responsible for the action. If an act cannot be denied, the strategy of evading responsibility can be used. This strategy has four variations: provocation, defeasibility, accident, or good intentions (Benoit & Henson, 2009). Provocation is to say that the crisis was a result of a wrongful act of another. With the defeasibility strategy, an organization would claim that there was a lack of information or control. The accident strategy is to say that the crisis was caused by a mishap. Last, organizations can claim that they had a good intention in spite of the crisis. The strategy of reducing offensiveness has six different forms. Bolstering occurs when the organization stresses good traits about itself. Minimization is an attempt to frame the act as not as serious as it seems. Differentiation occurs when the act in question is isolated from more offensive actions. Transcendence is when the act in question is justified by putting it in a favorable context. Attacking the accuser is a strategy used when the company in question wants to diminish the credibility of the ones complaining against it. Finally, through compensation the organization tries to reduce the negative feeling toward itself by offering the victim services or money. An organization can also use a corrective action strategy in which it promises to prevent recurrences of the problem and to fix the problem. Last, the organization can apologize, which is referred to as mortification.

Penn State's biggest challenge after the Sandusky scandal was recovering their reputation for honesty, integrity, and transparency (Carpenter, 2011). Before the scandal, Penn State enjoyed a good reputation of being one of the favorite targets of job recruiters (Marklein & Snyder, 2011) and ranked 10th in the collegiate sports royalty ranking out of 200 universities (Rovell, 2012). If these facts indicated strong social capital built by Penn State and its publics, we wondered how Penn State and the surrounding publics responded to repair their social capital. We were especially interested in their image restoration strategies after the scandal was investigated and Penn State received a sanction from National Collegiate Athletics Association (NCAA) and if the strategies were used in ways of strengthening social capital and PRSA ethics.

Based on the literature, four research questions are posited here:

RQ1: Did Penn State and their surrounding publics try to protect bonding social capital or bridging social capital in a crisis?
RQ2: How did Penn State and its surrounding publics utilize the three components of established social capital (i.e., network, social norm, and sanction) in a crisis?
RQ3: How did Penn State and their surrounding publics respond to the Freeh Report and the NCAA sanction?
RQ4: Do the responses of Penn State and their surrounding publics comply with the social capital building process and PRSA ethics?

Methods

The goal of content analysis is to investigate communication materials systematically. Quantitative content analysis has been frequently used, but sometimes it does not give enough textual consideration of the contents (Marying, 2004; Meng & Berger, 2008). Marying introduced qualitative content analysis, which is still systematic but does not quantify findings. We followed his approach and used a qualitative content analysis of 303 newspaper articles published between July 23, 2012, when the NCAA announced the sanction against Penn State, and September 24, 2013, when the NCAA reduced the length of the sanction for the first time. We used the keywords "Penn State" and "scandal" to search the LexisNexis Academic database. Five newspapers were chosen: *Philadelphia Inquirer* and *Pittsburgh Post-Gazette* had the most articles among newspapers in Pennsylvania, and *Daily News*, *USA Today*, and *The Washington Post* were the top three newspapers in terms of the number of news articles about this case outside the state.

Media's response, Penn State's response, and community's response were analyzed to see how Penn State and their surrounding publics tried to protect social capital. The three components of social capital introduced by Halpern (2005) were also coded: social network, social norms, and sanction. In addition, based on Putnam, Feldstein, and Cohen's (2004) explanation, we coded mentions or acts that reinforce exclusive identities and homogenous groups as bonding and mentions or acts that try to encompass people across diverse social groups as bridging. Professional values were coded based on descriptions in the PRSA member code of ethics (http://www.prsa.org/aboutprsa/ethics/codeenglish/#.VEqvIPnF_pU). Image restoration strategy was also coded based on the description given by Zhang and Benoit (2009).

A coding protocol was created and utilized to train three coders. After a 1-hour training session, all coders coded the same 30 articles. An additional 1-hour training and discussion session was held to ensure that the coders all agreed on the coding process before actual coding. After coding all articles, all data were aggregated in one document to be analyzed. The three coders then sorted out common themes and patterns from the coding separately. Last, the coders had a 2-hour discussion session to outline findings.

Data Analysis and Findings

Throughout the 303 articles, we found three recurring themes. First, we found that the Penn State community including alumni, students, faculty, and fans fought to protect their bonding social capital. Second, we found that Penn State paid excessively lopsided attention to bridging social capital toward a bigger community which includes the NCAA, higher education institutions in general, and organizations for preventing child sexual abuse. Third, Pennsylvania media focused much more on the conflict between Penn State and its community, while national media focused more on how Penn State responded to the recommendations of the NCAA and the Freeh report. Overall, Pennsylvania media were harsher to Penn State by reporting more negative opinions from the local community.

Protecting Social Capital

Halpern (2005) said that sanctions are communicated when neighbors find violations of unwritten rules of the neighborhood. After the

NCAA announced sanctions of Penn State's football program including a
$60 million fine and a postseason ban for 4 years and vacated all wins from
1998, Penn State's publics condemned the Freeh report and the NCAA's
decision on the sanction. For example, the Penn State faculty senate called
the sanction unjust to the university and to students (Moran, 2012a).
More interestingly, publics constantly expressed their disapproval of Penn
State's accommodation with the NCAA's decision. Specifically, this blame
was reported more in the Pennsylvania media (i.e., *Philadelphia Inquirer*
and *Pittsburgh Post-Gazette*). Roebuck (2012) reported that only 17% of
Pennsylvania voters approved of how Penn State's former president Graham
B. Spanier handled the investigation. Penn State alumni criticized the Penn
State board of trustees for rushing to judgment in firing Joe Paterno, the
former head coach, and claimed that the board wanted to find a scapegoat
(Infield, 2013; Schackner, 2012a). A former player also said that university pride was diminished because of ill-conceived decisions by Penn State
(Schackner & Tully, 2013). People also complained that Joe Paterno's statue
was taken down (Lopresti, 2012). Interestingly, sanctions were discussed
more in Pennsylvania media than in national media, which possibly indicates that Pennsylvania media were more involved with building and protecting the social capital of the state university.

At the same time, bonding activities of Penn State's publics were observed
in articles in both Pennsylvania media and national media. The Penn State
community expressed displeasure when coaches from all around the country came to recruit Penn State players after the sanction (Fitzpatrick, 2012).
Alumni gatherings for expressing concerns were organized. One alumnus
said, "I will not stop supporting the team. If anything, I will show up every
Saturday screaming louder to show them we are with them" (Tully, 2012a).
Former Penn State players sent emails to alumni asking them to sign a peti-
tion condemning the NCAA's decision (Russo, 2012). More than 1,000 fans
gathered and organized a pep band to greet players and cheer for them
(Armas, 2012). Local residents also said they were proud to support Penn
State football and annoyed by all national media talking about the scandal
(Lopresti, 2012). Pennsylvania senators insisted that the fine paid by Penn
State needs to be used in Pennsylvania ("State to fight NCAA's Penn State
sanctions," 2013). Even though some players left the team, more than 90%
stayed with the team after the sanction (Fitzpatrick & Anastasia, 2012). As
of July 2013, the number of donors actually went up compared to the previous year (Snyder, 2013a).

While publics of Penn State emphasized bonding, the social norms and
unwritten rules of Penn State and its community were also mentioned. The
community did not just express their love of the football program, however, they also expressed their support of Penn State academics (Graff,
2012; Kaplan, 2012). Imm (2012), an editor of the *Pittsburgh Post-Gazette*
and an alumnus of Penn State, said their chanting "May no act of ours
bring shame!" was not about their Penn State pride, but about Penn State
responsibility.

Comments and actions regarding bonding and sanctions were found more from publics around Penn State, not from Penn State officials. For Penn State officials, bridging efforts were more often observed. Right after the NCAA announced the punishment for Penn State, Penn State's spokesperson stated that any input from the outside would be welcomed (Couloumbis, 2012). Penn State tried to keep their focus on the bigger community by discussing child abuse, raising awareness, and fixing this social problem (Armas, 2013). They also hosted a conference about preventing child abuse (Moran, 2012b). Penn State officials showed that they were taking responsibility instead of making the issue disappear ("Reserve judgment on Paterno until trial of ex-PSU officials," 2012). They tried to listen to fans and removed the song Sweet Caroline from its play list during football games because of its lyrics "touching me and touching you" (Weiss, 2012). Throughout the analyses, we found that Penn State quietly followed decisions made by NCAA for the year.

Ethical Practice of Penn State's Officials

For the most part, Penn State officials followed PRSA professional values in addressing the nation, but they were very quiet toward the Penn State community, which can be viewed as unethical because it violates almost every PRSA professional value. However, Penn State officials were honest about their procedures for electing a new board of trustees (Snyder & Gammage, 2013), disclosed Penn State's financial situation (Berkowitz, 2012; Hickok, 2013; Schackner, 2012b), and shared with publics what they had learned about their problems (Couloumbis, 2012). They disclosed a confidential letter between Penn State and league officials as well (Schackner, 2013). Loyalty to its publics was also found. For example, the Penn State football team decided to put their names on their uniforms, breaking a tradition started by Joe Paterno (George, 2012).

Being silent is not in accordance with public relations professional values; it is exactly the opposite, thus unethical. Penn State, from time to time, did not say anything to its students or alumni. Officials declined to comment on publics' complaints about the NCAA's punishment (Moran, 2012a) and the former president's resignation (Wood, 2012). Penn State also did not respond to protesters who requested the board of directors to resign because of their poor handling of firing Paterno (Schackner & Tully, 2013) and did not comment on how they would handle Paterno's statue, which was removed right after the scandal was revealed (Tully, 2012b).

Image Restoration Strategies

The Penn State administration mostly used corrective action strategies, such as removing the statue of Joe Paterno from Beaver Stadium (Saffron, 2012), holding a conference on sexual abuse and trauma (Moran, 2012b), having the board of trustees take voting privileges away from the governor and university president (Snyder, 2013b), putting the former president on leave after he was charged with perjury (Wood, 2012), and implementing 116 of the 119 recommendations from the Freeh Report (Snyder, 2013c). Penn State also hired an academic integrity officer and a director of ethics and trained 16,000 employees about their responsibility to report child abuse (Anderson, 2013).

However, publics around Penn State did not want to accept responsibility. These other publics, including alumni, faculty, and fans, mostly used defensive strategies. The attorney for Paterno's family claimed that the Freeh report was totally wrong (Feiden, 2013; Siemaszko, 2013). The faculty senate also attacked Freeh and said his report was wrong on many issues (Moran, 2012a). Former president Graham Spanier sued the author of the Freeh report for slander (Ward, 2013). Finally, a Penn State alumnus who conducted his own review of the Freeh report shifted the blame to the Department of Welfare and Children and Youth Services by saying that they should have stopped Sandusky back in 1998 (Heltzel, 2012). Former players also organized a group to demonstrate their disagreement with the Freeh report (Snyder, 2013c).

Implications

Kirby-Geddes, King, and Bravington (2013) said that it is possible to investigate micro-levels of interplay between individuals and their community using the lens of social capital. At the same time, it is also possible to look at how these interplays influence society at a macro-level. We found micro- and macro-level interplays among publics of Penn State by observing what they did in the Jerry Sandusky scandal crisis using the lens of social capital. Penn State's publics tried to protect their social capital by emphasizing the cohesiveness and connectedness of the Penn State community. Various civic engagements such as gatherings, collecting petitions, protests, and social events were organized to protect their beloved university, which had established and provided bonding functions of social capital. These publics not only supported the university, they also did not hesitate to condemn and provide advice to university officials about how they handled the crisis. Pennsylvania media also played a significant role by reporting the conflict between Penn State and its publics more closely than national media. Lowrey, Brozana, and Mackay (2008) insisted that revealing community structure, listening to various parts of a community, and promoting community cohesiveness (i.e., helping a community find solutions) are all components of community journalism. We found that Pennsylvania media played this community journalism role by reporting various voices of Pennsylvanians. These activities of publics around an organization including local media repairing social networks and enforcing social norms by sanctions are good examples of how already established social capital works toward protecting social capital in a crisis. As Letki (2006) found, however, these activities of preserving social capital do not represent strong civic morality. This may show the "dark side" of social capital as Putnam (2000) and Ayios et al. (2014) pointed out. The activities the various publics engaged in served to strengthen social cohesiveness among people who supported Penn State but excluded many other publics including victims of sexual abuse.

Penn State officials, on the other hand, showed their commitment to ensuring corrective action, which would preserve civic morality. This can be a good example of bridging social capital. We found that these officials often did not respond to their own community but took action toward the bigger community. They sought help from the NCAA to get their legitimacy back. They followed directions and tried to bridge the gap between the Penn State community and victims of child abuse, the community that Jerry Sandusky hurt the most. This strategy could be considered effective, considering that the sanction given to Penn State was reduced much more quickly than expected (Moyer, 2013). In addition, enrollment at Penn State increased in 2013 ("Enrollment sees slight increase," 2013).

Conclusion

As bonding and bridging social capital are both related to the mental health of community residents who sometimes act exclusively to protect social connectedness (Almedom, 2005), publics around Penn State also tried to bond together and show support. At the same time, they showed the dark side of social capital. Pennsylvania senators' insisting on use of fines paid by Penn State only in Pennsylvania is one example of how bonding social capital can be exclusive. Penn State's apparent indifference to its supporters including students, alumni, fans, and local community, especially for their condemnation of how they handled the crisis, can be viewed as an unethical public relations process. Public relations professionals should have done a better job communicating with those publics. However, in terms of building a social capital, it was a good practice that Penn State focused much more on bridging social capital. At the macro-level, establishing civic institution such as "The Network on Child Protection and Well-Being" (http://protectchildren.psu.edu/) would bring more social trust from the broader community. Putnam et al. (2004) said that bridging "is about coming together to argue, as much as to share" (p. 279).

In addition, Putnam et al. (2004) said the relationship developed in the process of social capital building "can be reused to resolve other local issues that were not even visible to the initial watershed activists" (p. 270). It was not because Penn State's publics were no longer supporting Penn State that they condemned how the university handled the crisis. They kept showing their support, which indicated that the established social capital was strong enough. This is an evidence of how public relations professionals' building social capital on behalf of their organizations would benefit the organizations in a crisis. However, it is also important for them to focus on bridging social capital to ensure civic morality of an organization when bonding social capital is already established.

This study is limited in that we only looked at newspaper articles from five newspapers for 1 year. In addition, because we only looked at what the media reported, the true rationales behind the approaches and actions that Penn State officials took could not be identified. It is also uncertain if any bonding activities led by Penn State officials happened behind the scenes and how Penn State's focus on the wider community and bridging social capital influenced publics around Penn State. More survey or focus group studies need to be conducted to gain more in-depth information behind this case. However, our findings still illustrate how social capital established by a university and its football team was utilized by and benefitted a community in a crisis. More research on social capital in crises should provide useful insights and direction for organizations.

References

Almedom, A. M. (2005). Social capital and mental health: An interdisciplinary review of primary evidence. *Social Science and Medicine, 61*, 943–964.

Anderson, N. (2013, July 17). Penn State cites post-scandal strides. *The Washington Post,* p. A09.

Armas, G. C. (2012, July 31). Amid roster questions, fans rally for PSU team. *Pittsburgh Post-Gazette,* p. A8.

Armas, G. C. (2013, July 24). NCAA seeks dismissal of Paterno family suit. *Pittsburgh Post-Gazette,* p. B2.

Ayios, A., Jeurissen, R., Manning, P., & Spence, L. J. (2014). Social capital: A review from an ethics perspective. *Business Ethics: A European Review, 23*(1), 108–134. doi:10.1111/beer.12040.

Benoit, W. L. (1995). *Accounts, excuses, and apologies: A theory of image restoration strategies.* Albany, NY: State University of New York.

Benoit, W. L. (1997). Image repair discourse and crisis communication. *Public Relations Review, 23*(2), 177–186.

Benoit, W. L. (2000). Another visit to the theory of image restoration strategies. *Communication Quarterly, 48*(1), 40–44.

Benoit, W. L., & Henson, J. R. (2009). President Bush's image repair discourse on Hurricane Katrina. *Public Relations Review, 35*, 40–46.

Berkowitz, S. (2012, July 25). Penn State's finances may be pinched. *USA Today,* p. 1C.

Bourdieu, P. (1985). The forms of capital. In J. G. Richardson (Ed.), *Handbook of theory and research for the sociology of education* (pp. 241–258). New York, NY: Greenwood.

Carpenter, D. (2011). Penn State scandal: Image damaged; what can university do? *Associated Press.* Retrieved from https://www.yahoo.com/news/penn-state-image-damaged-university-123109412.html.

Clopton, A. W., & Finch, B. L. (2010). College sport and social capital: Are students "bowling alone?" *Journal of Sport Behavior, 33*(4), 333–366.

Coleman, J. S. (1988). The creation and destruction of social capital: Implications for the law. *Notre Dame Journal of Law, Ethics, and Public Policy, 3*, 375–404.

Coombs, W. T. (1999). *Ongoing crisis communication: Planning, managing, and responding.* Thousand Oaks, CA: Sage.

Coombs, W. T. (2007). Protecting organizational reputations during a crisis: The development and application of situational crisis communication theory. *Corporate Reputation Review, 10*(3), 163–176.

Couloumbis, A. (2012, November 15). Pennsylvania auditor general recommends post-Sandusky changes at Penn State. *The Philadelphia Inquirer,* p. B01.

Dodd, M. D., Brummette, J., & Hazleton, V. (2015). A social capital approach: An examination of Putnam's civic engagement and public relations roles. *Public Relations Review, 41,* 472–479.

Drape, J. (2016, January 22). Some charges against former Penn State officials thrown out. *The New York Times.* Retrieved from http://www.nytimes.com/2016/01/23/sports/ncaafootball/some-charges-against-former-penn-state-officials-thrown-out.html?_r=0.

Enrollment sees slight increase. (2013). [Press release]. Retrieved from http://news.psu.edu/story/291612/2013/10/16/academics/enrollment-sees-slight-increase.

Feiden, D. (2013, February 11). Not our Joe Paterno family's experts rip "flawed" probe. *Daily News,* p. 3.

Fitzpatrick, F. (2012, August 3). Penn State loses another player. *The Philadelphia Inquirer,* p. 1.

Fitzpatrick, F., & Anastasia, P. (2012, August 2). Pollard leaving Penn State for Rutgers, Fortt headed to Cal. *The Philadelphia Inquirer,* p. D01.

George, R. (2012, August 10). Penn State works to move past Paterno era. *USA Today,* p. 1C.

Graff, C. (2012, July 28). Paterno statue carted off to undisclosed location. *The Philadelphia Inquirer,* p. D03.

Halpern, D. (2005). *Social capital.* Malden, MA: Polity.

Harris, J. C. (1998). Civil society, physical activity, and the involvement of sport sociologists in the preparation of physical activity professionals. *Sociology of Sport Journal, 15,* 138–153.

Heere, B., & James, J. D. (2007). Sports teams and their communities: Examining the influence of external group identities on team identity. *Journal of Sport Management, 21,* 319–337.

Heltzel, B. (2012, November 24). Child protection group calls for more advocacy centers; Task force formed in response to Sandusky child abuse scandal to releave recommendations. *Pittsburgh Post-Gazette,* p. B1.

Hickok, G. M. (2013, January 8). Gorbett's folly. *Pittsburgh Post-Gazette,* p. B6.

Horky, T. (2013). Uses of sport communication in groups. In P. Pedersen (Ed.), *Routledge handbook of sport communication* (pp. 378–387). London and New York: Routledge.

Imm, J. (2012, November 18). Shameful denial. *Pittsburgh Post-Gazette,* p. B2.

Infield, T. (2013, January 26). 200 flock to King of Prussia in support of Paterno. *The Philadelphia Inquirer,* p. B04.

Kaplan, E. (2012, November 11). Penn State, a year after sex-abuse scandal. *The Philadelphia Inquirer,* p. E01.

Keenan, W. R., & Hazleton, V. (2006). Internal public relations, social capital and the role of effective organizational communication. In C. H. Botan & V. Hazleton (Eds.), *Public Relations Theory II* (pp. 311–338). Mahwah, NJ: Erlbaum.

Kirby-Geddes, E., King, N., & Bravington, A. (2013). Social capital and community group participation: Examining "bridging" and "bonding" in the context of a healthy living centre in the UK. *Journal of Community and Applied Social Psychology, 23*, 271–285. doi:10.1002/casp.2118.

Letki, N. (2006). Investigating the roots of civic morality: Trust, social capital, and institutional performance. *Political Behavior, 28*(4), 305–325.

Lopresti, M. (2012, October 30). Anguish in State College; Year into scandal, residents reflect. *USA Today,* p. 3C.

Lowrey, W., Brozana, A., & Mackay, J. B. (2008). Toward a measure of community journalism. *Mass Communication and Society, 11*(3), 275–299. doi:10.1080/15205430701668105.

Luoma-aho, V. (2009). Bowling together—Applying Robert Putnam's theories of community and social capital to public relations. In O. Ihlen, B. Van Ruler, & M. Fredrikson (Eds.), *Public relations and social theory: Key figures and concepts* (pp. 231–251). New York, NY: Routledge.

Marklein, M. B., & Snyder, A. (2011, December 14). Will Penn State grads have trouble finding jobs? *USA Today.* Retrieved from http://usatoday30.usatoday.com/money/perfi/college/story/2011-12-14/penn-state-reputation/51929992/1.

Marying, P. (2004). Qualitative content analysis. In U. Flick, E. V. Kardorff, & I. Steinke (Eds.), *A companion to qualitative research* (pp. 265–269). London: Sage.

Meng, J., & Berger, B. K. (2008). Comprehensive dimensions of government intervention in crisis management: A qualitative content analysis of news coverage of the 2003 SARS epidemic in China. *China Media Research, 4*(1), 19–28.

Moran, R. (2012a, September 5). Penn State incurs $17 million in costs from Sandusky scandal. *The Philadelphia Inquirer,* p. B01.

Moran, R. (2012b, August 15). Penn State sets conference on child sex abuse. *The Philadelphia Inquirer,* p. 1.

Moran, R. (2013, September 25). Penn State to regain scholarships. *ESPN.* Retrieved from http://espn.go.com/college-football/story/_/id/9716482/ncaa-reduce-penalties-penn-state-regarding-jerry-sandusky-child-sexual-abuse-matter.

Moyer, J. (2013, September 25). Penn State to regaini scholarships. *ESPN.* Retrieved from http://espn.go.com/college-football/story/_/id/9716482/ncaa-reduce-penalties-penn-state-regarding-jerry-sandusky-child-sexual-abuse-matter.

Palmer, C., & Thompson, K. (2007). The paradoxes of football spectatorship: On-field and online expressions of social capital among the "Grog Squad." *Sociology of Sport Journal, 24*(2), 187–205.

Pastoriza, D., Ariño, M. A., & Ricart, J. E. (2008). Ethical managerial behaviour as an antecedent of organizational social capital. *Journal of Business Ethics, 78*, 329–341. doi:10.1007/s10551-006-9334-8.

Pearson, S. (2012, November 8). Ex-Penn State president charged. *The Gazette,* p. A19.

Portes, A. (1998). Social capital: Its origins and applications in modern sociology. *Annual Review of Sociology, 22*, 1–25.

Public Relations Society of America (PRSA). (n.d.). *Public Relations Society of America member code of ethics.* Retrieved from https://www.prsa.org/AboutPRSA/Ethics/CodeEnglish/index.html#.VkHf4LerS01.

Putnam, R. D. (1996). The strange disapperance of civic America. *The American Prospect, 7*(24), 34–48.

Putnam, R. D. (2000). *Bowling alone: The collapse and revival of American community.* New York, NY: Touchstone.

Putnam, R. D., Feldstein, L. M., & Cohen, D. (2004). *Better together: Restoring the American community.* New York, NY: Simon & Schuster.

Putnam, R. D., Leonardi, R., & Nanetti, R. Y. (1994). *Making democracy work: Civic traditions in modern Italy*. Princeton, NJ: Princeton University Press.

Reserve judgment on Paterno until trial of ex-PSU officials. (2012, September 5). *USA Today*, p. 8A.

Roebuck, J. (2012, August 26). Poll finds disapproval of PSU's handling of scandal. *The Philadelphia Inquirer*, p. A18.

Rovell, D. (2012). Penn State merchandise still selling. Retrieved from http://espn.go.com/college-football/story/_/id/8243778/penn-state-nittany-lions-royalty-merchandise-numbers-surprise.

Russo, R. D. (2012, July 28). Harris, other former players defend Joe Paterno in email. *Pittsburgh Post-Gazette*, p. A3.

Saffron, I. (2012, July 23). Philadelphians approve of removal of Paterno statue. *The Philadelphia Inquirer*, p. A09. http://www.post-gazette.com/news/education/2014/03/08/PSU-trustee-Clemens-regrets-firing-Paterno/stories/201403080085.

Schackner, B. (2012a, November 11). PSU alums push to "find the truth"; Franco Harris leads group of 140 in lambasting grand jury, trustees. *Pittsburgh Post-Gazette*, p. A17.

Schackner, B. (2012b, November 28). Spanier package nearly $3.3 million. *Pittsburgh Post-Gazette*, p. A5.

Schackner, B. (2013, March 12). Law firm letter to PSU trustees angers some alumni. *Pittsburgh Post-Gazette*, p. B1.

Schackner, B., & Tully, J. (2013, September 21). PSU trustees shore up athletic program; University struggles to move past Sandusky scandal. *Pittsburgh Post-Gazette*, p. B1.

Siemaszko, C. (2013, February 9). Good Ol' Joe Wife tries to save Paterno's kid-sex tainted image. *Daily News*, p. 8.

Smith, J. M., & Ingham, A. G. (2003). On the waterfront: Retrospectives on the relationship between sport and communities. *Sociology of Sport Journal, 20*(3), 252–274.

Snyder, S. (2013a, July 8). Penn State on track to meet fund-raising goal. *The Philadelphia Inquirer*, p. B01.

Snyder, S. (2013b, January 18). Penn State trustees consider changes in board voting procedures. *The Philadelphia Inquirer*, p. B02.

Snyder, S. (2013c, September 22). Reminders of the past at PSU board meeting. *The Philadelphia Inquirer*, p. 1.

Snyder, S., & Gammage, J. (2013, June 29). Three to vie for leadership post on Penn State board. *The Philadelphia Inquirer*, p. B01.

State to fight NCAA's Penn State sanctions. (2013, January 2). *The Washington Post*, p. A03.

Taylor, M., & Kent, M. L. (2014). Dialogic engagement: Clarifying foundational concepts. *Journal of Public Relations Research, 26*(5), 384–398. doi:10.1080/1062726X.2014.956106.

Toma, J. D. (2003). *Football U: Spectator sports in the life of the American university*. Ann Arbor, MI: University of Michigan Press.

Tonts, M. (2005). Competitive sport and social capital in rural Australia *Journal of Rural Studies, 21*(2), 137–149.

Trust around the world. (2015). Retrieved from http://www.edelman.com/insights/intellectual-property/2015-edelman-trust-barometer/trust-around-world/.

Tully, J. (2012a, August 13). Penn State's families stay loyal, in lockstep; nearly a third of incoming freshmen have a relative who previously attended university. *USA Today*, p. 3A.

Tully, J. (2012b, November 5). Students lead in scandal's wake; Real change, symbolic steps taken at Penn State. *USA Today,* p. 4C.

Wann, D. L., & Polk, J. (2007). The positive relationship between sport team identification and belief in the trustworthiness of others. *North American Journal of Psychology, 9,* 251–256.

Ward, P. R. (2013, July 12). Spanier to sue Freeh; Ex-PSU president says report slandered him. *Pittsburgh Post-Gazette,* p. B1.

Weiss, D. (2012, August 28). Sour Caroline misguided Penn St. cuts Diamond. *Daily News,* p. 51.

Wood, S. (2012, November 1). Penn State puts ex-president Spanier on leave. *The Philadelphia Inquirer,* p. 1.

Zhang, W., & Benoit, W. L. (2009). Former Minister Zhang's discourse on SARS: Government's image restoration or destruction? *Public Relations Review, 35,* 240–246. doi:10.1016/j.pubrev.2009.04.004.

3 Communicating Social Responsibility Efforts

A Success Strategy for Nonprofits or a Shift from Stakeholders' Priorities?

Richard D. Waters and Holly K. Ott

From direct mail to blog posts, website articles to Facebook posts, companies are utilizing a variety of channels to communicate about their corporate social responsibility (CSR) efforts. No longer deemed an optional initiative, CSR has become an expectation among organizational leaders and stakeholders. Furthermore, scholars and practitioners continue to seek best practices for effective CSR messaging, whether that includes a strategic approach or an "anything goes" approach to program and communication efforts (Bortree, 2014). An increasingly examined aspect of CSR communication is public perceptions of CSR. That is, how and via which channels can organizations ethically and effectively engage in CSR messaging? Furthermore, what does the public most value with regard to organizational efforts to exhibit civic professionalism and contribute to the public good? As outlined by Kelly (1998), stewardship outlines four dimensions that provide a framework for keeping organizations focused on developing sound relationships through civic professionalism and working toward a common good.

CSR is broadly defined as the voluntary actions a company implements to pursue goals, with a responsibility to its stakeholders (Chandler & Werther, 2014). Building on Carroll's (1991) definition that focuses on the legal, ethical, and discretionary aspects of socially responsible behaviors, modern definitions emphasize a concern for people, profit, and the environment, commonly known as the "triple bottom line" (Coombs & Holladay, 2012) and a focus on ethics, diversity, environmental sustainability, and philanthropy (Chandler & Werther, 2014). However, to date, CSR research has focused on the socially responsible practices and communication practices of companies in the for-profit realm (Rumsey & White, 2009). Therefore, little is known about the role of the nonprofit organization and the impact of CSR efforts in the nonprofit sector.

Research has frequently shown that CSR has positive impact on organizations' reputations and community relations efforts, but this research has primarily focused on for-profit entities. Recent research has shown that nonprofit organizations—even though they also engage in CSR efforts—are hesitant to publicize these efforts formally for fear that it draws attention away from their missions. Using in-depth interviews with nonprofit leaders,

Waters and Ott (2014) found that nonprofits downplay the CSR behaviors in which they are engaged, both in terms of message strategy and the media channels used to communicate their CSR behaviors. Results from the study indicated that nonprofits preferred to communicate about their CSR efforts using less formal media channels, unlike the formal communication channels preferred by for-profit counterparts. The researchers suggest that nonprofits are faced with the challenge of balancing "stakeholder expectations, socially responsible behaviors, and following the crowd with a mission-first orientation" (Waters & Ott, 2014, p. 15).

However, a notable limitation of this study is that it provides only a one-sided view of nonprofit CSR. While the views of the nonprofit communication staff are certainly important, they reiterated during their interviews that they were relying on their gut instincts rather than data to support their conclusions. The interview participants rejected the notion that nonprofit and for-profit organizations alike reap the potential benefits, including enhanced reputation (Yoon, Gurhan-Canli, & Schwarz, 2006), stronger relationships with publics (Hall, 2006), greater legitimacy or admiration of the organization (Bortree, 2009), a positive impact on the bottom line (Joyner & Payne, 2002), or an increased level of purchase intention (David, Kline, & Dai, 2009). However, the researchers stressed that the positive impact of CSR messaging could not be ignored by nonprofit organizations and that more research needed to be done to understand its impact on nonprofit stakeholders.

This study seeks to fill the gap in our understanding of CSR communication by examining how individuals perceive CSR by nonprofits. Specifically, this study uses an experimental design to present CSR messaging in five different communication channels to test how adult populations evaluate the CSR messages from nonprofits in terms of the source credibility and message believability. By examining the different presentations of the same CSR messages, the chapter answers the titular question of whether CSR messaging is a successful strategy for nonprofits or if it distracts from the nonprofits' core messaging around their missions, programs, and services. Specifically, it raises the question of how much nonprofits should inform stakeholders about their efforts to contribute to the public good and how different communication strategies impact public perception of nonprofits with regard to civic professionalism.

Literature Review

CSR as Stewardship

As public relations becomes more entrenched with relationship management with organizational stakeholders as its guiding theoretical foundation, the notion of relationship growth and cultivation becomes critical for organizational success. Following patterns derived for the study of the organization-public relationship, Ki and Hon (2008) first examined relationship cultivation strategies that were derived from interpersonal communication literature. The impacts of these strategies were found to be less influential in the nonprofit organization-donor relationship than stewardship strategies derived from practitioner behavior (Waters, 2010). Stewardship was first proposed by Kelly (2001) and focuses on four specific behaviors that underline the norms of a mutually beneficial relationship with an organization's stakeholders.

The four dimensions of stewardship are reciprocity, which centers on the recognition of stakeholders who choose to become involved with the organization and demonstrating gratitude toward them; responsibility, which has been summarized as keeping promises made with stakeholders; reporting, which argues that it is not enough for an organization just to keep its promises, but it has an obligation to keep stakeholders informed of those promise-keeping efforts; and relationship nurturing, which highlights efforts to make sure that stakeholders' concerns and connections to the organization's behaviors are taken into consideration before decisions are made. Though derived from different sources, these four dimensions have a strong connection to the practice of CSR.

CSR

Freitag (2008) argues that public relations practitioners might be best positioned to develop an organization's CSR policies because of their relationship focus. Specifically, he argues that the public relations practitioner is trained to move beyond the simple economic and legal responsibilities that organizations have to creating meaningful relationships with an organization's external stakeholders through civic and moral actions that strengthen the community rather than only advancing the organization's self-interests. Although management may not be required to factor in additional responsibilities, Klonoski (1991) outlined both sides of the CSR debate and concluded that organizations that strive to develop roots within a community are more likely to be held in high esteem and supported by the public. At the core of these community roots are the promises that were made when the organization first began its operations—secure employment for residents, safe working conditions, workplace diversity, safe products and services, and ultimately strong guidance by the management team. These promises help keep an organization accountable to its stakeholders and keep them focused on being good stewards with their community. Public relations practitioners serve as the moral conscience of the organization by ensuring external stakeholders' voices are heard and actively discussed during decision-making meetings.

As described by stewardship literature, the promises made by organizations should not only be kept but also reported back to the stakeholders to ensure that external audiences are informed about the organizational actions and not left wondering whether the organization followed through on its promises. To become a transparent and open organization, informational updates on CSR initiatives must be done in a timely manner so commitment to the public good does not come across as a contrived afterthought. Seele and Lock (2015) argue that an organization may be socially responsible, but if it is not communicating its efforts to its stakeholders then it is failing them. Indeed, research has found that organizations receive a reputational boost from their CSR updates whether they are a formal, quantitative report or less formal, qualitative updates on specific actions (Press & Arnould, 2014).

The final dimension of stewardship focuses on relationship nurturing. In discussing the *pyramid of CSR*, Carroll (1991) argues that an organization's management team must consider the entire impact an organization has on its operating environment. Meeting its legal and fiduciary responsibilities are expected, but going beyond that is what makes an organization a good corporate citizen. As the relationship nurturing dimension of stewardship prescribes, public relations practitioners must work to ensure that during management meetings and times of decision making, the stakeholders outside the organization's walls are actively discussed and considered prior to decisions being made and actions being taken. Public relations serves as the organization's conscience so that stakeholders are kept close to the forefront of the organizational mind so that they adhere to the higher levels of CSR behavior and focus on a mutually beneficial relationship rather than one-sided involvement with stakeholders (Clark, 2000). It is through serving in the role as the ethical conscience that public relations practitioners can enhance the relationship between organizations and their publics by "incorporating an aspect of ethical analysis and responsibility often lacking in organizational decision making" (Bowen, 2008, p. 291). Therefore, with regard to relationship nurturing, scholars suggest that an ethical conscience supporting a socially responsible organization engenders trust with key publics (Bowen, 2004), thus supporting an argument for higher levels of transparency and communication about socially responsible efforts to stakeholders.

CSR Communication

Frequent open and accurate communication is a key characteristic of stewardship, and public relations practitioners must develop an effective CSR communication strategy to be good stewards to all of the organization's stakeholders. It has long been known that a well-derived communication strategy is a vital part of the CSR process (Coombs & Holladay, 2012; Manheim & Pratt, 1986). Furthermore, knowing what and how to communicate to meet consumer-publics' expectations is a challenge that companies continue to face as they develop their CSR communication strategy (Kim & Ferguson, 2014).

Scholars have examined several aspects of CSR communication, including what and how to communicate (Kim & Ferguson, 2014), message strategies (Morsing, Schultz, & Nielsen, 2008) and message channels (Pomering &

Dolnicar, 2009; Schlegelmilch & Pollach, 2005), the role of internal and external stakeholders in the communication process (You, Huang, Wang, Liu, Lin, & Tseng, 2013), and the role of third-party endorsers (Pomering & Dolnicar, 2009). With specific regard to message content and channels, previous research has examined various options of company-controlled media channels (e.g., advertising, company website, or social media) and uncontrolled media channels, such as news coverage or expert blogs (Morsing & Schultz, 2006; Schlegelmilch & Pollach, 2005) and CSR messaging strategies (Waters & Ott, 2014).

Tonello (2011) provided a proposed framework of CSR communication in regard to message content (e.g., commitment to the cause, impact, or fit), message channel (formal and informal channels), and contingency factors (e.g., stakeholder characteristics and company characteristics) that impact desired CSR communication outcomes. In support of previous research, Tonello (2011) highlighted the positive outcomes that CSR communication had on audiences when the proposed framework was followed effectively.

However, Waters and Ott's (2014) study that consisted of in-depth interviews with strategic communicators in nonprofit organizations found that the nonprofits represented in the study were more concerned with negative outcomes than the positive outcomes proposed by Tonello (2011). That is, for example, participants indicated a concern that CSR efforts could risk the loss of donor and volunteer support, thus expressing a concern that formal CSR messaging detracts from their missions, programs, and services, which could be a turnoff to potential donor publics.

With regard to CSR message channels, Morsing and Schultz (2006) found support for implicit forms of CSR communication over explicit forms of communication. That is, indirect CSR communication was seen as more plausible than the presentation of more formal, objective data. However, a recent study by Kim and Ferguson (2014) found that more formal channels (websites, promotion events, company CSR designated websites, and annual reports) were among the most preferred media channels for CSR communication. Less formal media, including social media channels, were among the least preferred by consumer-publics. The study questioned future CSR communication research that suggested that more controlled communication channels have lower credibility ratings among consumer-publics (Schlegelmilch & Pollach, 2005). Kim and Ferguson (2014) suggest that less formal, "uncontrolled media channels may increase CSR communication's credibility, but publics may prefer more direct and interpersonal company-controlled communication channels" (p. 16). Given previous studies' different perspectives on the level of formality, it is necessary for the current study to begin by assessing how a nonprofit organization's CSR messaging impacts the organization by first asking:

RQ1: To what extent does the use of a CSR message strategy by a nonprofit impact its reputation?

Source Credibility

Public relations research on CSR has largely ignored examining whether these messages are credible and believable by their audiences. Source credibility is the "extent to which the source is perceived as possessing expertise relevant to the communication topic and can be trusted to give an objective opinion on the subject" (Goldsmith, Lafferty, & Newell, 2000, p. 43). Haigh and Brubaker (2010) argue, "when a source is perceived by the audience to be credible, that source is much more persuasive than a source seen as uncredible or one for which credibility is indeterminate at the outset" (p. 456).

Source has frequently been measured along two dimensions, the media channel used for distributing a message and the individuals who are interviewed or featured in the message. For both dimensions, Sundar (1999) concluded that the most credible channels and sources can be characterized by their objectivity and fairness. Turning to the media channel, the outlets that are most often viewed as credible have high levels of accuracy, trustworthiness, and completeness of information (Flanagin & Metzger, 2000).

Previous research on CSR credibility has suggested that third-party, or independent, resources are perceived as more credible than communication directly from the company (Morsing & Schultz, 2006; Schlegelmilch & Pollach, 2005). Furthermore, Chebat, Filiatrault, and Perrien (2001) argue that source credibility and perceptions of trustworthiness impact audience attitudes. Given previous research that proposes that nonprofit organizations are likely to be seen as moving away from their missions by using a CSR strategy, a second research question was created:

> RQ2: Does the public perceive CSR messages from nonprofits different in terms of credibility based on the media channel used to disseminate those messages?

Message Believability

Another concept that is frequently examined in relation to source credibility is message believability. Meyer (1988) provided a believability index that included the following items: fair-unfair, unbiased-biased, tells the whole story-doesn't tell the whole story, accurate-inaccurate, and can be trusted-can't be trusted. Whether CSR messaging is deemed believable by audiences has an impact on its overall effectiveness because of our cognitive and emotional responses to the messages (Dillard & Peck, 2001). After finding consistent results in 17 separate tests, perceived message believability predicted the actual effectiveness of a message (Dillard, Shen & Vail, 2007). Results from the study provide implications for message construction and evaluation techniques in the field, particularly for nonprofit organizations considering CSR. If the messages are perceived to be believable, then the nonprofit could reap benefits from the CSR strategy. Therefore, the researchers propose the third research question:

RQ3: Does the public perceive CSR messages from nonprofits different in terms of believability based on the media channel used to disseminate those messages?

Finally, as this study seeks to determine whether CSR messaging is a strategy that should be used by nonprofits, the final research question asks:

RQ4: Are there general trends in relation to the channels used for CSR messaging that could positively impact nonprofit organizations' use of this strategy?

Method

To answer the four research questions, the researchers designed a 2×5 experiment that was carried out at three Bay Area festivals (agricultural, arts/cultural, and sexual health). Festivals were chosen where nonprofits had an active role in education and awareness at the festival through having a booth or table present each day at the festival. Prior to the festivals, stimuli were created around hypothetical organizations relevant to the festivals that discussed the organizations' overall CSR efforts.

The messaging was created so that it addressed the organizations' commitment to environmental efforts, diversity, and being a community partner. This message was presented in five different formats. More formal channels represented a news story from an independent newspaper, a formal letter that was prepared by the organization (similar to an executive letter that would appear in an annual report), and a website article that was housed on the organizations' websites. Less formal media channels represented a blog entry and a Facebook post. Given the different formats, it is important to note the overall word count varied with each format. The formal channels used more words than the less formal channels: news story (805 words), formal letter (415 words), website article (376 words), blog entry (352 words), and Facebook post (124 words). Each message had the same picture to eliminate any differing influence of visual communication with the formats.

At each festival, a team of graduate students stopped attendees and asked if they would evaluate social responsibility messages about the topic of the festival. At each festival, 750 individuals were targeted and response rates varied (agricultural = 24%, $n = 180$; arts/cultural = 38%, $n = 285$; sexual health = 15%, $n = 113$). Across all three festivals, the response rate from approached individuals was 25.7%. Students were instructed to approach any individual who approached them, provided the tablet they were assigned to was not being currently used by another participant. Age was the only disqualifying factor as individuals under the age of 18 were not allowed to participate given the difficulty of tracking parental consent in the festival environment. Once recruited, individuals read two pieces of messaging that were randomly chosen from CSR messaging across the five media channels.

After reading each message, the festival attendees were asked to assess the messaging for its overall credibility, which was measured through existing scales for source credibility (Gaziano-McGrath, 1986; Meyer, 1988), and message believability, which was based on Dillard and Peck's (2001) scales. Although these two concepts are often associated with one another, it is important to note that the credibility scale focused on the source itself (e.g., media format), while the message believability dimension focused on the actual rhetoric and words used to describe the organizations' CSR messaging. Additionally, a brief scale on organizational reputation (Walsh & Beatty, 2007) captured whether the organizations benefited in terms of their perceived reputation with the public based on their CSR messaging. For all three scales, the experimental stimuli were evaluated on a 7-point scale where 1 represented strongly disagree and 7 represented strongly agree. Using Cronbach's alpha, the scales were deemed to be reliable for both credibility (α = .82) and message believability (α = .89).

Results

Of the 578 participants, 353 (61.1%) were female while 225 were men (38.9%). The average age of the participants was 38.4 years (sd = 8.73 years). The 578 participants were representative of the Bay Area in terms of racial/ethnic composition based on the most recent U.S. Census of the area. Slightly more than one-third of the participants self-identified as Caucasian (n = 204, 35.3%), and those identifying as Hispanic/Latino represented the next largest group at 27.9% (n = 161). Asian/Pacific-Islanders (n = 108, 18.7%), African American/Blacks (n = 57, 9.9%), Middle Easterners (n = 15, 2.6%), and Native Americans (n = 11, 1.9%) also participated in the experiment. "Other" was chosen by 22 participants (3.8%). Note that the total does not equal 100% due to rounding.

Turning to the experimental measures and manipulated variables, no significant differences existed in the pooled samples from the three festivals for organizational reputation (F(2, 575) = 1.19, p = .303), source credibility (F(2, 575) = 2.12, p = .121), and message believability (F(2, 575) = 1.10, p = .334).

Table 3.1 presents the overall statistical summary for the study's three research questions as well as the individual cell count for each stimuli item across the three scales evaluating the messages. The study's first research question sought to determine whether the nonprofits received any reputational benefit from their CSR messaging. Overall, the nonprofits were perceived to have a positive reputation based on their CSR messaging (m = 4.38, sd = 1.09) given that the average was above the neutral point on the 7-point scale. Looking at specific media channels, the Facebook post and blog entry were found to have the biggest impact on the organization's reputation while focusing on CSR messaging in an executive letter one might find in an annual report negatively impacted the nonprofit's reputation. These differences were statistically significant based on a one-way analysis of variance (ANOVA) using a Tukey HSD post-hoc test to determine

Table 3.1 Summary Statistics for CSR Experiment

	Independent News Story	Executive Letter	Website Article	Blog Entry	Facebook Post
RQ1: Reputation					
Nonprofit Organization CSR Message	4.09 (1.11) *n* = 56	2.26 (1.14) *n* = 61	4.72 (1.63) *n* = 55	5.35 (1.08) *n* = 57	5.63 (1.35) *N* = 58
RQ2: Source Credibility					
Nonprofit Organization CSR Message	5.87 (1.05) *n* = 62	4.85 (1.43) *n* = 65	4.03 (0.96) *n* = 57	4.35 (1.38) *n* = 61	4.18 (1.52) *n* = 60
RQ3: Message Believability					
Nonprofit Organization CSR Message	6.02 (0.78) *n* = 66	4.39 (1.05) *n* = 47	4.17 (1.39) *n* = 59	5.34 (1.02) *n* = 56	4.34 (1.21) *n* = 61

Note: The results of this study are part of a larger study that compared the reputational impact, credibility, and believability of CSR messaging between nonprofits and for-profit organizations. Due to the authors' excision of the nonprofit data from the larger study, the sample size for each research question does not equal the total of the 578 participants in the study.

between group differences ($F(4, 282) = 66.05$, $p < .001$), which was based on the high reputational attributes associated with the blog entry and Facebook post as well as the low average received by the executive letter.

The study's second question sought to determine whether there was a difference in terms of source credibility for the CSR messaging based on the media channel. Again, overall the different media channels were deemed to be credible for nonprofit organizations ($m = 4.66$, sd = 1.27).

In terms of overall source credibility, the independent news story was by far the most credible outlet for CSR messaging ($m = 5.87$, sd = 1.05) and was followed by the executive letter ($m = 4.85$, sd = 1.43) and the blog entry ($m = 4.35$, sd = 1.38). The Facebook post ($m = 4.18$, sd = 1.52) and website article ($m = 4.03$, sd = 0.96) were slightly above the neutral points on the scale. A one-way ANOVA revealed that these differences were statistically different ($F(4, 300) = 20.29$, $p < .001$). The Tukey HSD post-hoc test revealed that these differences were primarily due to the strong credibility perceived for the independent news story and the executive letter.

The third research question sought to determine how the CSR messaging was evaluated in terms of its message believability. The overall believability of the CSR messages was positive for nonprofit organizations ($m = 4.85$, sd = 1.09). Similar to source credibility, the CSR messaging was most believable when presented by an independent news story ($m = 6.02$, sd = 0.92).

The blog entry was the next most believable message (m = 5.1, sd = 1.21), followed by the executive letter (m = 4.96, sd = 1.17), the Facebook post (m = 4.18, sd = 1.23), and the website article (m = 4.10, sd = 1.28). These differences were also statistically significant based on a one-way ANOVA test (F(4, 284) = 31.97, p < .001). The Tukey HSD post-hoc test revealed that these differences were significant due to the high evaluations of the independent news story and blog entry.

The fourth research question asked whether there were overall trends that could be identified from the experimental data and findings. First, it is evident that a nonprofit organization's reputation is enhanced when they engage in CSR messaging. The one caveat to that trend is that some message formats are more helpful than others as the nonprofit organization executive letter had a negative mean score based on the 7-point scale. That being said, the executive letters were perceived to be credible and believable. One of the most noticeable trends that was observed was that traditional media (e.g., non-web communications) was perceived to be a more credible source and had more believable messaging than web content presented in either Web 1.0 or Web 2.0 formats.

Specifically examining web content, there are mixed results in terms of what works best with CSR messaging. In terms of reputation, nonprofit organizations benefited from Web 2.0 tactics, blog entry, and Facebook posts. However, when turning to both credibility and believability, blog entries outperformed the other web tactics for both types of organizations. Facebook performed slightly better than the website article for message believability.

Discussion

This study attempted to provide some understanding of how nonprofits can use CSR messaging strategically to benefit them the most. Despite results from interviews with nonprofit communicators that expressed concern over implementing messages that might distract from their core mission and programs (Waters & Ott, 2014), the results of this study indicate that nonprofits should embrace CSR messaging though perhaps not across all media channels. Through the use of a controlled experiment, this study found that there were specific differences in how the public perceived CSR messaging for nonprofit organizations in terms of their believability and credibility based on different outlets. Additionally, the study found that CSR communication tends to have a more positive impact on the reputation of nonprofits.

Reputational Benefits

The notion that CSR efforts have positive impacts on how the public perceives an organization has found wide support in the private, for-profit sector (Bortree, 2009). In this study, CSR messaging was found to be evaluated favorably by those participating in the experiment for all media channels except for the formal, organizational letter written by the executive director. The findings indicate that nonprofits gained the biggest reputational boost based on less formal methods of CSR messaging, such as the Facebook post and the blog entry. If a nonprofit was going to engage in CSR, interview participants in Waters and Ott's (2014) study said that it would really need to be done in an informal manner so that these efforts were not seen as taking time and resources away from their missions and programs.

The results of the experiment echo the concerns of the nonprofit communicators. The more formal methods of communication (e.g., the independent news story, the executive letter, and the website article) were all found to have less of an impact on the nonprofits' reputation as the messaging posted to social media applications. The less formal blog and Facebook post had a significantly higher impact on the nonprofits' reputation. This reputational boost seems to be reflected in the findings as informal conversations about environmental efforts, commitments to diversity, and being a good community citizen were perceived to be more helpful to their reputation than when the same topics were presented in more formal publications. The findings support arguments for public relations practitioners to serve as the ethical conscience of an organization and for the need to employ two-way communication, as suggested by systems theory and excellence theory, to be viewed as ethical, socially responsible organizations among stakeholders. That is, a possible explanation for the reputational boost that is reflected more in the informal channels than the formal channels is that such channels allow for two-way dialogue, which scholars argue is more conducive to creating mutually beneficial relationships between an organization and its publics (Bowen, 2008).

Stewardship advocates would argue that for a nonprofit's stakeholders to become truly informed about the organization and its work, then the nonprofit public relations practitioner needs to inform them about the full range of activities at the nonprofit, including CSR initiatives. Fortunately, the experimental results provide a path for doing so. Rather than spending time and resources to develop formal reports, informal, prompt updates on Facebook about nonprofits' efforts should be made because it helps meet the responsibility and reporting requirements of stewardship. While they demonstrate the organizations' accountability to their stakeholders, social media updates also advance the overall social good in the organization-public relationship as the external stakeholders are kept informed about organizational behaviors. They were also viewed more favorably for the nonprofits.

Source Credibility

Public relations scholars have long advocated for its practitioners to push for programming and communication that enhance an organization's reputation but not at the sacrifice of a lasting relationship with their stakeholders (Ledingham, 2003). Through transparency and openness, stewardship also supports the notion of deeper relationship development with stakeholders so that they are more confident in the truthfulness of organizational messaging regardless of the medium. Furthermore, when organizations are viewed as ethical contributors to the public good, public perception is likely more favorable because of their efforts to report their socially responsible initiatives to key publics. White and Raman (1999) speculated that the Internet would bring credibility concerns for organizations, and the results of the current study appear to validate this thought. When looking at the source credibility measures, traditional media channels, such as the independent news story and the executive letter, were viewed more credibly by the experimental subjects than all forms of web communication. Callison (2001) noted that the public might have a negative view toward public relations materials, which can explain why the stimuli that was authored by an external journalist was evaluated more favorably than the four stimuli that were written by an organizational representative.

However, it is important to note that the executive letter outperformed the web content as well. The value placed on the executive letter by the participants in the experiment is significant because it runs counter to current literature that argues that interactive formats, such as the blog entry or Facebook post, should be favored because of the open dialogue opportunities that exist (Dozier, L. A. Grunig, & J. E. Grunig, 2013). This finding is supported by research from Waldman, Siegel, and Javidan (2006) who found that not only does addressing CSR programs by an organization's CEO or executive director instill more confidence in the organization's commitment to the social good, but it also encourages stakeholders to become more involved with the organization.

In public relations scholarship, there is a litany of research highlighting the continued megaphone approach to organizational messaging in the social web across Facebook, Twitter, YouTube, and other platforms. One explanation for the less credible evaluation of CSR messaging presented in blogs and on Facebook may stem from research indicating that the social web was created for and is used mostly for social interaction between friends, family members, and coworkers. As Vorvoreanu (2009) found, individuals did not want to connect to organizations on Facebook. Attempts at conveying CSR messaging on Facebook may be perceived as promotions or attempts at pandering to an audience that does not want to see the message in this environment. Therefore, an organization's credibility may be called into question, as stakeholders may perceive the organization's efforts as self-promoting and less than altruistic.

Another possible explanation for the lack of credibility can also be connected to the social web megaphone that many organizations use. By using Facebook, blogs, and other social platforms in a one-way manner, organizations rarely interact with their stakeholders when they comment on posts or share them with others. The relationship nurturing dimension of stewardship promotes organizations demonstrating that they are thinking about their stakeholders' concerns and questions by the use of a two-way symmetrical model (Bowen, 2008); ignoring their questions and posts on social media certainly is the opposite of nurturing the relationship. It is possible that the lack of credibility due to the placement of CSR on the web might be attributed to the stakeholders' expectation that the organization's messaging would not be addressed if it were questioned or challenged by outsiders. Whereas the independent news story would be vetted by an objective journalist and the executive director letter was formalized into organizational messaging, casual updates on Web 2.0 platforms might not have the lasting impact as more formal messages. Therefore, it may be easier to dismiss their credibility.

Message Believability

Given the overall high performance of the news story, it is not surprising that the externally authored news story also had the highest level of believability. It has been well-documented that organizational messages built into news stories are perceived to have higher believability because of the supposed research that went into developing the news story by the objective journalist (Cameron, Sallot, & Curtin, 1997). The perceived third-party endorsement of the organization's CSR messaging may have impacted the stronger perception of believability of the news story, but the organizations also had success with other organization-authored channels.

With the organization-authored website story and letter, the organizations can take control of their messaging to tell their CSR story. They are able to use the power of narrative story-telling to convey the impact of their CSR efforts. However, the presentation of these efforts may result in mixed evaluations. While the letter was perceived to be third most believable message, the website article was last though it was still favorable. In the study, the executive letter highlighted the nonprofit's CSR efforts but it also talked about other organizational successes, such as programmatic, volunteer management, and fundraising. The website story focused exclusively on the CSR efforts. Perhaps the believability of the letter was enhanced because it placed these efforts contextually against the primarily focus of the nonprofit, whereas the website story may have been seen as giving the CSR efforts a higher priority within the overall management of the organization than the stakeholders thought it deserved.

The interactive Web 2.0 format was thought to be more believable by the experimental subjects than the static website story. This finding may have been hinted at in the interviews that Waters and Ott (2014) summarized. Nonprofit communicators felt that informal discussions about CSR would be best for their organizations. With the blog, the nonprofit organizations are able to put together their CSR story in a manner that is not formally introduced in an annual report, a white paper, or other official organizational publication that might include the executive letter.

The blog allows the organization to highlight its efforts and answer individuals' questions and reactions to the topic in a casual manner. Butcher (2009) notes that nonprofits are more experimental with social media and have used these channels more than for-profit and government agencies. She speculates that the adoptions of Web 2.0 technologies by social media organizations rest in their need for support by a variety of stakeholders to not only fund their programs and services but also to deliver them. Blogging allows the nonprofit to connect with supporters to have conversations about items that ultimately impact the organization's behaviors without the need to formally become a critical component of the organization (Miller-Stevens & Gable, 2013). This can help explain why the blog messaging was more believable for the nonprofits because the subjects may have been anticipating their ability to reach out and discuss CSR messaging with the nonprofits.

Conclusion

CSR has long been studied by scholars and has been touted as a strategic endeavor by organizations that can help secure long-term support from stakeholders. It has become an expectation among corporate leaders based on research demonstrating positive attitudinal and behavioral outcomes for organizations that promote their CSR work. This study found that nonprofit organizations should embrace CSR, but should be strategic in how they choose to communicate their socially responsible behaviors. Nonprofits should consider not only the type of communication and the message channels they use to disseminate information but also how different strategies impact the relationship between organizations and key stakeholders. Building and nurturing relationships impacts an organization's credibility, believability, and ultimately the degree to which public perceive its efforts to exhibit civic professionalism. Traditional media tended to be perceived more credibly and had more believable messages than those disseminated over the Internet; however, traditional media messages focused on CSR did not have as strong of an impact on the nonprofit organization's reputation.

The five experimental stimuli all used the same language to describe the CSR efforts of the hypothetical nonprofit organizations the participants examined. The formats differed, but the messages were largely the same and included the same visuals. Even though we are in an age where virtual communication is pervasive and organizations are encouraged to embrace social media, overall web content did not perform as well as the newspaper story authored by an external journalist in terms of credibility and believability. Social media efforts were valued by nonprofit stakeholders, but so were more traditional forms of communication in varying amounts. Nonprofit organizations should embrace CSR communication.

While the reservations of those interviewed in Waters and Ott's (2014) study may impact stakeholders to some extent, the stewardship opportunities that exist in CSR communication outweigh the risks as evidenced by the results of this research. Being able to say thank you and publicly recognize those supportive publics in an organization's community will lead to more lasting relationships with stakeholders and a more welcoming attitude toward the organization by the community (Leeper, 1996). Thanking stakeholders for their involvement is one of the most important actions that an organization can use to demonstrate its focus is not organization-centric; instead it is one that recognizes the organization has a commitment to those who directly engage with the organization as well as the greater public good. Keeping the promises made to stakeholders during the good and bad organizational times and reporting back to the community regularly and openly about the organization's operations will result in supportive behaviors from the public (Kim & Reber, 2008). These efforts to inform stakeholders about organizational initiatives and actions reiterate the value placed on accountability and transparency, two characteristics of moral organizational behavior supporting a common good. Finally, the practice of public relations and CSR cannot exist under the relationship management paradigm without keeping stakeholders close to the organization's mind. Public relations practitioners act as the moral conscience of the organization by expressing the concerns, needs, and wants of external stakeholders during internal deliberations so that decisions and actions are made after careful consideration of external stakeholder relationships and the desire of the organization to remain a good community citizen (Kelly, 2001).

Limitations

Though this study was carried out using a controlled experimental design, it is important to note that there are limitations that should be acknowledged when interpreting the results of the study. First, the study examined organizations in the context of festivals representing the arts and humanities, sexual health, and agriculture subsectors. Ultimately, this represents only a small portion of industries represented in the nonprofit sector. Nonetheless, the results demonstrate consistencies across these three very different sectors. Additionally, this study ultimately only examined five media types. The media spectrum is vastly more complex than simply looking at an independent news story, a business letter, a website article, a blog entry, and a Facebook post. The study does not look at audio or video, which certainly have a strong hold over audiences in both the traditional media (e.g., television and radio) and Internet (e.g., viral videos). Additional research should be conducted to confirm whether the medium is the message or whether CSR messaging really trumps the delivery channel.

Future Research

Most CSR research tends to focus on the overall impact of the programming by organizations rather than the actual communication and messaging of the efforts. This study helps bring new light into CSR communication practices, and as such hopefully brings about new streams of research by the CSR community. It would be helpful to move the experiment to the "real world" to determine whether the perceived credibility and believability of the messaging actually result in tangible benefits to the organizations, such as increased sales, donations, or greater engagement on social media platforms. It would also be beneficial to determine whether the incorporation of stewardship strategies to demonstrate CSR practices results in greater perceptions of an organization's commitment to social good and civic professionalism; with that evidence, research on public relations strategy could determine how different message frames emphasizing an organization's moral responsibility result with increased public engagement. Ultimately, for nonprofit organizations, this study highlights that there may be some advantages for nonprofit organizations that decide to pursue CSR messaging. Perhaps the results from the 2014 study come from a few loud voices among these organizations' supporters and do not reflect the overall attitudes toward the nonprofits socially responsible, non-mission-specific endeavors. Future research can clarify this picture and hopefully strengthen the support for the adoption of a CSR strategy by the nonprofit sector.

Acknowledgments

The authors wish to thank the Arthur W. Page Center for Integrity in Public Communication for their sponsorship of this research as part of the 2012–2013 Legacy Scholars Program.

References

Bortree, D. S. (2009). The impact of green initiatives on environmental legitimacy and admiration of the organization. *Public Relations Review, 35*(2), 133–135.

Bortree, D. S. (2014). The state of CSR communication research: A summary and future direction. *Public Relations Journal, 8*(3).

Bowen, S. A. (2004). Organizational factors encouraging ethical decision making: An exploration into the case of an exemplar. *Journal of Business Ethics, 52,* 311–324.

Bowen, S. A. (2008). A state of neglect: Public relations as "corporate conscience" or ethics counsel. *Journal of Public Relations Research*, *20*(3), 271–296.

Butcher, L. (2009). Nonprofit organizations outpace businesses in use of social media. *Oncology Times, 31*(21), 39–40.

Callison, C. (2001). Do PR practitioners have a PR problem? The effect of associating a source with public relations and client-negative news on audience perception of credibility. *Journal of Public Relations Research, 13*(3), 219–234.

Cameron, G. T., Sallot, L. M., & Curtin, P. A. (1997). Public relations and the production of news: A critical review and a theoretical framework. *Communication Yearbook, 20,* 111–155.

Carroll, A. B. (1991). The pyramid of corporate social responsibility: Toward the moral management of organizational stakeholders. *Business Horizons* (July/ August), 39–44.

Chandler, D., & Werther Jr., W. (2014). *Strategic corporate responsibility: Stakeholders, globalization, and sustainable value creation.* Los Angeles, CA: SAGE Publications.

Chebat, J. C., Filiatrault, P., & Perrien, J. (2001). Limits of credibility: The case of political persuasion. *Journal of Social Psychology, 130*(2), 157–167.

Clark, C. E. (2000). Differences between public relations and corporate social responsibility: An analysis. *Public Relations Review, 26*(3), 363–380.

Coombs, W. T., & Holladay, S. J. (2012). *Managing corporate social responsibility: A communication approach.* Chichester, UK: Wiley-Blackwell.

David, P., Kline, S., & Dai, Y. (2009). Corporate social responsibility practices, corporate identity, and purchase intention: A dual-process model. *Journal of Public Relations Research, 17*(3), 291–313.

Dillard, J. P., & Peck, E. (2001). Persuasion and the structure of affect: Dual systems and discrete emotions as complementary models. *Human Communication Research, 27*(1), 38–68.

Dillard, J. P., Shen, L., & Vail, R. G. (2007). Does perceived message effectiveness cause persuasion or vice versa? 17 consistent answers. *Human Communication Research, 33*(4), 467–488.

Dozier, D. M., Grunig, L. A., & Grunig, J. E. (2013). *Manager's guide to excellence in public relations and communication management.* New York, NY: Routledge.

Flanagin, A. J., & Metzger, M. J. (2001). Internet use in the contemporary media environment. *Human Communication Research, 27*(1), 153–181.

Freitag, A. (2008). Staking claim: Public relations leaders needed to shape CSR policy. *Public Relations Quarterly, 52*(1), 37–40.

Gaziano, C., & McGrath, K. (1986). Measuring the concept of credibility. *Journalism Quarterly, 63*(Autumn), 451–462.

Goldsmith, R. E., Lafferty, B. A., & Newell, S. J. (2000). The impact of corporate credibility and celebrity credibility on consumer reaction to advertisements and brands. *Journal of Advertising, 29*(3), 43–54.

Haigh, M. M., & Brubaker, P. (2010). Examining how image restoration strategy impacts perceptions of corporate social responsibility, organization-public relationships, and source credibility. *Corporate Communications, 15*(4), 432–468.

Hall, M. R. (2006). Corporate philanthropy and corporate community relations: Measuring relationship-building results. *Journal of Public Relations Research, 18*(1), 1–21.

Joyner, B., & Payne, D. (2002). Evolution and implementation: A study of values, business ethics and corporate social responsibility. *Journal of Business Ethics, 41*(4), 297–311.

Kelly, K. S. (1998). *Effective fund-raising management.* Mahwah, NJ: Lawrence Erlbaum.

Kelly, K. S. (2001). Stewardship: The missing step in the public relations process. In R. L. Heath (Ed.), *Handbook of public relations* (pp. 279–290). Thousand Oaks, CA: Sage.

Ki, E.-J., & Hon, L. C. (2008). A measure of relationship cultivation strategies. *Journal of Public Relations Research, 21*(1), 1–24.

Kim, S., & Ferguson, M. T. (2014). Public expectations of CSR communication: What and how to communicate CSR. *Public Relations Journal, 8*(3), 1–22.

Kim, S.-Y., & Reber, B. H. (2008). Public relations' place in corporate social responsibility: Practitioners define their roles. *Public Relations Review, 34*(4), 337–342.

Klonoski, R. J. (1991). Foundational considerations in the corporate social responsibility debate. *Business Horizons* (July–August), 9–18.

Ledingham, J. A. (2003). Explicating relationship management as a general theory of public relations. *Journal of Public Relations Research, 15*(2), 181–198.

Leeper, K. A. (1996). Public relations ethics and communitarianism: A preliminary investigation. *Public Relations Review, 22*(2), 163–179.

Manheim, J. B., & Pratt, C. B. (1986). Communicating corporate social responsibility. *Public Relations Review, 12*(2), 9.

Meyer, P. (1988). Defining and measuring credibility of newspapers: Developing an index. *Journalism and Mass Communication Quarterly, 65*(3), 567–574.

Miller-Stevens, K., & Gable, M. J. (2013). Lobbying in the virtual world: Perceptions in the nonprofit sector. *Nonprofit Policy Forum, 4*(1), 47–63.

Morsing, M., & Schultz, M. (2006). Corporate social responsibility communication: Stakeholder information, response and involvement strategies. *Business Ethics: A European Review, 15*(4), 323–338. doi:10.1111/j.1467-8608.2006.00460.x.

Morsing, M., Schultz, M., & Nielsen, K. U. (2008). The "Catch 22" of communicating CSR: Findings from a Danish Study. *Journal of Marketing Communications, 14*(2), 97–111.

Pomering, A., & Dolnicar, S. (2009). Assessing the prerequisite of successful CSR implementation: Are consumers aware of CSR initiatives? *Journal of Business Ethics, 85,* 285–301.

Press, M., & Arnould, E. J. (2014). Narrative transparency. *Journal of Marketing Management, 30*(13–14), 1353–1376.

Rumsey, G. G., & White, C. (2009). Strategic corporate philanthropic relationships: Nonprofits' perceptions of benefits and corporate motives. *Public Relations Review, 35*(3), 301–303. doi:10.1016/j.pubrev.2009.05.005.

Schlegelmilch, B. B., & Pollach, I. (2005). The perils and opportunities of communicating corporate ethics, *Journal of Marketing Management, 21,* 267–290.

Seele, P., & Lock, I. (2015). Instrumental and/or deliberative? A typology of CSR communication tools. *Journal of Business Ethics, 131*(2), 401–414.

Seitanidi, M. M., & Crane, A. (2008). Implementing CSR through partnerships: Understanding the selection, design, and institutionalisation of nonprofit-business partnerships. *Journal of Business Ethics, 85*(2), 413–429.

Sundar, S. S. (1999). Exploring receivers' criteria for perception of print and online news. *Journalism and Mass Communication Quarterly, 76*(2), 373–386.

Tonello, M. (2011, April 26). What board members should know about communicating corporate social responsibility. Retrieved from http://blogs.law.harvard.edu/corpgov/2011/04/26/what-board-members-should-know-about-communicating-corporate-social-responsibility/.

Vorvoreanu, M. (2009). Perceptions of corporations on Facebook: An analysis of Facebook social norms. *Journal of New Communication Research, 4*(1), 67–86.

Waldman, D. A., Siegel, D. S., & Javidan, M. (2006). Components of transformational leadership and corporate social responsibility. *Journal of Management Studies, 43*(8), 1703–1725.

Walsh, G., & Beatty, S. E. (2007). Customer-based corporate reputation of a service firm: Scale development and validation. *Journal of the Academy of Marketing Science, 35*(1), 127–143.

Waters, R. D. (2010). Increasing fundraising efficiency through evaluation: Applying communication theory to the nonprofit organization-donor relationship. *Nonprofit and Voluntary Sector Quarterly, 40*(3), 458–475.

Waters, R. D., & Ott, H. K. (2014). Corporate social responsibility and the nonprofit sector: Assessing the thoughts and practices across three nonprofit subsectors. *Public Relations Journal, 8*(3), 1–18.

White, C., & Raman, N. (1999). The world wide web as a public relations medium: The use of research, planning, and evaluation in web site development. *Public Relations Review, 25*(4), 405–419.

Yoon, Y., Gurhan-Canli, Z., & Schwarz, N. (2006). The effect of corporate social responsibility (CSR) activities on companies with bad reputations. *Journal of Consumer Psychology, 16*(4), 377–390.

You, C., Huang, C., Wang, H., Liu, K., Lin, C., & Tseng, J. (2013). The relationship between corporate social responsibility, job satisfaction and organizational commitment. *International Journal of Organizational Innovation, 5*(4), 65–77.

4 A Rising Tide Lifts All Boats? The Constitutive Reality of CSR in Public Relations

Ashli Q. Stokes

If stakeholder dialogue, integrity, and transparency are key components in being considered an ethically sound company (Ulrich, 2008), 2014 was a tough year for Duke Energy, the nation's largest utility. In February, coal ash, the toxic waste produced from burning coal in power plants to produce electricity, spilled from a retired power plant into the Dan River in Eden, North Carolina. The third largest spill in U.S. history, more than 30,000 tons of coal ash and up to 27 million gallons of contaminated water dumped into the Dan, coating 70 miles of the river with waste filled with chemicals, including arsenic, lead, and mercury (Chapel Hill Herald, 2014; Tomsic, 2015). Duke Energy waited a day to tell people about the spill, downplayed the damage, and took 6 days to seal off the leaking pipe. Ten days after the spill the state issued two health advisories warning residents to avoid direct contact with the water and from eating its fish (Chapel Hill Herald, 2014; Starnes, 2014). More than a dozen community and environmental groups rallied against the company, and by March, the U.S. government launched a criminal investigation. Meanwhile, as Duke Energy's CEO Lynn Good was receiving a "Businesswoman of the Year" award, the Associated Press reported that Duke Energy lobbyists pushed the state's legislature to shield the corporation from coal ash cleanup. Nevertheless, North Carolina, led by Governor Pat McCrory, crafted legislation that set a 15-year timeline for Duke Energy to close its 32 ash ponds and named a new commission to analyze its hazard rankings (Wilmington Star-News, 2014). In August, the state legislature passed a bill requiring it, with critics complaining that state officials worked with the former 29-year Duke employee and shareholder McCrory to fine Duke a paltry $99,111 (Chapel Hill Herald, 2014). The Department of Environment and National Resources continued to move to fine Duke Energy $25 million for groundwater pollution (Fayetteville Observer, 2014), a historic amount. Despite ongoing backlash against the company, by September, Duke Energy was named to the Dow Jones Sustainability North America Index for the ninth consecutive year. Still, by spring 2015, it pleaded guilty to violations of the Clean Water Act and agreed to pay penalties of $102 million in a federal settlement (Dalesio, 2015). Throughout the crisis, some applauded Duke Energy's sense of responsibility surrounding the spill, noting that it did not try to "pass the buck," but other observers complained, calling Duke Energy a "bully" that relied on special interests and attempted to have consumers, and shareholders, cover the costs of the spill (Stahl, 2014; Starnes, 2014). As 2014 came to a close, criticism stemming from the incident continued, and as one reporter groused, "Let's face it, Duke Energy could use a public relations makeover about now" (Wilmington Star-News, 2014, p. 10).

To write about Duke Energy's corporate social responsibility (CSR) efforts in light of this public relations controversy may seem to be somewhat of an oxymoron (Cloud, 2007), but the "Duke Energy case" provides a clear example of the challenges that make executing successful CSR programs difficult. That is, by its very nature as an electricity manufacturer, Duke Energy has a tall order in developing its CSR program. Unlike choosing where to eat, selecting an insurance provider, or deciding which car to purchase, many consumers in North Carolina must turn to Duke Energy if they want to power their energy needs through traditional methods. Indeed, the expectation for ethical and moral behavior is heightened when people have little choice of providers in an industry that may contribute to air and water pollution, environmental spills, injuries, and death. As Spence (2011) argues, people demand CSR from energy companies perhaps more than any other industry, and they bear the difficult burden of proving their actions will not cause harm. This chapter assesses Duke Energy's efforts to respond to the coal ash issue to illustrate how designing strategically effective but also socially responsible messages presents a difficult challenge for such industries. Duke Energy's efforts stand as an example of the generative, but difficult, nature of CSR as a practical and academic concept. Companies in certain sectors must make a "tighter fit" between the values they profess and the practices in which they engage if they want to implement a successful CSR program. Corporations simultaneously shape public expectations about the practice of CSR even as they communicate their CSR goals, and for certain companies, communicating broad CSR initiatives may invite skepticism and public distrust due to the nature of business.

To explain why CSR continues to be particularly challenging for certain industries, the chapter first briefly outlines the relationship between public relations and CSR. Several scholars (Coombs & Holladay, 2007; Freitag, 2008; Wilde, 2012) argue that public relations should lead the CSR effort, due to its focus on establishing relationships and establishing goodwill, rather than marketing products and services. Spangler and Pompper (2011) point out that ideally, PR links top management with constituents, such that practitioners help align interests of the organization with those of stakeholders. When viewing CSR through a constitutive lens, we see how public relations does indeed have the opportunity to serve this important ethical role in organizational life. I draw specifically on constitutive rhetorical scholarship (Stokes, 2013) to show why designing strategically effective but also socially responsible messages presents a difficult challenge for certain industries such as energy. After briefly describing a rhetorical methodology, I analyze one example of Duke Energy's CSR messaging to explain how its professed values and its actions do not align. I use this example to argue that constitutive rhetorical approaches help point out the gaps between CSR practice and potential.

CSR, Public Relations, and the Need for Constitutive Approaches

CSR study involves several disciplines, including business, organizational communication and management, marketing, corporate communication, and public relations; as a result, defining CSR is "like trying to map sand dunes in a desert" (Coombs & Holladay, 2012, p. 81). It is possible, however, to trace generally the outlines of the concept. One of the field's pioneers, Carroll (1979, 1991, 1999) argues that CSR encompasses the economic, legal, ethical, and discretionary expectations that society has of organizations. It is both a philosophy and process that concerns the role of business in society, but it stresses the idea that businesses "use their expertise and other resources to improve society" (Coombs & Holladay, 2012, p. 81). From a CSR standpoint, corporations change their behavior not because they are required to legally but because they seek to meet societal standards for public behavior; still, the "allure of profit" sometimes causes corporations to act in an irresponsible or even inhumane manner (Coombs & Holladay, 2012). CSR does not substitute for regulation, but if done well, CSR programs may limit government involvement, manage competition from nongovernmental organizations (NGOs) and the like, and reduce risk (Craig, 1999; Schoeneborn & Trittin, 2013). In general, then, CSR "is the voluntary actions that a corporation implements as it pursues its mission and fulfills its perceived obligations to stakeholders, including employees, communities, the environment, and society as a whole" (Coombs & Holladay, 2012, p. 82).

There are a variety of typologies and categories used to assess CSR initiatives. Some discussions of CSR divide its programs into the normative case, where organizations implement programs for pure philanthropy, and the business case, where organizations use it to increase profit and improve their reputation, or mixed-motives, which is a combination of both (Wilde, 2012). Similarly, Morsing and Schultz (2006) divide CSR into types of strategies that are more instrumental, focusing on effectiveness and seeking to maximize an organization's strategic goals, while others seek more involvement from stakeholders regarding corporate behavior.

These authors argue that CSR needs to develop more toward the stakeholder involvement strategy, integrating the perspectives of NGOs, activists, and the like. Instead of focusing on CSR goals, Coombs and Holladay (2012) use another schema to divide CSR into five traditional types: philanthropy, cause promotion, cause marketing, social marketing, and volunteering. Although each of these typologies note varying levels of importance of "outside" voices, an instrumental view still predominates, meaning all of these schemas tend to privilege a view of CSR that seeks communication effectiveness (Schoeneborn & Trittin, 2013).

Many of these studies see CSR through this instrumental lens (Schoeneborn & Trittin, 2013). Such "transmission views" of CSR tend to imply that "information and meaning are transmitted in 'packages' from one sender to one or more receivers" (Schoeneborn & Trittin, 2013, p. 194). Instead, scholars such as Christensen and Cheney (2011) argue that communication constitutes an organization, whereby it is involved in an ongoing meaning-making process. Applying a constitutive view of CSR allows us to understand organizations as created by conflicting voices, by people who "talk the communicative reality they speak of into being" (Schoeneborn & Trittin, 2013, p. 194). It recognizes that organizational boundaries flex and incorporate views of third parties like NGOs and other stakeholders. It sees "non-human entities" such as texts, scripts, and so on, as also constitutive of organization. Importantly, constitutive views suggest that an organization not only uses CSR to achieve strategic goals but also to "invoke notions of ethics and responsibility within the entire organization" (Schoeneborn & Trittin, 2013, p. 195).

Indeed, in the constitutive view, communication is more than a transmitter or container, such that CSR becomes a "continuous process through which social actors explore, construct, negotiate, and modify what it means to be a socially responsible organization" (Christensen & Cheney, 2011, p. 491; Cheney and McMillan, 1990). From a constitutive view, whether CSR becomes practically meaningful "depends on the extent to which it is resonant with and becomes connected to other communicative practices, especially those geared to profitability" (Schoeneborn & Tritten, 2013, p. 204). This perspective is about more than making the "business case" argument for CSR that is cited so widely; instead, it suggests that organizations pay attention to a variety of voices so that they can balance profit motives with corporate citizenship ones. In a constitutive view, activists using awareness campaigns, along with media attention and public concern, all exert pressure on corporations and gain an organizational audience, as much as the "internal" voices inside an organization's inner workings.

One of the most interesting components of constitutive views about CSR is that they value all sorts of organizational talk. Even instances of "greenwashing," "cheap" or "aspirational" talk by an organization still drive organizational change (Schoeneborn & Tritten, 2013). Thus, Duke Energy can talk about being "responsible" by closing the coal ash plants and adopting more environmentally sensitive and progressive practices; but, through its talk, it creates "raw material" for constructing the organization's and society's expectations about it (Christensen, Morsing, & Thyssen, 2010). Communication in this view is performative, creating a "creeping commitment" to CSR-driven organizational activities (Schoeneborn & Tritten, 2013, p. 194). Constitutive viewpoints argue that imitation and talk have value; that is, "if corporations see other corporations achieving positive outcomes such as increased profits, more favorable reputations and positive media coverage when they pursue CSR initiatives, they may try to mimic the corporation, and more societal good will be done" (Coombs & Holladay, 2012, p. 86). From an ethical and moral standpoint, then, we cannot substitute corporate for government efforts to address social problems, but how successful corporations talk about CSR may influence other corporations, along with governments, to address an issue in a more positive, ethically sound manner (Stokes, 2013). By understanding this generative nature of CSR language, constitutive views get us beyond thinking how CSR simply helps organizations become more "effective." Whether it emanates from outside or inside an organization, pressure to act responsibly may alter an organization's CSR behavior along with society's expectations. It is public relations' job to monitor and interpret these voices. One way to perform this monitoring is through constitutive rhetorical criticism.

Constitutive Rhetorical Criticism

A constitutive rhetorical method looks closely at how public relations shapes discursive activity by framing our perceptions of, as well as our discussions and expectations about, society. It explores how public relations texts help populate our culture with messages that encourage certain meanings over others. Jasinski (1997, 1998) asserts that the repeated use of a particular idiom allows people to conceive of events in a particular way. Similar to framing research, if something is construed repeatedly as a "conspiracy," for example, then alternative understandings are constrained (Entman, 1993).[1] Thus, if Duke Energy stresses "safety," publics come to expect corporate policies to then reflect this viewpoint. Constitutive rhetorical criticism helps examine how Duke Energy helps shape the public discourse surrounding coal ash safety and electricity production in general. The perspective also shows how its efforts have implications for ethically sound corporate practices and disciplinary CSR scholarship.

Constitutive rhetorical criticism helps analyze Duke Energy's CSR efforts because it describes, analyzes, interprets, and evaluates the persuasive, and sometimes subtle, uses of language (Campbell & Burkholder, 1997; Hart, 1990). Rhetorical criticism helps people better understand the messages with which they interact by illustrating how "anybody in a given time and space might have experienced a rhetorical transaction," and by helping to make people aware of how they experience symbolic action (Brummett, 1984, p. 102). For this case, the *key words, metaphors, and themes* were identified in one particularly strong example of Duke Energy's CSR communication surrounding its coal ash response: its widely distributed "Letter to the People of North Carolina" (text included below) published on March, 24, 2014, in newspapers throughout the state, including the Charlotte and Raleigh markets. Although the letter stands as but one example of Duke Energy's CSR effort, a closer look at its language demonstrates a gap between the potential and reality of CSR communication for certain industries.

Duke Energy's Letter, Duke Energy's CSR Reality

Surrounded by a public relations crisis of this magnitude, it is tempting to assess Duke Energy's letter as strategic damage control. An instrumental or transmission view would evaluate this effort by how well it helped stem the tide of legislation and regulation. Clearly, it would be difficult to argue or "prove" how one such letter had discernible outcomes regarding Duke Energy's fate, but more than that, simply analyzing how well the letter helps achieve Duke Energy's strategic goals omits an important part of the story from a CSR perspective. It is equally compelling to analyze the letter for how it evokes notions of ethics and responsibility that gradually cultivate public expectations of CSR. There are three themes about CSR that the letter invokes through its aspirational language: a particular view of stakeholders and the public, an understanding of what constitutes corporate action in responding to a crisis, and the role of corporations vis-à-vis the public.

A key theme of the letter's language involves its view of its stakeholders. In the letter, Duke Energy, too, is a "citizen" of North Carolina, a member of the team, a neighbor, and part of the community. When the letter notes that Duke Energy has been "serving the Carolinas for more than 100 years … and call(s) North Carolina home," it leaves the door for public forgiveness, or at least acceptance, open. Metaphorically, a team member can miss the shot, and a neighbor can wait too long to mow the yard. Duke Energy can mess up and still be allowed membership in the community. Thus, when the letter notes that as "your neighbor" it is responsible for "restoring power to your home after a storm, strengthening our state by attracting top jobs and businesses, and contributing financial support and volunteer time to import-ant community projects," it becomes more human and thus forgivable. By positioning itself in this manner, it becomes more difficult to ostracize Duke Energy from the North Carolina community, even though it has violated standards of responsible behavior.

Invoking this view of its relationship to its public also gives Duke Energy some latitude in addressing the crisis. It may be "taking immediate action to ensure the safety of its ash basins companywide" and "developing a plan for long-term management," but the specifics of these actions and details of the plan are allowed to remain vague. If its position as a neighbor is established, then a certain level of trust can be granted, such that it can tell readers "we care deeply about getting this right" without showing what this level of care translates into specifically. Similarly, a neighbor/part of the community is perhaps given more latitude to fix a problem, whereby Duke Energy can note how each site is "unique" and "complex" and needs time to rectify.

Duke Energy's language invoking these two themes is not necessarily problematic, but it does require evaluation. It is the case that Duke Energy has been a long-standing part of the Carolinas' economy and that solv-ing a problem correctly does indeed require time. Mistakes do happen and solutions may be complex. What is more concerning from a constitutive view, however, is how Duke Energy's language signifies its position or status

To the People of North Carolina:

Duke Energy has been serving the Carolinas for more than 100 years. We are a great team – more than 13,000 employees, 8,600 retirees and our families call North Carolina home.

We believe our responsibility to provide safe, reliable and affordable electricity is a noble mission, and our employees are proud of our work. We are your neighbors and we carry out our mission day in and day out – maintaining our system, restoring power to your home after a storm, strengthening our state by attracting jobs and businesses, and contributing financial support and volunteer time to important community projects.

Following the events of the last few weeks, we want to regain your confidence. We are taking immediate action to ensure the safety of our ash basins companywide and are developing a plan for long-term management, including closure. Our highest priority is the safe operation of all of our facilities and the health and well-being of our communities.

Each ash basin site is unique and will require complex measures that will take time. Our work continues with all stakeholders, including our state regulators, to find the right solutions that position North Carolina for the future.

Duke Energy is proud to be part of North Carolina. We consider it a privilege to serve you, our customers. We want you to count on us for reliable power, safe operations and a strong commitment to the environment. We care deeply about getting this right.

Sincerely,

Lynn Good, President and Chief Executive Officer

This message paid for by Duke Energy shareholders.

Figure 4.1 Letter to the People of North Carolina. Source: Duke Energy.

within society. Duke Energy may claim it is a North Carolina neighbor, but metaphorically speaking, it has the biggest house on the street and is President of the Neighborhood Association. Its mission is "noble," it is "proud," of its work, and it wants to "regain" customers' confidence. The assumption here is that its stakeholders view manufacturing electricity in the same lofty terms, that they trust Duke Energy and approve of its business operations. This language belies the tenuous position Duke Energy occupied for years among activists and the media, where it was often discussed as an untouchable corporate giant that was shielded from environmental reform through its political and legal connections (Jarvis, 2014). Still, talk is aspirational, such that Duke Energy can argue it is working *with* stakeholders, *with* regulators, to "*find* the right solutions" to the coal ash problem. Duke Energy remains powerful in this language. It is not told *what* to do, it works *with* regulators and the public to arrive at what needs to be done to solve the problem.

Discussion

In the end, state regulators did pursue this more "neighborly" approach to handling Duke's Energy's behavior. Duke Energy's aspirational positioning prevailed and it received a punishment befitting its position of power. The original state fine of $25 million was cut to $7 million, and Duke Energy settled the lawsuit. Duke Energy remained, in essence, Duke Energy. Although the 2014 Coal Ash Management Act required groundwater assessment and closure and remediation of certain ponds, activists argued that the bill allowed Duke Energy to leave its coal ash in 10 of 14 sites. The Southern Environmental Law Center, for example, decried the bill, arguing it left people downstream from the plants in North Carolina at risk. It claimed that the bill "seeks to weaken existing law and protect Duke Energy from taking responsibility for its coal ash waste" (Legal Monitor, 2014). The historic spill and landmark fine against the company became just another corporate cautionary tale, despite the EPA's rating 29 of Duke Energy's 37 coal ash ponds as "high hazard," meaning that failure could cause loss of life, economic loss, and environmental and infrastructure damage. This case distills why some scholars argue that CSR remains problematic. Duke Energy's CEO claimed that the bill "gives Duke Energy direction to move forward with a stronger standard for the management of coal ash at our facilities" (in Legal Monitor, 2014), but even coupled with fines and settlements, there is no serious change in Duke Energy's status quo. Some CSR scholars argue that stakeholder input is essential in granting public acceptance of a business (Lehtimaki, Kujula, & Heikkinen, 2011), but as this case shows, stakeholders may express dissatisfaction and outrage without satisfactory resolution. As one women living near a coal ash pond complained, "Our people have heart attacks and breathing problems. They're dealing with this big mountain of coal ash in their face. This is a civil rights issue just as much as environmental and health one" (Plus Media Solutions, 2014).

When evaluating how well Duke Energy relied on the principles of CSR to demonstrate its responsibility to community and society, then, it does not embody the concept of CSR as outlined earlier in this essay. Recall that CSR ideally drives corporations to use their resources to improve society because of their obligations to communities, environment, and society, along with shareholders (Coombs & Holladay, 2012). This case reveals that Duke Energy failed to pay attention to the concerns of a variety of voices, and its aspirational talk of being a good neighbor did not provide fully the raw material for driving civic-minded business practices. In fact, there were many hints that Duke Energy was not having the type of discussions that would drive changes in how it addressed its environmental responsibilities. In an interview, for example, Duke Energy's CEO revealed that following another, larger spill in Tennessee back in 2008, Duke had implemented an inspections process, which revealed that the pipe that failed on the Dan River was expected to have "less longevity." The EPA also warned Duke Energy about that particular pipe. Nevertheless, since those reports advised that the pipe would leak before it failed, Duke Energy was left unprepared when the pipe just simply collapsed without leaking. As Governor McCrory complained following the accident, "I don't think Duke even knew what was underneath some of their dams and knew the structural issues… the record's been quite poor. Because frankly, it's been out of sight, out of mind" (in Stahl, 2014). Further, 2 years before the spill, engineers at the Dan River plant requested $20,000 from Duke Energy to use a robotic camera to inspect the drainage pipes, but were denied twice, even after a top manager pleaded for the funds (Nbcnews.com, 2015). For years, environmental groups had tried to get regulators to hold Duke Energy accountable for its coal ash pollution, but each time, the North Carolina Department of Environment and Natural Resources (DENR) blocked the lawsuits. Thus, instead of monitoring the pipes effectively, listening to employees, and evaluating activists' charges, which would have been a textbook public relations CSR response, Duke Energy did not follow these principles. Instead, by May 2015, it faced the largest federal criminal fine in North Carolina history, $68 million in fines and $34 million on environmental projects and land conservation projects in North Carolina and Virginia.

From a constitutive viewpoint, for Duke Energy to operate more with the public good in mind highlights the difficulty of CSR as it attempts to bridge the gap between theory and practice. Aspirational talk is cheap (and can be useful), but changing lobbying practices, agreeing to more regulation, meeting with stakeholders, and capping/lining ash ponds so that they do not leak in the first place is not. As Stahl (2014) points out, due to intense lobbying, there are no federal regulations on coal ash disposal, and states themselves are responsible for overseeing these powerful utility companies. For Duke Energy to effectively bridge the gap between talk and practice, then, since constitutive talk is generative, discussions with its communities and employees would be better integrated into company environmental policy. As CEO Lynn Good said herself in an interview with 60 Minutes following the incident, "It was an accident. It didn't work the way it should have worked. It didn't meet our standards or our expectations" (in Stahl, 2014, para. 1). Had it listened more carefully, Duke Energy could have avoided the crisis (NBCnews.com, 2015). Similar to issues management approaches that argue that crisis is avoided through proactive management of issues prior to reaching crisis phases, constitutive approaches stress that you cannot wait until the coal ash in flowing to try and change the dialogue about an energy company's decisions. Duke Energy's decisions surrounding coal ash reveal that responsible action would have required the company to not only change its monitoring activities, it would have required that it, for example, would have listened to stakeholders worried about the basins many, many years before the accident occurred. As such, to help build the CSR enterprise, Duke Energy and similar companies must rely on public relations in its original, fundamental role as boundary spanner and bridge between company and publics. Far from being the way a company "covers up" or "spins" an issue, public relations, in its truest rhetorical sense, would help Duke Energy build CSR programs in ways that contribute to a more fully functioning society (Heath, 2006).

Conclusion and Implications

This chapter began by arguing that instrumental analyses of CSR are incomplete. It used only one example of CSR communication to do so, but given space limitations, it was chosen to best reflect the advantages of employing a constitutive rhetorical approach. The Duke Energy case highlights the notion that in some cases CSR remains a corporate ideal, not evidence of societal improvement. Taking a closer look at Duke Energy's letter shows how little has changed in how Duke Energy considers its stakeholders in conducting its business. For some industries, CSR seemingly remains an "add on," whereby public opinion is considered, but not holistically integrated, and certainly not privileged. In some business models, it makes sense that stakeholder involvement drives more corporate decision making; right now, it is trendy and profitable, for example, to show how your burrito business is better for your health and better for the environment than its competitors. Currently, Duke Energy and others do not need to operate by the same playbook. Consumers may desire more environmentally conscious energy choices but there is not a driving economic case to do so. Until Duke Energy and like companies rely on public relations to drive management decisions instead of only communicating them, they are unlikely to serve the public good as much as the shareholder one. Sense must be made of diverse voices as the world and workplace become more interconnected, and public relations must help stress dialogue and adjustment of different perspectives for the best interests of society, rather than self-interest (Heath, 2000; Waymer & Heath, 2007). As Spence (2011) points out, meeting ethical expectations, along with legal ones, "may turn out to be every bit as important to companies in the long run as laws and regulations" (p. 61). Duke Energy does have a long record of excellence in North Carolina, employing almost 30,000 citizens and resting at number 26 on the 2013 100 Best Corporate Citizens list (Nahigyan, 2014). Committing to aligning its profit-seeking motives more closely with the public's environmental expectations will require fundamental changes that could be far reaching, but change will happen gradually, not all at once. A rising tide may lift all boats, but for certain industries, it is slow to come in.

Note

1. This method is described in Stokes (2005) and Stokes (2013), as well.

References

Brummett, B. (1984). Rhetorical theory as heuristic and moral: A pedagogical justification. *Communication Education, 33*, 97–107.
Campbell, K. K., & Burkholder, T. R. (1997). *Critiques of contemporary rhetoric.* New York, NY: Wadsworth.
Carroll, A. B. (1979). A three-dimensional conceptual model of corporate performance. *Academy of Management Review, 4*, 497–505.
Carroll, A. B. (1991). The pyramid of corporate social responsibility: Toward the moral management of organizational stakeholders. *Business Horizons, 34*, 39–48.
Carroll, A. B. (1999). Ethics in management. In R. Frederick (Ed.), *A companion to business ethics* (pp. 141–152). Malden, MA: Blackwell.
Chapel Hill Herald. (2014, March 16). The burden of toxic cleanup. Retrieved from http://www.lexisnexis.com.
Cheney, G., & McMillan, J. J. (1990). Organizational rhetoric and the practice of criticism. *Journal of Applied Communication Research, 18*(2), 93–114.
Christensen, L. T. and Cheney, G. (2011). Interrogating the communicative dimensions of corporate social responsibility. In Ø. Ihlen, J. Bartlett, & S. May (Eds.), *The handbook of communication and corporate social responsibility* (pp. 491–504). Oxford, UK: Wiley.
Christensen, L. T., Morsing, M., & Thyssen, O. (2010). The polyphony of corporate social responsibility: Deconstructing transparency and accountability and opening for identity and hypocrisy. In G. Cheney, S. May, & D. Mumby (Eds.), *The handbook of communication ethics* (pp. 457–473). New York, NY: Routledge.
Cloud, D. L. (2007). Corporate social responsibility as oxymoron: Universalization and exploitation at Boeing. In S. May, G. Cheney, & J. Roper (Eds.), *The debate over Communication Theory and CSR* (pp. 219–231). New York, NY: Oxford University Press.
Coombs, T. W., & Holladay, S. J. (2007). *It's not just PR: Public relations in society.* Malden, MA: Blackwell.
Coombs, T., & Holladay. S. (2012). Book highlight—Conceptualizing corporate social responsibility. *Global Business and Organizational Excellence,* July/August, 78–97.
Craig, R. T. (1999). Communication theory as a field. *Communication Theory, 9*, 119–161.
Dalesio, E. P. (2015, September 11). Duke, Feds to settle pollution lawusuit. *The Associated Press.* Retrieved from http://www.fayobserver.com/news/business/

duke-feds-to-settle-pollution-lawsuit/article_7f6ea6c4-7b5c-54c3-9f9d-08df7425a128.html.

Entman, R. M. (1993). Framing: Toward clarification of a fractured paradigm. *Journal of Communication, 43*, 51–58.

Fayetteville Observer. (2014, August 27). Editorial: This coal-ash chapter ends fairly well. Retrieved from http://lexisnexis.com.

Freitag, A. R. (2008). Staking claim: Public relations leaders needed to shape CSR policy. *Public Relations Quarterly, 52*(1), 37–40.

Hart, R. (1990). *Modern rhetorical criticism.* Glenview, IL: Scott, Foresman, and Company.

Heath, R. L. (2000). A rhetorical perspective on the values of public relations: Crossroads and pathways toward concurrence. *Journal of Public Relations Research, 12*, 69–91.

Heath, R. L. (2006). Onward into more fog: Thoughts on public relations' research directions. *Journal of Public Relations Research, 18*, 93–114.

Jarvis, C. (2014, November 19). Lawyers in governor's lawsuit also represented Duke Energy. *Charlotte Observer.com.* Retrieved from www.charlotteobserver.com.

Jasinski, J. (1997). Instrumentalism, contextualism, and interpretation in rhetorical-criticism. In W. Keith & A. Gross (Eds.), *Rhetorical hermeneutics* (pp. 195–224). Albany: SUNY Press.

Jasinski, J. (1998). A constitutive framework for rhetorical historiography: Toward an understanding of the discursive (re)constitution of "Constitution" in *The Federalist* Papers. In K. J. Turner (Ed.), *Doing rhetorical history: Concepts and cases* (pp. 72–92). Tuscaloosa, AL: University of Alabama Press.

Legal Monitor Worldwide. (2014, August 22). Coal ash bill ratified in Raleigh. Retrieved from http://lexisnexis.com.

Lehtimaki, H., Kujula, J., & Heikkinen, A. (2011). Corporate responsibility in communication: Empirical analysis of press releases in a conflict. *Business Communication Quarterly, 74*, 432–449.

Morsing, M., & Schultz, M. (2006). Corporate social responsibility communication: Stakeholder information, response and involvement strategies. *Business Ethics: A European Review, 15*(4), 323–338.

Nahigyan, P. (2014, March 11). Duke Energy has North Carolina in its pocket. *Nation of Change.org.* Retrieved from http://nationofchange.org.

NBCnews.com. (2015, May 14). Prosecutors: Duke Energy could have avoided Dan river spill in. North Carolina. *NBCnews.com.* Retrieved from http://www.nbc-news.com.

Plus Media Solutions (2014, December 22). EPA's first-ever coal ash rule leaves communities to protect themselves. Retrieved from http://www.lexisnexis.com

Schoeneborn, D., & Trittin, H. (2013). Transcending transmission. *Corporate Communications: An International Journal, 18,* 193–211.

Spangler, I. S., & Pompper, D. (2011). Corporate social responsibility and the oil industry: Theory and perspective fuel a longitudinal view. *Public Relations Review, 37*(3), 217–225.

Spence, D. (2011). Corporate social responsibility in the oil and gas industry: The importance of reputational risk. *Chicago-Kent Law Review, 59*, 59–85.

Stahl, L. (2014, December 14). The spill at Dan River. *CBSnews.com.* Retrieved from http://www.cbsnews.com/news/duke-energy-on-coal-ash-waste-at-dan-river/.

Starnes, R. (2014, February 28). Coal ash poses threat on Yadkin. *The Stanley News and Press.* Retrieved from http://www.lexisnexis.com.

Stokes, A. Q. (2005). Metabolife's meaning: A call for the constitutive study of public relations. *Public Relations Review, 31*(4), 556–565.

Stokes, A. Q. (2013). You are what you eat: Slow Food USA's constitutive public relations. *Journal of Public Relations Research, 25,* 68–90.

Stokes, A. Q., & Waymer, D. (2011). The good organization communicating well: Teaching rhetoric in the public relations classroom. *Public Relations Review, 37*(5), 441–449.

Tomsic, M. (2015, September 29). NC, Duke Energy settle lawsuit over coal ash pollution. *WFAE.org*. Retrieved from http://wfae.org.

Ulrich, P. (2008). *Integrative economic ethics*. Cambridge, UK: Cambridge University Press.

Waymer, D., & Heath, R. L. (2007). Emergent agents: The forgotten publics in crisis communication and issues management research. *Journal of Applied Communication Research, 35,* 88–108.

Wilde, C. (2012). For the game. For the world: A public relations approach to corporate social responsibility and global mega-events. Unpublished Masters Thesis.

Wilmington Star-News. (2014, March 19). Duke Energy Lobbyists. Retrieved from http://www.lexisnexis.com.

Part II

Moral and Civic Responsibility in Theory and Practice

5   Public Relations Postures of Organizational Civic Responsibility

Christie Kleinmann

Until the mid-20th century, the primary role of an organization in society was the maximization of organizational profit. Maximizing profit was not only considered a legitimate goal, but also a responsible use of organizational resources (Friedman, 1962; Heath & Ryan, 1989; Kim & Choi, 2012). This role was then widened to consider the ethical ramifications of business decisions on society. Organizations came to recognize that ethical responsibility was just as important as fiscal responsibility (Davis, 1967). Today, civic responsibility is best understood from a public relations perspective as it is built on the relationship between an organization and its community (Clark, 2000). The need for organizations to establish themselves as good corporate citizens in society has led to an increased focus on how organizations manage their relationships with society (Burchell & Cook, 2006; Devin & Lane, 2014; Du & Vieira, 2012).

Relationships are the core of civic responsibility, and public relations professionals are the managers of these relationships. "Never before in history has the field of public relations been as affected by the social climate in which it operates because never before has the social climate demanded so much of the individual practitioner" (Parsons, 1993, p. 50). Public relations advocates for the organization and mediates for society. L'Etang (1994) argued that organizational civic responsibility is the practice of symmetrical public relations in order to build positive relationships with societal stakeholders. Public relations professionals understand the needs and interests of both the organization and society and are able to provide moral guidance in the organization's responsible conduct to society. As a result, public relations professionals direct the organization's civic engagement with society (Pearson 1989b). Thus, in this study, civic responsibility is operationalized as the management of the relationship between the organization and society. This research then examines how public relations professionals manage the organization's civic responsibility with society.

Passive Organizational Civic Relationships

A review of the public relations literature on civic responsibility reveals two broad relational approaches to civic responsibility, a passive civic relationship approach and an active civic relationship approach. Both approaches construe civic responsibility as a relationship management function of public relations, but differ in their type of response. In the passive approach, organizations respond to societal ills as they become known, while organizations in the active approach engage in a continuous dialogue with society to identify and respond to societal needs.

Passive organizational civic relationships include an adherence to rules and regulations from external guiding agencies. External groups define and determine appropriate action that organizations must follow, and an organization reacts to these regulations in order to avoid a rule infraction. Often organizations adopt a "no harm" civic responsibility outlook ensuring no harm comes to society. However, Esrock and Leichty (1998) found when civic responsibility is approached in this manner, civic-minded efforts typically end at the fulfillment of the law. Organizations who seek "no harm" rarely extend beyond corporate compliance.

A second passive civic relationship approach recognizes the need to comply with external regulations, but also believes that the organization must "do good" in society because of its prominence and/or success (Badaracco, 1998). Because the community has helped the organization succeed, the organization feels indebted to the community. In response, the organization completes a variety of "good deeds" to repay the debt. For example, an organization may donate to a charity or provide resources for a community initiative. While these activities benefit the community, the organization follows a self-centered approach with its primary concern on creating continued benefit for itself (Esrock & Leichty, 1998; Fitzpatrick & Gauthier, 2001; Kim & Choi, 2012). This self-interest approach prioritizes organizational needs and wants above the good deeds of society and believes that such good deeds will promote continued organizational success. Thus, the organization moves beyond the minimum of corporate compliance, but retains organizational priority when managing civic relationships.

Despite the organizational self-interest approach, civic responsibility activities can positively affect society. Doing good in society still benefits society, regardless of the internal motive (Martinson, 1994). However, if an activity would benefit society but not the organization, the organization would not typically perform the good deed. Such an activity represents the use of civic responsibility as a tool for image building, so that even the act of donating to a Little League baseball program is strategically construed to build the organization's image or create misdirection from organizational issues (Heath & Ryan, 1989). Despite this priority, Kim and Choi (2012) found that many stakeholders view the motive of civic engagement programs neutrally. As a result, civic activities, even from an organizational self-interest motive, may not be viewed as such by society.

Organizations with a passive civic relationship choose to respond to societal issues as the issues become known and engage in those that will bring the greatest benefit to the organization. Yet, why organizations choose to respond to select societal issues may reflect a deeper concern. The ultimate failure is not the organization's self-interest, but the use of this self-interest as a baseline to make civic decisions (Martinson, 1994). The often competing interests of the organization and society result in an imbalanced relationship that always leans in the organization's favor.

Active Organizational Civic Relationship

Public relations professionals also guide organizations in active civic relationships. In these relationships, civic responsibility moves beyond an organization's response to society and becomes a means to engage society. The organization works *with* society; the organization dialogues *with* society; and the organization engages *with* society to develop symmetrical relationships.

Active organizational civic relationships approach civic responsibility from a symmetrical relationships perspective. These organizations seek to identify and when possible, collaborate with societal stakeholders that align with the organization's mission (Dahlsrud, 2008; Devin & Lane, 2014; Pedersen, 2006). They use dialogue to engage societal stakeholders in mutually beneficial relationships that highlight the shared needs and expectations of each (Amaeshi & Crane, 2006). Together, the organization and societal stakeholders create a shared understanding of the civic responsibility that directs the organization's behaviors and determines if societal needs have been met (Devin & Lane, 2014).

The active organizational civic relationship approach demonstrates a conceptual shift in the orientation of the organization and society from an organizational self-interest to a societal interest. However, the symmetrical relationship between an organization and society often places the public relations professional in a balance of loyalties. Practitioners simultaneously serve dual roles as organizational advocate and societal mediator. As organizational advocate, the practitioner shares a heightened interest in the organization's needs, but the opposite may be true as a society mediator. Potentially conceived as conflicting loyalties, the public relations practitioner walks a tenuous balance of organizational priority and societal priority that some believe defies resolution (Pearson, 1989). The active organizational civic relationship approach addresses this tension by advocating a duty to society as the primary focus of a public relations professional. Although often considered idealistic, this approach places the good of society as the highest priority of an organization (Parsons, 1993; Seib & Fitzpatrick, 1995; Sullivan, 1965). The primary question an organization must address is how this activity will positively or negatively impact society (Seib & Fitzpatrick, 1995). The question can only be answered through dialogue with diverse viewpoints beyond the organization. Thus public relations professionals manage the tenuous balance of loyalties through dialogue considering the diverse viewpoints, interests, and rights of others (Parsons, 1993).

This research utilizes the passive and active approaches to organizational civic responsibility to examine the practice of civic responsibility in sport organizations. Sport is one of the most visible institutions in America and one of the most active in societal concerns. Collegiate athletes in the National Collegiate Athletic Association (NCAA) and the National Association of Intercollegiate Athletics (NAIA) regularly perform civic engagement programs with their sports teams. At the professional level, sports organizations develop comprehensive civic engagement programs, such as NBA Cares, to help meet societal needs. Because of their active civic engagement, it is important, then, to understand how sports public relations professionals approach civic responsibility.

This study sought to understand how sports professionals define civic responsibility and their role in related activities. The goal was to determine if sports professionals identify a role in the organization's civic responsibility and if so, to examine how they managed its activities. Two exploratory research questions guided the study: How do sports public relations professionals define their role in civic responsibility? How do sports public relations professionals manage civic responsibility?

Qualitative interviews were utilized in order to gain deep understanding of the sport organization's approach to civic responsibility, the public relations professional's role in these activities, and the guideline and/or motive used to direct these activities. By doing so, the sports professionals provided rich context and personal insight that helped clarify the type of civic responsibility approach used and for what purpose. Twenty sport public relations professionals initially responded to the research inquiry. Of those, one professional did not to participate due to the study's focus on civic responsibility; two were unable to arrange interview times due to their schedules; and several did not participate due to lack of time. Therefore interviews were conducted with 12 full-time sports professionals.

These practitioners represented a broad spectrum of sports organizations including NCAA and NAIA collegiate sports programs and professional teams from the NBA, MLB, and NASCAR. In-depth interviews were conducted in person with three participants and via telephone for nine participants. The use of telephone interviews allowed the study to include participants within a larger geographical region. The interviews averaged 30 minutes and reached the point of redundancy. Interview data were transcribed and analyzed thematically in order to identify the main themes. Two coders analyzed the data independently and resolved minor differences dialogically by clarifying the emerging themes.

Humans use posture to position themselves in their environments. Whether standing, sitting, or lying down, humans adopt postures based on the activity and the internal and external factors involved. Organizations also have postures, or ways they position themselves in relation to their environment. Reflective of human posture, organizations assume multiple postures in response to internal and external environmental pressures. Using the civic relationship approaches found in the literature, this research sought to identify the organizational postures sports organizations use during civic responsibility activities. Four postures or themes of civic responsibility emerged from the research: the posture of contractual-obligation, the posture of consumerism, the posture of concession, and the posture of communion. Following Hon and Brunner (2000), these postures represent a continuum from a basic acceptance of civic responsibility with the posture of contractual-obligation to an idealistic practice of civic responsibility with the posture of communion. All of the interviewees identified contractual-obligation as a foundational posture for their civic responsibility. Beyond this posture, organizations did not identify with a single posture, but illustrated a fluid usage of the different postures. As a result, organizations exhibited different postures. Often the same organization illustrated multiple postures within a single program. In particular, organizations fluctuated between the postures of consumerism and concession. When employing primarily media relations strategies, organizations often illustrated a consumerism posture, but they assumed a concession posture most often when discussing community relations strategies. This variation between the two postures seems to reflect the balance of needs between organizations and the publics that is inherent in public relations. The final posture, the posture of communion, often appeared as an ideal of civic responsibility to which practitioners aspired. While a third of the participants discussed the ideal of this posture, only one provided an example of the posture of communion. Future research should examine the movement of organizations between the postures in order to determine if a certain situation facilitates the assumption of a certain posture. The following will explain each posture and its usage in civic responsibility.

Posture of Contractual-Obligation

The posture of contractual obligation is a rules-based approach that seeks compliance with external regulations that govern the organization. The goal of this posture is to follow the rules and to create no harm to society. Public relations professionals in this posture focus on knowing the rules, understanding the rules, and creating procedures to help the organization follow the rules. The posture emerged as a meta-posture, meaning that it encompasses an aspect of every other posture. For example, a sports organization with a consumerism posture would first assume a posture of contractual-obligation in order to ensure fulfillment of the external laws and regulations. Success, in this posture, is measured by the lack of organizational rule infractions.

As with the passive organizational civic relationship approach, organizations in the contractual-obligation posture do not perform civic actions beyond the fulfillment of the law (Esrock & Leichty, 1998). The organization considers laws and regulations as its civic responsibility to society and does not expect recognition for organizational compliance. Rather the assumed benefit of this posture is an absence of organizational attention.

For example, sports organizations are guided externally by a variety of regulatory bodies, such as the Health Insurance Portability and Accountability Act (HIPPA) and the Family Educational Rights and Privacy Act (FERPA). Both of these federal mandates aim to protect and regulate the release of personal information. All of the participants in this study attested that these guidelines form the foundation of their practice. One practitioner said, "With the HIPPA rules, we don't announce any kind of injury unless we get permission from the student athlete. We get with our trainers and the doctors before the season even starts and get permission from them to even say what we need to say. There are a lot of rules." Organizations in the posture of contractual-compliance follow external and personal guidelines in order to avoid negative publicity or potential harm to organizational credibility. In addition to external regulations, sports practitioners identified truthfulness as a necessary aspect of their societal obligation. One interviewee said, "We are obligated to always be truthful. I say that not just because of a personal code, but also to keep yourself and your organization out of trouble. That's first and foremost."

As a result, sports public relations professionals identify this posture as an overarching posture that governs their jobs. Although organizations exhibited other postures in their civic responsibility activities, every decision was first filtered through this meta-posture to ensure the organization maintained compliance. Interestingly, these sports professionals believed that they have a unique contractual-obligation to society because of their organization's success and due to sports esteemed place in society. One practitioner said, "We have a responsibility to give back to the community. Because of the resources that a company our size has, we can really add to the quality of life all around." Another interviewee added, "When you do well and you provide something for so many people that they love (sports), you need to give back to your community. And you hope that every day feels that way no matter what business they're in. You hope that they feel if they're successful that they should be doing their part to give back." This extension of contractual-obligation illustrates the continuum-nature of the postures. Sports organizations assume a greater contractual-obligation due to their influence and success. This extension of perceived obligation leads to the next posture on the continuum, the posture of consumerism.

Posture of Consumerism

The posture of consumerism exhibits a "what's in it for me" organizational philosophy toward civic responsibility. The organization positions itself above society, indicating that organizational concerns are primary. This posture is analogous to organizational self-interest, a passive civic organizational relationship approach that performs only those actions that bring benefit to the organization (Fitzpatrick & Gauthier, 2001; Kim & Choi, 2012). All civic responsibility decisions are filtered through a consumeristic lens of organizational gain. One practitioner characterized this gain as an organization's return on investment. He said, "We are not taking advantage of fans, but we are offering them things that really do benefit them, as well as benefit us. Being a business, you do have to have some return on your investment. Some things you do because it's the right thing to do, but you still have to have a return on your investment." Thus, societal concerns may be met, but only if the activity brings greater benefit to the organization (Heath & Ryan, 1989).

The goal of the posture of consumerism is publicity. The organization uses good deeds as a means to create and maintain a positive image in society. Often these activities stem from a reactive response to organizational negativity, using good deeds to reposition the organization in a positive light. For example, one sports public relations professional recounted using civic activities as a means to offset poor game performance or athlete misconduct. Another participant added, "People tend to buy a product more if they know the (organization) gives back to the community. Hopefully, despite our athletic performance, they'll be loyal fans to us because they know that we're really committed to this community."

Sports organizations in the posture of consumerism do good things for society (Martinson, 1994). They engage in singular efforts to shelter the homeless, feed the hungry, and care for the sick. Society benefits from the organization's actions in this posture; yet, the central focus of the consumeristic organization is the organization. Every civic decision is made from a posture of organizational priority. One practitioner described a public relations strategy that was originally developed for civic responsibility activities, but used primarily to promote revenue. "The priority is always on ticket sales. Community relations is placed as a last priority because (management) wants to communicate to a season ticket holder a new pricing plan ... I know our company in particular understands the importance of the philanthropy of social responsibility, but when it comes right down to it, it's not always a priority." Another professional underscored the priority of the organization in civic responsibility, saying, "My number one priority is the (organization). I have to think about my organization first." As a result, organizations are unable to build long-term symmetrical relationships. Two-way asymmetrical communication occurs in feedback loops to assess if the civic activity created organizational benefit. If so, the organization will continue two-way communication to maximize organizational gain. Noticeably absent, however, is a dialogue between the organization and society on shared needs and opportunities.

Posture of Concession

The posture of concession positions the organization equally or a bit lower than society. The organization recognizes a responsibility to society and often provides slightly higher priority to society than to itself. In this posture, the organization utilizes dialogue with societal stakeholders to identify the needs of society and to strategically meet those needs (Amaeshi & Crane, 2006).

Through dialogue, the posture of concession is built on the tenets of symmetrical relationships. Organizations engage with their environment to identify societal issues and needs that align strategically with the organization's mission (Dahlstrud, 2008; Devin & Lane, 2010; Pederson, 2000). Sports professionals developed organizational guidelines and philosophies for civic engagement to determine which needs best fit the organization. Through consistent application, these practitioners believed that their civic efforts were more symmetrical because they brought mutual benefit to both parties. One practitioner said that the organizational philosophy helped her meet community needs, but also ensured that these activities aligned strategically with the public relations goals and objectives of the organization. Another practitioner noted that these guidelines helped his sports organization make a strategic long-term difference in society rather than a singular impact on a particular need.

Often organizational management in this approach adopted a "lived out loud" approach to civic responsibility. One professional explained that his organization doesn't believe in simply writing a check, but encourages employees to become personally involved. "We get 20 hours of charity work each year. Whatever charity, (management) just wants you to become a part of it. Take a few hours out of your day, whatever it is, and become a part of it." Leaders in these organizations would exemplify the organization's civic philosophy in their personal life, often serving as a catalyst for new civic endeavors. Sports professionals described community care days as lived out loud opportunities for employees, athletes, and management to serve the community side by side. One sports professional expressed that her manager's lived out loud approach inspired her to identify additional methods for the organization to assist the community. One participant said, "It's promoted from the top down, and I honestly believe that when the person at the top encourages you, and you see their involvement with Boards and clubs and charities, then it's something you want to get involved with. I think that is why we (employees) all feel like it is not an obligation, but something you feel like you want to be a part of." Through leading by example, these leaders create a civic-minded culture that empowers employees and athletes to become involved in civic responsibility. As a result, the sports professionals within this posture describe employees, athletes, management, and societal stakeholders as partners in meeting societal needs.

Reflective of the active organization civic relationship, acts of civic responsibility within the posture of concession flow from strategic directives and organizational culture, resulting in mutually beneficial relationships with others in society (Esrock & Leichty, 1998; Fitzpatrick & Gauthier, 2001). One professional explained her organization's guiding principles were used in all aspects of operation. "(Our manager) gave us the principles and asked that we use them to guide daily work activities in order to be accountable and socially responsible, to reflect integrity, and to keep the focus on our publics." Mutually beneficial relationships include the expectation for mutual benefit. The organization expects to receive benefit from its relationships with others in society, and others in society expect to receive benefit from the organization. Sports public relations professionals noted that the opposite is true as well. Concession is also an expectation of a mutually beneficial relationship. Practitioners recognized that sport organizations may actually provide greater relational concession than society due to sports organizations' prominence. One professional said, "Everyone has an opportunity and maybe a responsibility to improve whatever community that you're living in. A high profile organization, such as ours, has the opportunity to have much more of a positive impact on community and society." This belief reflects the idea that prosperous businesses owe something to society because of their success (Badaracco, 1998). Rather than providing a sense of obligation, sports practitioners believed that these concessions created opportunity to have increased positive impact on society and bring long-term benefit to the organization. One sports practitioner described a large community event that the organization presents each Christmas. All of the proceeds of this event are given to select community partners or to meet current community needs. The practitioner admitted that the event was costly in terms of financial and personal resources and sometimes reduced the organization's focus on other strategic endeavors. However, the practitioner said that the value of the event could not be overstated in its significance to community relationships and positioning the organization as a good community citizen.

Concessions are not always large scale but can also represent the accumulation of smaller concessions. For example, one sports practitioner described a reading program the sports organization developed with a community children's center. Organizational employees and athletes would donate their time to read books to the children and spend time at the center. The practitioner explained that it would be very easy to use this activity as a publicity opportunity, but she did not do so. She explained that inviting the media to these events would shift the focus from the community center and its needs to the sports organization. She said, "A strategy we've tried is for nonprofits that we align with to write the news release. We give them information, but then the media pitch and everything comes from them on their letterhead so that it doesn't sound as self-serving. This is how we're accomplishing a goal together in our community. It seems to be a win-win." Despite this concession, the sports practitioner emphasized that these types of opportunities bring associated benefits to an organization. Although the organization might not publicize these events, others unintentionally do through social media or word of mouth, providing unsolicited third-party endorsements that positively impact the organization. Thus, the posture of concession allows for benefits as well as concessions in the relationship. The organization expects to make greater concessions than society and receive less benefit in the short term of the relationship; however, the organization also expects a return on the civic investment over the long term that positively impacts the organization.

Despite the acts of concessions toward society, organizations in the posture of concession retain a sense of organizational importance. Sports professionals identified the organization, not society, as their primary responsibility. The posture of concession acknowledges this balance. An organization may make short-term concession in a relationship, but never concedes to the point of causing detrimental harm to the organization. One practitioner said that meeting community needs was important, but he worked for the organization. "Frankly I'm not an independent journalist. My salary is paid by the (organization), so I try to find the high points for our team, athletes, or coaches and include those in the article. I sometimes say jokingly that I do a lot of creative writing. Not that I put anything dishonest, but you've got to find something, even if it's one thing." This practitioner illustrated the tenuous balance of loyalties public relations professionals face between the organization and society. While this practitioner acknowledged the importance of society, he could not bring harm to his organization through his efforts to do good. Thus sports professionals indicate that there is a baseline of costs in the organization's relationship with society. Organizations expect to accrue costs in the relationship, as well as benefits, but the costs cannot fall below the organization's ability to remain healthy and fiscally viable. If costs exceed the benefits of the relationship, the organization may end the associated civic activities with societal stakeholders.

Finally, organizations in the posture of concession express a shared sense of responsibility to society. While the posture of consumerism views civic responsibility as a means to gain success, organizations in the posture of concession believe civic responsibility is the organization's responsibility because of its success. As a result, the organization seeks symmetrical relationships that provide mutual long-term benefit to both the organization and society.

Posture of Communion

The final posture, the posture of communion, positions society directly above the organization, indicating that societal interests are primary to organizational interests. The goal, in both the short and long term, is the benefit of society. An organization seeks to achieve this goal through continuous dialogue, or communion, with society in order to identify and understand its needs. Communion extends beyond the strategic directives that guide organizational relationships and include the identification of needs outside of the scope of the organization's strategic philosophy of civic responsibility. Sports professionals characterize civic activities within this posture as the right thing to do. One practitioner explained that when considered objectively, activities from the posture of communion do not make business sense.

For example, one sports professional recounted that the local high school had to close school in the middle of the school year due to the presence of black mold. The sports organization, however, opened its facilities to the high school for the remainder of the school year and assumed all operational costs of the facility. She said, "Nobody even questioned it; nobody even though about if it was going to cost extra money, or anything like that. It was just the right thing to do, so we did it." Strategically, the sports professional admitted that the decision did not make business sense. The activity was outside the scope of organizational objectives and would create a financial burden for the organization. Yet, the sports professionals described the decision as the right thing to do. "It was pretty neat to be honest with you. Nobody here knew exactly how that was going to work out, but it was great. And everybody felt like it was so cool that we were able to do that for them." Through its civic response, this sports organization did not receive immediate mutual organizational benefit, not even through short-term publicity. Yet, the sports practitioner recalled that the experience created meaningful personal relationships among sports employees, students, teachers, and parents that still continue today.

The posture of communion runs counter to traditional business models and is often conceived as an idealistic approach to civic responsibility (Parsons, 1993; Seib & Fitzpatrick, 1995; Sullivan, 1965). Organizations are willing to accrue costs below its baseline of costs and not receive mutual benefit in return. As a result, the posture of communion is an unnatural long-term organizational posture. Only one sport organization exhibited this posture, and did so as a singular event. The remaining sports organizations did not illustrate the posture of communion at all. Rather, the posture of communion is one that sports professionals aspire to reach as an organization and in their work with others. One professional described the job of helping young athletes accept their status as role model in terms of the posture of communion. Although the professional did not provide an example of this posture in action, she attributed it as the goal of her work. She explained, "I think most athletes know they are held as role models, but I've heard a couple of athletes say on occasion 'I don't' care what you think. I'm not a role model. I don't want to be a role model.' But, because of celebrity, if you will, there is a responsibility … One of my duties is helping (athletes) realize what an impact and influence they do have and what role that they're going to have for the rest of their career and that they need to take it seriously. That is probably one of my most important roles." As a result, the posture of communion did not have wide occurrence in this study; yet, discussion of the posture and its singular occurrence indicated a profound impact on how the organization and its employees understand themselves and their relation to civic responsibility.

In conclusion, this research examined how sports public relations professionals manage the organization's civic responsibility to society. Conceptualized as a relationship management function, these professionals identified four public relations postures to an organization's civic responsibility: a posture of contractual obligation, a posture of consumerism, a posture of concession, and a posture of communion. Each of these postures illustrates how public relations professionals engage society and create relationships with societal stakeholders. As organizational goals change, the organization's postures toward society change. The postures also indicate the organization's philosophy toward civic responsibility. From a "do no harm" posture to a "do the right thing" posture, the public relations postures of civic responsibility represent the various approaches organizations use to navigate the complex environmental landscape and understand their responsibility to society.

Due to the study's qualitative nature, the findings only represent the public relations experiences of the participating sports public relations professionals. While these professionals represent a broad range of sports organizations, future research should consider the larger occurrence of these postures in sports as well as other organizational types. Additional research should consider how situational context impacts an organization's civic responsibility posture. In particular, sports professionals noted the use of civic responsibility activities in conjunction with sports performance. Future research might examine the relationship between athletic performance and the civic responsibility postures. Finally, additional research should identify the use of the posture of communion and examine its potential connection with athletes as role models.

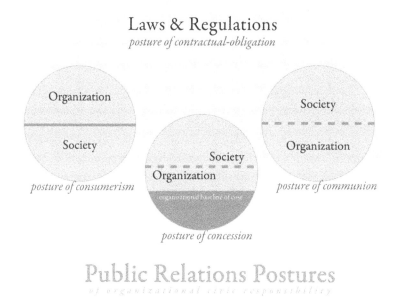

Figure 5.1 Diagram of the Public Relations Postures of Organizational Civic Responsibility.

References

Amaeshi, K. M., & Crane, A. (2006). Stakeholder engagement: A mechanism for sustainable aviation. *Corporate Social Responsibility and Environmental Management, 13,* 245–260.

Badaracco, C. H. (1998). The transparent corporation and organized community. *Public Relations Review, 24*(3), 265–272.

Burchell, J., & Cook, J. (2006). It's good to talk? Examining attitudes towards corporate social responsibility dialogue and engagement processes. *Business Ethics: A European Review, 15*(2), 154–170.

Clark, C. E. (2000). Differences between public relations and corporate social responsibility: An analysis. *Public Relations Review, 26,* 363–380.

Dahlsrud, A. (2008). How corporate social responsibility is defined: An analysis of 37 definitions. *Corporate Social Responsibility and Environmental Management, 15,* 1–13.

Davis, K. (1967). Understanding the social responsibility puzzle: What does the businessman owe to society? *Business Horizons, 10,* 45–50.

Devin, B. D., & Lane, A. B. (2014). Communicating engagement in corporate social responsibility: A meta-level construal of engagement. *Journal of Public Relations Research, 26,* 436–454.

Du, S., & Vieira, E. T. (2012). Striving for legitimacy through corporate social responsibility: Insights from oil companies. *Journal of Business Ethics, 110*(4), 413–427.

Esrock, S. L., & Leichty, G. B. (1998). Social responsibility and corporate web pages: Self presentation or agenda-setting? *Public Relations Review, 24*(3), 305–319.

Fitzpatrick, K., & Gauthier, A. (2001). Toward a professional responsibility theory of public relations ethics. *Journal of Mass Media Ethics, 16,* 193–212.

Friedman, M. (1962). *Capitalism and freedom.* Chicago, IL: University of Chicago Press.

Heath, R. L., & Ryan, M. (1989). Public relations role in defining corporate social responsibility. *Journal of Mass Media Ethics, 4*(1), 21–38.

Hon, L. C., & Brunner, B. (2000). Diversity issues and public relations. *Journal of Public Relations Research, 12*(4), 309–340.

Kim, Y., & Choi, Y. (2012). College students' perception of Philip Morris's tobacco-related smoking prevention and tobacco-unrelated social responsibility. *Journal of Public Relations Research, 24,* 184–199.

L'Etang, J. (1994). Public relations and corporate social responsibility: Import issues. *Journal of Business Ethics, 13,* 111–123.

Martinson, D. L. (1994). Enlightened self-interest fails as an ethical baseline in public relations. *Journal of Mass Media Ethics, 9*(2), 100–108.

Parsons, P. H. (1993). Framework for analysis of conflicting loyalties. *Public Relations Review, 19*(1), 49–57.

Pearson, R. (1989). Beyond ethical relativism in public relations: Coorientation, rules, and the idea of communication symmetry. In L. A. Grunig & J. E. Grunig (Eds.), *Public relations research annual* (Vol. 1, pp. 67–86). Hillsdale, NJ: Lawrence Erlbaum Associates.

Pearson, R. (1989b). Business ethics as communication ethics: Public relations practice and the idea of dialogue. In C. H. Botan & V. Hazelton (Eds.), *Public relations research* (pp. 111–131). Hillsdale, NJ: Lawrence Erlbaum Associates.

Pedersen, E. R. (2006). Making corporate social responsibility (CSR) operable: How companies translate stakeholder dialogue into practice. *Business and Society Review, 111*(2), 137–163.

Seib, P., & Fitzpatrick, K. (1995). *Public relations ethics.* Fort Worth, TX: Harcourt Brace.

Sullivan, A. J. (1965). Values in public relations. In O. Lerbinger & A. Sullivan (Eds.), *Information influence and communication: A reader in public relations* (pp. 412–439). New York, NY: Basic Books.

6   Hope for the Future

Millennial PR Agency Practitioners' Discussion of Ethical Issues

Tiffany Derville Gallicano and Kelli Matthews

A survey of 808 Public Relations Society of America (PRSA) members concluded that practitioners younger than 30 were less likely than any other age category to talk with management about a questionable decision, and they were more likely than any age group to stand by and do nothing about poor organizational decisions (Berger & Reber, 2006). Furthermore, practitioners with fewer than 10 years of experience were less likely than their peers to talk with management about an inappropriate decision. In terms of how practitioners express dissent, those younger than 30 were the least likely of any age group to articulate dissent and were more likely to use antagonistic/latent dissent (i.e., talking with people inside the organization who are unlikely to make a difference) than any other age group (Berger & Reber, 2006). Berger and Reber (2006) offered the following explanation:

> The lack of will among young practitioners and early-career practitioners to rock the boat is understandable. They are working to curry favor with their superiors and build a career. They, therefore, do not want to make trouble through dissension. (p. 197)

Berger and Reber's (2006) research is supported by a study of Millennial public relations agency practitioners. Most respondents to the survey preferred to "avoid an issue rather than take a stand" and "for those who took a stand, more followed the boss' orders than not" in the hypothetical scenarios presented to participants (Curtin, Gallicano, & Matthews, 2011, p. 13). Berger and Reber explained, "Educators and professional organizations can play a role ... by teaching students and new practitioners the value of dissent to an organization, as well as teaching appropriate dissent tactics in specific scenarios." Although extant literature addresses a range of ethical issues (e.g., Fitzpatrick & Bronstein, 2006; Parsons, 2008; Seib & Fitzpatrick, 1995), research is needed to examine the pressing ethical issues that entry-level practitioners face today from the perspectives of entry-level practitioners. Textbooks offer contemporary examples of ethical issues; however, some ethical issues do not become public enough to make it into books.

In this study, fresh examples of common ethical issues from the perspectives of Millennial public relations agency practitioners are explored for several reasons. First, the resulting data can help educators, employers, and industry groups understand which issues to focus on when training students and agency employees. Also, educators, employers, and industry groups can use the recent real-world examples as powerful teaching tools for people who have not encountered ethical issues yet, especially given that people are most likely to retain ethics lessons that incorporate concrete stories with unexpected information, rather than abstract discussions of principles and generic issues (see Heath & Heath, 2007). Improved training could lead to increased confrontation regarding ethically questionable decisions by management and ultimately, more responsible decision making by organizations. In addition to using this study's results as a training tool for students and new agency employees, public relations agencies can use the results as a form of environmental scanning to identify potentially weak areas they might need to fortify through various tactics such as all-staff meetings, ethics advisories, ethics courses for all employees, and organizational codes of ethics.

This study not only provides contemporary examples of common ethical issues but also investigates Millennials' opinions about how the profession could improve ethical decision making. Millennials tend to have the least amount of institutional authority in their organizations, so it is especially important to see what can be done from their perspectives to facilitate ethical decision making.

Literature Review

Frameworks for Ethical Decision Making

Public relations practitioners have a professional civic duty to make decisions that are ethical. Two broad frameworks for ethical decision making include deontology and teleology.

People solely using deontological reasoning believe that the ends never justify the means—the morality of how an outcome is achieved determines the ethicality of the decision (Curtin & Boynton, 2001). For example, it is never virtuous to lie, regardless of the desirability of the expected results. Deontologically based decisions are made without regard to how the organization will benefit and without regard to pressures from workplace politics, personal ambition, and concerns about job security (Bowen, 2005). Teleology, on the other hand, is an approach to determining the ethicality of a decision based on the good outcomes that can result from it (Curtin & Boynton, 2001). For example, PETA's objectification of women to attract attention to animal rights could be justified through a teleological approach to ethics. Virtuous public relations practitioners would be wise to examine the ethicality of both the means and the expected outcomes of a decision (Bivins, 2009).

A preliminary study suggested that many Millennial agency practitioners use a deontological approach to ethics and often rely on transparency as a guiding principle (Curtin et al., 2011). Respondents to this survey perceived that they had a significantly better relationship with their agency employers when they also thought that their workplaces gave them the autonomy to make ethical decisions, which supports Bowen's (2005) deontological model. Several Millennials in the study, however, applied a teleological approach by judging whether the outcomes would be potentially harmful.

Ethical codes also provide a general framework for ethical decision making. Although they do not appear to be useful to seasoned public relations practitioners (Lee & Cheng, 2011, also see the discussion by Curtin & Boynton, 2001), nearly half of the Millennial agency respondents to a survey expressed that the PRSA Code of Ethics is a helpful resource (Curtin et al., 2011). Employers need to enforce their codes of ethics and should be specific with their guidelines (e.g., Curtin & Boynton, 2001; Seib & Fitzpatrick, 1995).

Approaches for Influencing Ethical Decision Making

Practitioners need to learn how to effectively influence ethical decision making in organizations to give themselves a voice (which improves job satisfaction) and to improve organizational decisions (Garner, 2009; Kang, 2010). Not surprisingly, an ethical orientation is a key dimension of public relations leadership and best practices (Bowen, 2004; Kang, 2010; Meng, 2012). To influence ethical decisions in an organization, a public relations practitioner must have the ear of senior management and be persuasive (Berger & Reber, 2006). Public relations practitioners have identified effective ways to persuade senior management. The top three approaches that are also acceptable to employers (i.e., approaches that avoid unsanctioned tactics such as leaking information to the media) include rational argument, coalition building with other employees, and pressure (e.g., ignoring a supervisor's request or being assertive until management listens; Berger & Reber, 2006). Public relations practitioners commonly express dissent in response to unethical courses of action; in fact, in a survey of PRSA members, a little more than half of all respondents expressed that they would always object to unethical decisions (Berger & Reber, 2006).

Research Questions

Preliminary research about student public relations interns lends insight into ethical issues in the workplace at the entry level. Interns conveyed their concerns about media relations (e.g., maintaining fairness and integrity in the face of intense media interest in a story), client relations (e.g., being tempted to inflate measurements of success), observations of ethical breaches and not knowing what to do, and issues unique to nonprofits as ethical issues they faced (Lubbers, Bourland-Davis, & Rawlins, 2007/8). More in-depth research is needed in the focused context of public relations agencies to understand the pressing ethical issues Millennials confront, how they make meaning of them, and how they respond to them. Therefore, the following research questions are investigated:

RQ1: What ethical issues do Millennials confront in their PR agencies?
   Recent research has focused on seasoned professionals' perspectives about how to improve ethical decision making (e.g., Lee & Cheng, 2011). To complement existing research, this study provides a view from the bottom rung of the ladder:
RQ2: How do Millennial agency practitioners think the profession could improve ethical decision making in the industry?

Method

To explore the research questions, five asynchronous online discussions with approximately 10 people per group were conducted through Focus Forums, and one person participated by email to help obtain a more diverse sample ($N = 51$ participants). There are several advantages to asynchronous online discussion groups. The lack of face-to-face interaction and the assignment of a pseudonym mean that participants can share more openly than they might otherwise do, which is especially important for discussions of sensitive topics (Houston, 2008; Oringderff, 2004; Valaitis & Sword, 2005). Asynchronous online discussion groups tend to result in deeply reflective monologues, in addition to more disclosure of personal stories and emotions than would occur in a face-to-face focus group (Graffigna & Bosio, 2006). The balance of talk tends to be more equal in an asynchronous online discussion group, and every participant responds to every question asked (Graffigna & Bosio, 2006).

   Drawbacks of this method include the lack of visual and verbal signs to convey meaning, the risk that participants will be so comfortable that they will lack discretion and tact when interacting, access issues could exclude people from participation, and there is no way to verify that people are who they say they are (Oringderff, 2004). Fortunately, participants' meanings seemed to be straightforward, follow-up questions were asked as needed, there were no problems with participants lacking discretion or tact, and Millennials who work for PR agencies are unlikely to have Internet access challenges (i.e., they could even participate from their phones).

Study Procedures

Participants were asked demographic questions when they registered for the study, including the year when they were born to confirm that they were Millennials. Next, participants received log-in information and a confidential name based on a color and number (e.g., Blue5), which appeared next to all comments, along with an avatar (i.e., an animal or object) of the participant's choice. Each participant received a computer-generated password to log in to the group. The data were protected by bank-level encryption security. The online discussion groups were conducted through Focus Forums. This interface involved a discussion board that was organized by tabs. Participants were required to answer questions in order and were not allowed to see future questions. They were not able to see anyone's answer to a question until they had responded. Once they had responded, they could read and comment on other people's answers, and they later responded to our follow-up questions.

The asynchronous discussion groups required approximately an hour a day from participants for 3 days; some participants reported that they spent 90 minutes a day. Each day focused on a theme. Due to space constraints, the abundance of communication participants provided, and the desire to incorporate rich details to achieve quality, this study includes data from the second day, which was focused on ethics. The first day was focused on organizational culture.

Recruitment and Demographics

For a prior component of this study (see Gallicano, Curtin, & Matthews, 2012), a survey was conducted and respondents were invited to participate in a discussion group that would include a $100 incentive. Of the 51 discussion group participants, 40 volunteered from the survey. The survey recruitment involved an email from PRSA to members with 2 years of experience or fewer, and the survey recruitment included solicitation via Twitter, Facebook, and blogs. The remaining spots were filled through word of mouth by participants who had already signed up, and the last few spaces were filled by the researchers' former students who worked for agencies.

About 78% of the participants were women and about 22% were men. Approximately 75% were Caucasian (29 women and 9 men), 12% were African-American (5 women and 1 man), 8% were Asian (4 women), almost 4% were Latino (2 men), and nearly 2% were Caucasian-Latino (1 man). All participants were age 27 or younger. Responses were analyzed through descriptive codes, followed by interpretive codes and pattern codes (see Miles & Huberman, 1994).

Results

RQ1: What Ethical Issues Do Millennials Confront in Their PR Agencies?

The ethical issues described by Millennials are offered below in order of prominence, beginning with the issues most commonly discussed. The most significant pressure participants faced involved breaches of responsibility to clients in attempt to look better, maximize profits, or both. Breaches of responsibility included helping competitors, committing malfeasance, overpromising, using the "bait and switch," padding media coverage, covering up mistakes and bad news, and wrongfully billing.

Helping competitors

Numerous participants discussed situations in which there was a temptation to share private client information:

> A coworker of mine was asked by a former boss who was now at a competing agency for some confidential client documents to help with a pitch for a competitor. All I can figure out is she wanted to impress this former boss or in some way felt an obligation because she shared the documents. In the end, she got fired.

Several participants identified the possibility of helping competitors and addressed the problem by not sharing insider information:

> Knowing that I had insider knowledge on the competition, I know that it would be wrong to share that. … In the end, I did participate in the new business pitch. I still feel like this was, in part, not ethical. But I also was careful not to share any of the "insider information" I had on my client and on the new business prospect.

Participants had various views about whether insider information could be shared. For example, one participant wrote

> We have, on two different occasions, retained on an account team an individual who had worked for a competitor to that account less than a year earlier. This type of information sharing does not sit well with me, but as a relative junior there is little I can do. I understand that this is commonplace in the industry and is actually looked upon as a selling point in certain new business situations, but it does seem unethical to me.

Committing malfeasance

Many participants discussed their discomfort with malfeasance:

> My agency's worst offense in my opinion is knowingly selling services and products that a client does not need. I understand the pressure of profitability in a rough economy, but ultimately the services a client does not need will only work to hurt the agency/client relationship and hinder our results. … My agency needs to stop this practice.

Some people, such as the participant featured above, positioned their discomfort in terms of long-term effectiveness, and others positioned the issue in term of ethics: "Pitching them things or services they don't need just to get money for our agency is unethical in my opinion."

In addition to stories in which agencies committed malfeasance, other stories showed agencies that at least initially resisted it or fired employees for it. For example, one participant discussed her agency's unsuccessful attempts to dissuade a client from public relations services that would result in a "very low return on investment." The agency ultimately complied with the requests to avoid losing the account. The Millennial involved reflected, "I thought this situation was both damaging to us and to our clients. It is our job as public relations professionals to advise on the best strategy, not to blindly carry out requested tasks." Although this agency attempted to dissuade the client, another participant noted that her agency embraces the mantra that "the client is always right." In another case, a participant discussed a supervisor who the agency fired for "upselling the client on something they did not want and would probably not work" and then "stringing them along" by lying about the results. The participant noted, "She should have been fired earlier."

Overpromising

Overpromising can occur throughout the client relationship, beginning with the client pitch: "I feel we overstate our capabilities in order to win business. Just because everyone does it, doesn't make it right." Another participant commented, "You should never overpromise, but it can happen in your aim to please the client." He noted that in situations where he is not confident with an immediate recommendation, he has learned to respond to the client by stating, "I'm not sure. I'll need to explore that more to see if this (option, campaign, tactic) will work here." He added, "Clients usually don't want to hear this or they are at least surprised when they do." Some participants discussed their success with keeping their agencies from overpromising by talking with their managers:

> I sometimes take issue with the way my managers change the words of my emails to the client. ...I think my managers sometimes hedge on how frank they are with the client about a journalist's interest. ... The last time I was concerned about the manner in which we were presenting an opportunity to the client, I expressed my concerns to my manager and the email was rephrased to language I felt more comfortable using.

Using the bait and switch

In addition to misleading some clients about what can be accomplished, some clients have also been misled about which person on the account team performs the bulk of the client work:

> This is a hugely unethical practice that is very commonplace in the large agency world. The old bait and switch with personnel assigned to a particular client. This is also a practice that ends up costing agencies a lot of money in client turnover. Again, thinking short term and unethically affects the bottom line in the long run.

Padding media coverage

Several participants expressed their objection to what they referred as padding coverage:

> Padding coverage happens too much. There is so much pressure to make the numbers bigger than the year before, even if budgets have been cut. It's too bad, because when we go along with this, we are watering down the field of PR by making things about numbers of hits and impressions, not about relationships and thought leadership.

Another participant agreed: "To me, a robot syndicating my press release is not coverage. To become a 'hit,' at the very least I think a release must pass through an editor's eyes."

Covering up mistakes and bad news

Several participants also discussed cover-ups:

> A coworker never sent the appropriate prep materials for a media opportunity that was scheduled with the client the next day, and the client blew up, very angry, that such a basic account management step wasn't executed. The client called the president of my company and the president told my coworker to lie and say that he did send the document, must've just gotten lost. I think lying is lying and it isn't necessary.

Another cover-up involved a printing error on materials in various countries:

> I was told that if the other countries hadn't noticed the error yet, that there was no need to reprint the materials or notify the client. I continued to bring up the fact during internal meetings and with co-workers that we should reprint the materials. Although we did not reprint all the countries, we did reprint a few of the countries.

Wrongfully billing

One participant addressed a situation in which her agency shifted funds between accounts:

> Supervisors purposely alter a correct budget that I have sent to fit within the guidelines. When I bring up that we're not able to do the project for the budget laid forth, they will say, "We'll transfer the money from another bucket." Granted I'm not in the position to deal with our client budgets closely, this seems like this could come back and bite us if a real audit was performed by the client.

Following the most discussed area of ethical conflict, which involved breaches of responsibility to clients, the next most commonly discussed issue involved astroturfing and disguised environmental scanning.

Astroturfing and disguised environmental scanning

Many participants offered an astroturfing story that is similar to the one below:

> When a client or my organization lands some great media coverage, my boss wants me to make comments online as if I were a third party. He's suggested that I use an alias and try to hide my connection. At first I just told him no. It just made me uncomfortable. But after a few times, I worked to find an alternative. One of these is that I offer to find someone not connected who would genuinely be impressed or interested and ask them to comment. This has worked well. I don't feel bad for bringing the story to the attention of those people, and my boss gets his desired result of positive comments.

Some participants also identified this type of situation as unethical but refused to perform the work: "I refused to do the tasks because I said that I didn't think it was an ethical choice. They just asked someone else to do the task." Just one participant expressed approval of astroturfing, and she wrote the following response to a participant who was against it:

> On the flip side, I find myself doing a lot of defending [of] my clients from other interest groups/competitors/etc. who are manipulating facts for their own gain. Maybe I'm drinking the Kool-Aid, but that's one aspect of my job where I do take a lot of pride. ...I get to set the record straight about what the company is doing. ... Because others are manipulative, you have to be too—just to even the playing field.

Also, one participant discussed disguised environmental scanning:

> We had a client dealing with layoffs ... the news was leaked. One of the team VPs asked me to monitor lots of message boards online in addition to regular news and social media. For some of the message boards, you had to be a member to gain access, and my VP asked me to create an account with my personal email address.

The practitioner explained, "I was not a big fan of this personally, but there wasn't a lot of time to give my feedback, and what really guided my decision of whether or not to disagree with this, was that this particular VP is pretty mean and also has some bearing on my advancement opportunities." She also added that she complied with the request because she "didn't have to lie" about who she was and did not have "to call someone up pretend to be [someone else]."

*Giving gifts without transparency and purchasing ad space
with editorial demands*

Another common issue addressed by participants involved gift giving to the media, bloggers, and consumers:

> One ethical conflict I confront on a daily basis is transparency. I work with many different teams that often involve paid spokespeople or bloggers who were given free product. I feel that while I always put my best foot forward, not all of my colleagues and media I work with follow the same guidelines, and it frustrates me.

This participant relies on helpful senior executives to gain influence:

> Unfortunately, without a VP attached to my name, I sometimes face struggles that people don't value my POV [point of view]. Fortunately, I always have the support of my older mentors/supervisors who are not just looking out for my well-being but the agency's too.

Examples involving the media included cases in which editors would request gifts in exchange for product placement. In addition, a participant discussed pressure her friend faced to demand editorial placement due to advertising purchases: "A friend/co-worker of mine who recently got laid off… was told to call publications that the client advertised in and basically hint that because they had advertising they owed the client editorial space, as well." Her friend refused, and the VP relented: "I think she too knew that it was completely inappropriate for her to suggest this. When the junior staffer threw out the word 'unethical,' I think our VP got the hint and dropped it."

Ghostwriting

Participants had mixed opinions about whether ghostwriting was acceptable. A Millennial shared her story about dissuading her agency and client from ghost blogging:

> When developing a new media strategy for a client, we were intending to have our spokesperson start a travel blog about a trip they were taking. In planning sessions, the client desired to control the message and wanted us to draft the blog posts, approve them with the spokesperson, and then post them. I interjected during these discussions and insisted that the blog be genuine, insisting that no one could tell the story like the person himself. I explained in length how blogs are a conversational medium and a clear deception like this, if found out, would not be well received. Eventually, everyone agreed and the project went on to be a grand success.

He also emphasized that it was important to get influential senior executives on his side: "It was a very hard fought battle that lasted for at least three meetings. I was forced to get other people on the account team on my side (more senior people, primarily) who had more impact on the client." The client initially resisted because "they wanted to retain control; they were very concerned about getting off message and having the spokesperson say things that were factually inaccurate. They also thought that they could provide more brand focused messages if they controlled the content." The Millennial was successful and noted, "The primary client contact and I joke about that little clash now, he is 20 years my senior, and says that I taught him a good lesson on that one." Another Millennial defended ghostwriting:

> The client is consulted at every step of the writing process, they must approve of the final product, and I have done extensive research to write in a voice true to the client and to the campaign. Although the words are mine, they cohesively reflect the ideals of the organization and the thoughts of the person I am writing for.

After a participant complimented the rationale above, the Millennial who wrote the justification explained how she arrived at the decision: "I read a few articles (and blog entries!) on the topic, and my current opinion is a result of this research."

Voting for clients in contests

A few participants discussed their discomfort with requests to vote for clients in contests:

> Colleagues frequently send out emails asking everyone to go to X website and vote for our client. I don't feel voting for our client is ethical for two reasons. 1) If this person wasn't my client, I wouldn't be voting for them. 2) There's no way for me to disclose when I'm voting that I work for that client.

All three participants explained that they ducked the situation and did not address it with managers: "If I don't want to speak the truth, but I don't want to tell a lie, it comes in handy. Although it does carry its own implication." One participant pointed out that employee voting is "padding the stats" and might suggest that the agency isn't really doing its job "to increase visibility for the company."

Performing work that conflicts with personal beliefs

A handful of practitioners discussed issues that resulted from conflicts with ideology. For the few cases about ideology that were mentioned, participants agreed that it was important to represent the other side, "similar to a law-yer defending a client," which could be performed by "creating materials that are true," despite ideological differences. Another participant's agency screened out new hires based on "how they would feel working on a client where they might have to, for example, pitch a publication such as Playboy."

RQ2: How Do Millennial Agency Practitioners Think the Profession Could Improve Ethical Decision Making in the Industry?

Although some participants adopted a futile perspective, believing that people are "already set in their moral ways," the most common response was to call for more training by educators, employers, and associations such as PRSA.

Educators

Many participants emphasized the importance of ethics in the public rela-tions curriculum: "It should be taught in the schools. I've noticed that stu-dents who are taught ethics in their college courses are a lot more likely to be ethical than those who are not." Another participant noted, "Continue to hold ethical courses in school; I believe the generation of practitioners with PR degrees have a better understanding of ethics."

PRSA

In addition, participants asked for additional leadership from PRSA, such as holding "some type of annual ethics 'class' presented online or by video from PRSA that agencies could present for free." One participant criticized her local chapter for not doing more to focus on ethics: "Our industry should start making ethics part of the conversation if they want to improve them. When's the last time you went to a luncheon and the topic was ethics?" Another participant praised her local chapter for its annual ethics meeting: "Our local PRSA chapter does one program each year on ethics. It's usually great subject matter—and relevant."

Employers

Participants' responses demonstrated a range of efforts by agencies to assist employees with ethical decision making. Many participants explained that they have an ethics training as part of their employee ori-entation. Also, participants praised their agencies for annual ethics classes and tests, especially those with real cases and "situations where your cli-ent or boss may ask you to do something you don't agree with." Another participant noted, "It's good to have regular reminders to always act with integrity" and "recognize what the proper decision should be." Other participants did not see as much effort by their agencies: "I feel after answering all of these questions that maybe my agency doesn't discuss ethics often enough. And if every agency did so, it wouldn't be a question as to whether something is right or wrong—it would just be second nature." Several participants also explained their interest in training to "make it clearer where we should draw the line and what we should do." One participant added, "Ethics are incorporated into our review metrics (judged on honesty, integrity, etc.)," which she said shows that "the company takes this very seriously."

Although several participants thought their employers did not need to engage in additional efforts, others disagreed: "My company does not make us review a code of ethics after orientation, and I saw someone else did. I think that is a good idea." Similarly, respondents who did not have reminders about ethics or check-ins did not seem to retain their initial employer training: "When I was initially hired I was presented with a large employee handbook and required to sign the last page agreeing to the contents. I am sad to say that I have little recollection as to what was included." Several participants expressed the following suggestion: "It would be great if we had regular sessions, probably on a yearly basis, at our agency to address ethics in communications."

Participants were about evenly split on the usefulness of establishing ethics codes at the employer level. A participant who found her agency's code to be useful explained, "I consider it valuable in terms of understanding where our agency's position is on things like interacting in social media space, how we represent sponsors, etc. ...That way, there's no room for misunderstandings or discrepancies." Some participants expressed that their ethics code was not a resource they used, but "it is nice that it is written out and expressed... I appreciate that." Others thought their ethics code was "too broad," "too long," or not useful, especially because it "fails to address how to work with new media."

Motivation for training

Several participants focused on the importance of motivating practitioners to attend training opportunities, whether these opportunities come from graduate classes, local PRSA meetings, conferences, or employers. As one participant summarized, "The trick... is how to interest people in participating in the first place." Another participant noted that it is imperative for senior staff to attend, as well as juniors: "Agencies and employees need to play a better role educating ALL staff (not just juniors, sometimes senior staff have developed bad habits and don't realize that industry standards have changed) as the primary driver of ethical change." Another participant commented, "I think the more we can publicize the effects of poor ethical decision making, the better. ...Let's debate what's right, what's wrong and why."

Training tips

Many participants focused on the importance of "real-life" examples: "There should be real-life case studies (even if given anonymously by changing agency and client names) so that people can get a *real* sense of how ethical dilemmas play out and how they affect everyone involved." Similarly, a participant stated, "Practitioners should walk through real situations (stressing real), talk about the range of options, share the different thought processes, and come up with a group solution." Participants also suggested scenarios that "pit their will to do good communications work against their will to profit." They also expressed interest in understanding "how managers make ethical decisions."

In addition, there was a focus on the need to understand the ethical course of action for social media issues: "With the rise of social media as a dominant outlet for our industry. …we need to be well versed in the emerging media and the hypothetical dilemmas that may arise." One practitioner disagreed, explaining that companies and agencies will learn the ethics of social media as they get punished for transgressions, such as "the fake Wal-Mart blog created by another agency a few years ago."

Discussion

Ethical Issues in Agencies

The results of the first research question point to the persistence of a variety of ethical issues, especially those involving client management and social media. Other areas include gift giving, ghostwriting, voting for clients in contests, and performing work that conflicts with personal beliefs. One possible reason why client management was the most significant source of ethical problems for participants is that people think they can get away with it, which reinforces the importance of the recommendation to hold individuals accountable for their decisions (Lee & Cheng, 2011). Some agencies hold their employees accountable for poor client management practices, which was evidenced by participants' descriptions of people getting fired. The potential concealment of unethical client management practices suggests that clients might consider asking more questions of their agencies based on the problems described in the results, such as confirming who is doing which work on an account team.

Requests for Support

In response to the second research question, many Millennials focused on the importance of ethical training by educators, employers, and public relations associations, although some participants did not think further training would help. Some Millennials explained that the content of ethics classes and codes must be consistent with what an agency actually does, which is the same view that many senior public relations executives expressed in a recent study (see

Lee & Cheng, 2011). One reason why ethics codes and classes can be useful to Millennials is that they can use the content to persuade their supervisors to do the right thing. Previous research suggests that Millennials want to be mentored and groomed for senior positions (Gallicano, 2013), so approaches that tie ethical training into mentorship and professional development are advised.

Dissent

Although Millennials sometimes observed ethical infractions, in many cases (even outside of social media), they stood their ground, which provides good news in light of research that suggests that practitioners under the age of 30 are less likely than other generations to express dissent (Berger & Reber, 2006). This study provides preliminary evidence that many young practitioners stand their ground at times, even if young practitioners speak out less often than seasoned professionals. The contextual details of this study explain why young practitioners speak out less often, beyond the initial explanation offered by Berger and Reber (2006) about not wanting to rock the boat. In addition to this explanation, young practitioners also speak out less often when they perceive a decision to be out of their hands, which could help explain why Millennial respondents to a survey tended to duck ethical issues when possible (Curtin et al., 2011). The lack of control some Millennials perceive with ethical issues can also hurt the relationship they have with their employers (Curtin et al., 2011), which is not surprising given the importance of mutual control to many organization-public relationships. Thus, it is important for employers to encourage employees to voice their ethical concerns.

Social media dissent

Given that Millennials tend to identify social media leadership as a defining characteristic of their generation of practitioners and are eager to leverage this experience into opportunities to make a difference (Gallicano, 2013), it is also not surprising to discover that most respondents hold their ground on social media issues, despite research suggesting that many tend to avoid confronting employers about other ethical issues (Curtin et al., 2011). As one participant explained, the industry is slowly beginning to figure out where to draw the line on social media issues and is primarily doing so as public relations practitioners observe others receiving negative publicity for particular tactics.

Forms of rational argument

This study builds upon Berger and Reber's (2006) framework for dissent in the workplace by fleshing out the area of rational argument in a way that is easy to recall. This contribution is important because it can help employees consider a range of arguments available to them when expressing dissent through rational argument, and it is useful for teaching public relations leadership. Three forms of rational argument are presented below, and they can be used in isolation, or they can be combined.

As found in this study, one form of rational argument is to show an employer how he or she can get the same results or better results by using an ethical solution. A shorthand name for this line of rational argument is the *better path* argument. The path is inherently better because it is ethical, it does not jeopardize the organization's reputation, and it can deliver at least the same quality of results. Public relations students can practice the application of this approach by examining ethical situations they might face and by looking for creative solutions that can be used in a better path argument.

Another line of argumentation for rational appeals can be referred to as the *safe path* argument. This argument is a fear appeal that involves explaining the damage that can occur to the organization's immediate success, long-term success, or both when people find out what happened. This line of argument can be especially useful for persuading people who are unmoved by direct appeals to moral or ethical concerns. Ideally, this argument should be accompanied by concrete examples of similar situations in which an organization was caught and suffered from the results. It is not surprising, then, that several participants suggested that ethics trainings focus on real-world examples of the damaging outcomes that resulted from various unethical decisions.

An additional line of argumentation for rational appeals can be referred to as the *moral path* argument. The moral path argument involves making appeals based on moral principles, ethics, or both. This line of argumentation can be especially effective with people who have publicly expressed their commitment to ethics through their words, actions, or both. Merely objecting to a decision because it was unethical worked well for some of our participants; however, in a couple cases, the questionable decision was still implemented because a supervisor asked someone else to do it. In these cases, a better path argument, safe path argument, or both could have also been used to try to dissuade the supervisor. People using a moral path argument can consider their employers' ethics codes, public relations association codes, public relations models for ethical decision making (e.g., Bowen, 2005; Lieber, 2005), and extant discussions about public relations ethics (e.g., Bivins, 2009; Fitzpatrick & Bronstein, 2006; Parsons, 2008; Seib & Fitzpatrick, 1995).

Many participants' responses showed a commitment to deontological reasoning, such as objecting to lying and wanting to be transparent with social media use, which supports results from Curtin et al.'s (2011) study. Several participants successfully used the moral path by incorporating deontological reasoning in their rational appeals, which suggests a shared commitment between several Millennials and their supervisors to ethical solutions. There were exceptions, such as a participant who advocated for astroturfing and a participant who thought it was fine to use insider knowledge to benefit a competitor if no legal document was signed about keeping the information confidential.

Distributed Public Relations

In a better path appeal, a Millennial was able to turn down his boss' request to engage in astroturfing by offering to find people who genuinely like his client and asking them to post comments in response to his client's media coverage. This practice is close to the concept of distributed public relations, so this study proposes an extension to distributed public relations, which Kelleher (2007) defined as the "intentional practice of sharing public relations responsibilities among a broad cross-section of an organization's members or employees, particularly in an online context" (p. 98). Distributed public relations can be extended by including not only members (i.e., of a nonprofit) and employees but also consumers (i.e., for companies). A public relations practitioner who asks consumers to promote a client, of course, should also request that the consumers explain that the client encouraged them to engage in the promotion, disclose any conflict of interest, and disclose any incentives that they received. Transparency is critical with online public relations.

Limitations and Future Research

As a qualitative study, the results cannot be generalized; nevertheless, saturation with the research questions was achieved, which suggests a thorough identification of prominent themes. By having Millennials identify the ethical issues they faced, as opposed to triangulating the data through participant observation, this study's identification of ethical issues is constrained by Millennials' ability to recognize them. Similar to the study by Lubbers et al. (2007/8), some participants stated that they had never faced an ethical issue, which could suggest a failure to recognize ethical problems. Future research could incorporate participant observation to identify issues that participants might overlook, which could result in additional ethical issues for the industry to explore. Additional research is also needed to explore the ethical issues that are unique to other public relations contexts. Also, participants themselves called for research that connects ethics with effectiveness. Although studies relating these areas exist, additional research is needed, along with outreach efforts to publicize these studies.

This study provides some ethical "bright spots," not the least of which is Millennial participants' ability to identify ethical problems that are posed by various courses of action. The first step in the ethical decision-making process is to define the ethical issue(s) a course of action raises (Bivins, 2009). That identification allows the practitioner to consider the resources available to him or her and to think through the dilemma in the appropriate context. Millennials in the study appear equipped to start that process, but they do not always have the training or experience to take the next step. Through ethics education that includes real-life scenarios, regular training, and, ultimately, management support, Millennials can feel empowered to speak up and influence meaningful change in their agencies.

The authors thank the Public Relations Society of America Foundation and the University of Oregon for funding this study.

References

Berger, B. K., & Reber, B. H. (2006). *Gaining influence in public relations: The role of resistance in practice.* Mahwah, NJ: Erlbaum.

Bivins, T. (2009). *Mixed media: Moral distinctions in advertising, public relations, and journalism.* New York, NY: Routledge.

Bowen, S. A. (2004). Expansion of ethics as the tenth generic principle of public relations excellence: A Kantian theory and model for managing ethical issues. *Journal of Public Relations Research, 16*(1), 65–92.

Bowen, S. A. (2005). A practical model of ethical decision making in issues management and public relations. *Journal of Public Relations Research, 17*(3), 191–216. doi:10.1207/s1532754xjprr1703_1.

Bowen, S. A. (2010). Almost a decade later: Have we learned lessons from inside the crooked E,Enron? *Ethical Space, 7*(1), 28–35.

Curtin, P. A., & Boynton, L. A. (2001). Ethics in public relations: Theory and practice. In R. L. Heath (Ed.), *Handbook of public relations* (pp. 411–422). Thousand Oaks, CA: Sage.

Curtin, P. A., Gallicano, T. D., & Matthews, K. (2011). Millennials' approaches to ethical decision making: A survey of young public relations agency employees. *Public Relations Journal, 5*(2), 1–21.

Fitzpatrick, K. R., & Bronstein, C. (Eds.). (2006). *Ethics in public relations: Responsible advocacy.* Thousand Oaks, CA: Sage.

Gallicano, T. D. (2013). Relationship management with the Millennial Generation of public relations agency employees. *Public Relations Review, 39*(3), 222–225. doi:10.1016/j.pubrev.2013.03.001.

Gallicano, T. D., Curtin, P. A., & Matthews, K. (2012). I love what I do, but… A relationship management survey of Millennial Generation public relations agency employees. *Journal of Public Relations Research, 24*(3), 222–242. doi:10.1080/1062726X.671986.

Garner, J. T. (2009). Strategic dissent: Expressions of organizational dissent motivated by influence goals. *International Journal of Strategic Communication, 3*(1), 34–51.

Graffigna, G., & Bosio, A. C. (2006). The influence of setting on findings produced in qualitative health research: A comparison between face-to-face and online discussion groups about HIV/AIDS. *International Journal of Qualitative Methods, 5*(3), 55–76. Retrieved from http://ejournals.library.ualberta.ca/index.php/IJQM/article/view/4370/3801.

Heath, C., & Heath, D. (2007). *Made to stick: Why some ideas survive and others die.* New York, NY: Random House.

Houston, M. (2008). Tracking transition: Issues in asynchronous e-mail interviewing. *Forum: Qualitative Social Research, 9*(2), 1–22.

Kang, J.-A. (2010). Ethical conflict and job satisfaction of public relations practitioners. *Public Relations Review, 36*(2), 152–156.

Kelleher, T. (2007). *Public relations online: Lasting concepts for changing media.* Thousand Oaks, CA: Sage.

Lee, S. T., & Cheng, I.-H. (2011). Characteristics and dimension of ethical leadership in public relations. *Journal of Public Relations Research, 23*(1), 46–74. doi:10.1080/1062726X.2010.504790.

Lieber, P. S. (2005). Ethical considerations of public relations practitioners: An empirical analysis of the TARES Test. *Journal of Mass Media Ethics, 20*(4), 288–301.

Lubbers, C., Bourland-Davis, P., & Rawlins, B. (2007/8). Public relations interns and ethical issues at work: Perceptions of student interns from three different universities. *PRism, 5*(1&2), 1–10.

Meng, J. (2012). Strategic leadership in public relations: An integrated conceptual framework. *Public Relations Review, 38*(2), 336–338. doi:10.1016/j.pubrev.2012.01.004.

Miles, M. B., & Huberman, A. M. (1994). *Qualitative data analysis* (2nd ed.). Thousand Oaks, CA: Sage.

Oringderff, J. (2004). "My way": Piloting an online focus group. *International Journal of Qualitative Methods, 3*(3), 69–75.

Parsons, P. J. (2008). *Ethics in public relations: A guide to best practice.* London, UK: Kogan Page.

Seib, P., & Fitzpatrick, K. (1995). *Public relations ethics.* Fort Worth, TX: Harcourt Brace.

Valaitis, R. K., & Sword, W. A. (2005). Online discussions with pregnant and parenting adolescents: Perspectives and possibilities. *Health Promotion Practice, 6*(4), 464–471. doi:10.1177/1524839904263897.

7 Public Relations and Development

Ethical Perspectives on Communication for Societal Effectiveness

Amanda Kennedy, Sifan Xu, and Erich J. Sommerfeldt

In recent years, a small but vibrant stream of literature has stressed the role of public relations in enhancing community or societal effectiveness (e.g., Heath, 2006; Sommerfeldt, 2013b; Starck & Kruckeberg, 2001; Taylor, 2010). Such works have argued that public relations is not only used by corporate forces to increase profit and enhance organizational legitimacy, but by governments and nongovernmental organizations (NGOs) for purposes such as nation building (Taylor & Kent, 2006) and aiding civil society initiatives (e.g., Sommerfeldt, 2013a; Sommerfeldt, 2013b; Sommerfeldt & Taylor, 2011; Taylor, 2011). An intrinsically related area in which public relations can arguably contribute to societal effectiveness is development communication.

However, theories and topics germane to development communication remain significantly underdeveloped in public relations scholarship. As Sriramesh (2012) has explained:

> Communication for Development (C4D) is a field in which public relations has played a significant role, but that role has not been studied with much depth and included in the body of knowledge. Information campaigns have been a mainstay of work by international agencies in the developing world at least since the middle of the twentieth century with the establishment of the United Nations and its agencies such as the FAO, WHO, UNICEF, and UNESCO. ... They also use public relations strategies and techniques for these purposes even if they do not use the term public relations, instead using the more generic term public communication or public information to describe their activities. (p. 9)

As argued by Sriramesh (2012), despite the inherent connections between public relations and development communication practice, limited research has viewed public relations through the lens of development communication—or vice versa. Although a handful of public relations scholars have explicitly acknowledged development communication and argued for an interrogation of the relationship between these two fields (Dutta-Bergman, 2005; Paquette, Sommerfeldt, & Kent, 2015; Sriramesh, 2009), much of the public relations literature relevant to development communication has only implicitly discussed it. Though this small body of literature has theorized the role of public relations in (re)creating civil society, nation building, and a fully functioning society, it often fails to identify such activities as part of development communication and, more importantly for the present work, neglects the ethical questions inherent to a public relations role in development practice. Moreover, scholars and practitioners of development communication have resisted associating development practice with public relations, stating that development communication "… is not public relations or corporate communication" (Communication Initiative, 2007, p. xxxiii).

This chapter will interrogate the linkages between the two disciplines by exploring the ethical implications for a public relations role in development communication. A focus on the ethical role of public relations in development is timely. As public relations' influence grows and reaches increasingly remote and diverse cultural pockets in all corners of the world, and as public relations practice becomes further implicated in the new global economy, it is crucial (as well as moral) to envisage an ethical role for public relations in globalization and development work (Bardhan & Weaver, 2011; Curtin & Gaither, 2007; Dutta, Ban, & Pal, 2012; Dutta & Pal, 2011; Dutta-Bergman, 2005). Initial forays into the ethics of public relations in development have relied on dominant ethical theories like deontology for guidance (e.g., Paquette et al., 2015). We intend to argue that future efforts in this vein should also engage critical and "nondominant" or "alternative" ethical frameworks, resisting a narrow focus on Western approaches that have traditionally dominated public relations theory.

If public relations scholars are to integrate development communication into the public relations body of knowledge, we must be fully aware of the ethical dimensions of such a project. As such, the chapter begins with a brief review of ethical theories in extant public relations research, and then turns to a discussion of ethical questions in development practice. The final sections elucidate the ethical and moral implications of public relations research in development.

Ethics in Public Relations

Although public relations scholarship on ethics is growing, much ground is left to cover. Some popular topics in public relations literature relevant to ethics include professional codes of conduct (e.g., Huang, 2001; Hunt, 1993; Kim & Ki, 2014; Olasky, 1985), ethical duties of practitioners and practice (e.g., Place, 2010; Ryan & Martinson, 1983), merits of normative symmetrical and/or dialogic communication (e.g., Bowen, 2004; Dutta & Pal, 2010; J. E. Grunig, 2006; Kent & Taylor, 2002), and corporate social responsibility (e.g., Benn, Todd, & Pendleton, 2010; L'Etang, 1994). Dominant, formal ethical philosophies adopted in public relations scholarship are often deontological (duty and rules based; means matter more than the ends) (e.g., Bowen, 2004; Bowen & Heath, 2005; Paquette et al., 2015; Place, 2010) or utilitarian (do the least harm and the most good for the most people) (e.g., Messina, 2007). These philosophies are traditionally marked by normative, rationalistic, masculine, and Western values such as justice, detached objectivity, and universality (Holtzhausen, 2012).

Alternatively, less dominant ethical philosophies seen in public relations research have been grounded in critical, feminist, and postmodern theories—for example, postcolonial approaches (e.g., Bardhan & Weaver, 2011; Curtin & Gaither, 2007; Dutta & Pal, 2011; Dutta-Bergman, 2005), feminist ethics of care (Coombs & Holladay, 2013; Holtzhausen, 2012; Surma & Daymon, 2014), and postmodern ethics (Holtzhausen, 2012). These approaches are more subjective, situated, and embodied than their dominant counterparts (e.g., deontology). Further, champions of nondominant ethics have argued they are better suited for public relations research and practice than dominant approaches traditionally assumed to provide normative ethical guideposts for the field (e.g., Holtzhausen, 2012; Surma & Daymon, 2014). Still, critical, feminist, and postmodern ethics are overshadowed and marginalized in public relations literature by the more detached, rationalistic, and masculine approaches such as deontology (Holtzhausen, 2012). With this basic understanding of public relations' ethics in mind, we turn to a short discussion of two important ethical issues identified in the development literature.

Ethical Questions of Development

Like public relations, development communication has been inconsistently defined, and definitions have evolved over the decades. Yet, these changing definitions provide insight into the major ethical quandaries of development work. Early definitions, such as that offered by Quebral (1975), reflect the economic focus of development communication, who described it as "the art and science of human communication applied to the speedy transformation of a country from poverty to a dynamic state of economic growth and makes possible greater economic and social equality and the larger fulfillment of human potential" (p. 2). Others characterized development as a "widely participatory process of social change in a society, intended to bring about both social and material advancement, including greater equity, freedom, and other valued qualities for the majority of people through their gaining greater control over the environment" (Rogers, 1976, p. 225).

Given these contrasting definitions, Deneulin (2014) suggested that what actually comprises "development" is a central question of development ethics. Although the scholarly field of development has moved away from a "modernization" paradigm, one that views communication as a means to achieve ends, to a more "participatory" and dialogic view of the practice (cf. Paquette et al., 2015), most contemporary development projects continue to be primarily modernistic. Many development programs operate under the assumption that development is a process in which every society needs to complete a series of stages in order to become modern, indicated usually by economic growth as defined in capitalist, free-market contexts (Beltran, 2006). In contrast, participatory definitions of development highlight sustainability, social change, liberation, and empowerment (Servaes & Lie, 2013). Debates about development goals and how people should live are directly related to the issue of the very definition of development.

Second, many have questioned the ethics of actual communication practice in development work. Modernistic development programs conceptualize communication as the one-way transfer of information, or more bluntly, "the manipulation of messages and people for the purposes of directed development" (Servaes & Lie, 2013, p. 9). The participatory paradigm, by contrast, advocates a two-way, horizontal, bottom-up dialogic process, where community members are seen as active participants of development. Goulet (1995) thus argued that development ethics should focus on the "means of the means," writing that "ethics must somehow get inside the value dynamisms of the instruments utilized by development agents and itself" (p. 25). Expanding on this notion, Dower (2010) argued that there is no ethical development without ethical means. In other words, the means of communication express certain values. As argued by Paquette et al. (2015), to focus on the means is to find inherent value in the people involved in the communication process, whereas to focus on the ends implicitly devalues publics' roles.

The ethics of communication tactics in development are further complicated by questions of scale: to what extent should beneficiaries or publics be involved in the project? To that point, Herzog (1991) elegantly suggested:

> The answer rests on one's understanding of development and of communication. If physical well-being is enough, then participation could be considered optional. But, if development implies changing people, as well as physical conditions, then participation becomes critical. Furthermore, the answer rests in part on one's understanding of communication. If communication is understood to be a human process by which we share meanings and create symbolic reality and from symbolic reality we take action to transform concrete reality, then development communication has a particular obligation to increase people's ability to deal symbolically with their reality, and thereby create the possibility of a more human existence. This suggests a second meaning for development communication—development of the full human potential for communication. (p. 216)

As can be seen above, complicating examinations of development communication ethics are two seemingly separate issues—development ethics and ethics about communication that serves development goals.

A Role for Public Relations in Development?

In response to the rapid spread of globalization, there has been much conversation about the importance of locally tailored communication in global public relations practice, or "glocal" (global/local) public relations (Holtzhausen, 2012; Lim, 2010; Verčič, L.A. Grunig, & J. E. Grunig, 1996). Many scholars have espoused theories about why and how to tailor large-scale public relations programs of global organizations to local communities (e.g., Lim 2010; Motion, Haar, & Leitch, 2012). Some have argued that glocal public relations should be attentive and beneficial to indigenous cultures (Vujnovic & Kruckeberg, 2010) and give agency to subaltern publics (Dutta-Berman, 2005). Relatedly, scholars have also recognized the possible complications and ethical implications of Western practitioners' engagement with local, indigenous populations, prompting some critical, cultural, and postmodern orientations in global public relations theory (e.g., Bardhan, 2003; Curtin & Gaither, 2007; Dutta-Bergman, 2005; Holtzhausen, 2011).

Despite the claims of Sriramesh (2012), Paquette et al. (2015), and others who have explicitly noted the role of public relations in development practice—and more implicit connections offered by others (e.g., Sommerfeldt, 2013b; Taylor, 2010)—development communication scholars and practitioners have by and large rejected the notion that public relations is a central part of development campaigns (e.g., Servaes, 2008). Public relations is scarcely mentioned by development scholars and practitioners, and only then when discussing the information-dissemination phases of campaigns, as illustrated in the following comment: "We may find a small budget for 'promotion' of the overall project, which is more related with public relations than with development communication" (Gumucio-Dagron, 2008, p. 79). While development scholars primarily conceive of public relations as solely restricted to the one-way, information-dissemination components of development projects, public relations researchers have argued for a more participative role for public relations in interactions with development project beneficiaries and in building relationships among development actors such as NGOs (e.g., Paquette et al., 2015; Sommerfeldt, 2013b; Taylor, 2011).

Notwithstanding the contestations of development scholars, public relations strategies and techniques are clearly an active part of many development campaigns, particularly in diffusing information to targeted publics (Sriramesh, 2012). However, if public relations can be interpreted as a communicative means through which social realities can be improved (Dutta & Pal, 2010), interrogations of the two-way, relationship-oriented aspects of public relations in development should be pursued. In keeping with the theme of this book, the "moral responsibility" of public relations, or questions about the ethics of public relations in development, vary depending on which role one ascribes to public relations practice—that of information diffuser, or that of relationship builder. However, we understand public relations not as encompassing only one-way *or* two-way communication, but as necessarily constituted by both. Indeed, as Taylor (2010) noted, functional and co-creational approaches to communication in civil society efforts are not irreconcilable. Thus, one- and two-way communication should be conceptualized as interrelated and intrinsic to public relations, not separate and independent models of practice. With this point in mind, the next section takes up the challenge of examining the ethical considerations of both roles in practice.

Ethical Problems and Possibilities for Public Relations as Development Communication

If public relations is to assume a greater role in development communication—both in scholarship and in practice—certain ethical implications and imperatives must be addressed, some of which have already been introduced into the public relations body of knowledge by critical and/ or global scholars in the field (e.g., Bardhan & Weaver, 2011; Curtin & Gaither, 2007; Dutta et al., 2012; Dutta & Pal, 2011; Dutta-Bergman, 2005; Edwards, 2011; Holtzhausen, 2012; Paquette et al., 2015; Sriramesh, 2012). The following discussion outlines some theoretical and practical approaches to public relations as development work already present in extant public relations literature, as well as introducing some new concepts (for public relations theory) that we propose may help guide ethical and effective public relations practice for development.

Culture-centered Dialogue and the Subaltern

First, the practice and theory of public relations has long-standing ties to (Western) corporate and capitalist interests—ties that present worrisome implications for development communication practice. If the goal of development communication is social justice, capitalistic public relations practices in developing states might have conflicting interests and questionable assumptions about the ontology of "development" (Dutta-Bergman, 2005; Dutta & Pal, 2011). Indeed, global public relations has often been critiqued for its neoliberal agenda and role in Westernization via globalization (Bardhan & Weaver, 2011; Dutta & Pal, 2011; Holtzhausen, 2011). Even public relations under the guise of such noble projects as nation building and civil society efforts (e.g., Sommerfeldt, 2013b; Taylor, 2000; Taylor & Doerfel, 2003) has been accused of being self-interested and as ultimately having ulterior motives that hinge on the dispersion of capitalism and Western values and commodities (Dutta-Bergman, 2005). Wilkins (1999) noted that approaches adopted by many development projects are highly related to what is considered desirable by the private sector, concluding that "characterizing social change within a commercial structure resonates with globalization trends privileging the role of multinational corporations as dominant institutions" (p. 63), and "the transition toward privatizing public programs may be more disruptive than beneficial to the process of social change" (p. 64).

However, more civic-minded and participatory models of public relations that attempt to engage, for example, subaltern publics in true dialogue are more amenable to the emancipatory and altruistic impulses normative in development communication (Dutta et al., 2012; Dutta-Bergman, 2005). Subaltern studies and culture-centered approaches (Dutta et al., 2012; Dutta & Pal, 2010, 2011) to public relations as development communication ideally eschew primarily corporate and neoliberal interests for more liberatory communication practices that privilege marginalized voices, embrace resistance, and are grounded in the everyday experiences of oppressed people and their cultural and structural realities.

For example, Dutta and Pal (2010), drawing from seminal subaltern studies scholars such as Spivak and Guha, suggested a subaltern studies approach to theorizing and engaging in dialogue with subaltern publics disconnected from the traditionally defined global public sphere. Dutta and Pal argued that such dialogue offers a "framework for sincerely listening to subaltern voices in ways that challenge the transnational hegemony, disrupt neoliberal knowledge structures, and seek to transform neoliberal policies underlying global inequalities both locally and globally" (p. 362). Relatedly, Dutta et al. (2012) articulated a culture-centered approach to public relations, privileging bottom-up constructions of knowledge and challenging normative Western concepts of democracy, capitalism, and civil society. We argue that this culture-centered approach to dialogue grounded in subaltern studies and postcolonial theory is one ethical strategy for engaging marginalized publics in development work. Dialogue with disenfranchised publics perhaps foremost requires "the turning of the lens on the self" (Dutta & Pal, 2010, p. 381)—in other words, sincere ethical dialogue begins with critical self-reflexivity, acknowledgement of Western privilege and the erasure or cooptation of subaltern subjects in neoliberal projects of globalization and development, and interrogations of our own assumptions based on Western epistemologies and normative ideas of what constitutes hegemonic concepts such as "development" and "subaltern." In short, an acute self-consciousness on the part of communication practitioners of development work, along with respecting subaltern autonomy and privileging subaltern knowledge, is essential to ethical communication with marginalized publics and should precede and significantly influence public relations as development work.

Relatedly, conceptualizations of publics in "developing" nations in public relations literature (often referred to as "beneficiaries" in the development literature) have frequently been simplistic and misguided at best (Dutta & Pal, 2010). Shallow understandings of faraway publics may result from etic ("outside-in") research approaches scored with Western assumptions about society and normative public relations practices (Bardhan, 2003). Alternatively, emic ("inside-out") research on publics in marginalized settings can equip practitioners and scholars with better-attuned cultural knowledge, providing for more ethical and effective communication strategies for social justice and parity.

Feminist and Postmodern Ethics for Development Public Relations

Closely tied to subaltern, culture-centered, and emic methodologies discussed above, certain feminist theories and ethics are useful here. For instance, standpoint epistemologies operate on the assumption that knowledge is grounded in everyday lived experiences of, for example, women and subjugated people (Harding, 1987, 2004; Hartstock, 1987). Further, Haraway (1991) wrote about the concept of "situated knowledges," arguing that knowledge is always situated or obscured, yet constituted by the knower's social position. Taken literally, feminist standpoint theory and situated knowledges grounded in everyday material realities articulate a need for physical closeness to or immersion in a particular location (e.g., a subaltern community) to genuinely understand or "know" a community, its culture, subjects, and needs.

Further, a feminist ethic of care might be applicable in development communication scenarios. Feminist ethics of care—in contrast to classical masculine values of justice, rationality, universality, and objectivity characteristic of, for example, deontological and consequentialist ethical theories—situate values such as interdependence, vulnerability, emotionality, and attentiveness and responsiveness to others' needs as morally superior (Gilligan, 1982). Similarly, some postmodern philosophers have put forth theories of morality and ethics for which responsibility to the Other—and respect for heterogeneity and (social, cultural, etc.) *difference* in Others—is pivotal (e.g., Bauman, 1993). If motivated by a feminist ethic of care (Gilligan, 1982) and commitment to social change (Harding, 1987), along with a postmodern ethic of responsibility to the Other and Otherness (including a respect for cultural differences) (Bauman, 1993), communication practitioners should deploy "insider" cultural knowledge to work toward ends dictated by particular needs of the community—and *not* mechanically operate under Western rubrics of "development" and "modernization" that characterize most contemporary development communication efforts.

Another related point of ethical contention in public relations as development communication has been addressed by transnational and Third World feminist critics and concerns the Eurocentric and patriarchal underpinnings of the very construct of "development." For example, Mohanty (2003) pointedly argued that subscribing to a "developed/developing/development" vocabulary is "a move that constitutes nothing less than unjustifiably confusing development with the separate path taken by the West in its development, as well as ignoring the directionality of the power relationship between the First and Third World," and further, "since no connections are made between First and Third World power shifts, the assumption is reinforced that the Third World just has not evolved to the extent that the West has" (p. 40). According to Mohanty and others, these assumptions drive the idea that Western development work is inherently positive and coming to the rescue of poor, "underdeveloped" Third World communities by ushering them into the global economy. This paternalistic impulse in development communication may be checked if development practitioners use the afore-mentioned methods of culture-centered dialogue wherein self-reflexivity and a genuine desire to understand the Other is key (Dutta et al., 2012; Dutta & Pal, 2010). Acknowledging these Eurocentric and patriarchal tendencies may help scholars and practitioners question Western assumptions about "development," to conduct emic research that privileges subjugated knowl-edge (Bardhan, 2003), and to recognize the limits of situated knowledge (Haraway, 1991).

(Post-)Colonial Ethics and Development Public Relations

In addition, closely related to the culture-centered, feminist, and postmod-ern interventions discussed above, critical theories of (post-)colonialism[1] and Western imperialism are also useful in problematizing normative discourses and practices—and engaging questions of ethics—in public relations and development communication. According to Chrisman and Williams (1993), while the terms are often conflated, *colonialism* may be more precisely understood as a specific time in history marked by "the [formal] conquest and direct control of other people's land" (and thus *post*-colonialism generally assumes and refers to the period and state of affairs after the end of colonialism), while *imperialism* can be defined as "the globalization of the capitalist mode of production, its penetration of previously non-capitalist regions of the world, and destruction of pre- or non-capitalist forms of social organisation" (p. 2). They went on to explain that, while the term "post-colonialism" implies that the global community has moved beyond formal colony-colonizer structures, many critical (post-)colonial scholars argue that the world indeed remains in the throes of colo-nialism vis-à-vis Western imperialism, or "continuing Western influence, located in flexible combination of the economic, the political, the military and the ideological (but with over-riding economic purpose)" (Chrisman & Williams, 1993, p. 3).

   In short, (post-)colonial studies and imperialist critiques interrogate the politics of power and knowledge, especially how dominant knowledge is produced about the "Other" (e.g., Third World nations and people) and, in turn, reproduces imperialistic power (Chrisman & Williams, 1993). Inasmuch, (post-)colonial critics presume a very real presence of Western power and control in Other or "developing" nations—*Western imperialist* forms of power and control, ubiquitous even in the most well-intentioned development efforts (Chrisman & Williams, 1993; Mohanty, 2003; Said, 1978; Spivak, 1990).

By the same token, many scholars of (post-)colonial studies have written about *decolonization*—decolonizing subjugated people and nations (e.g., Fanon, 2004); decolonizing methodologies (e.g., Smith, 2012); decolonizing theory, education, and academe (e.g., Mohanty, 2003; Said, 1978); and decolonizing knowledge and episteme (e.g., Santos, Nunes, & Meneses, 2008), are just some examples of emancipatory discourses in critical, feminist, postmodern, and (post-)colonial theory. To put it simply, decolonizing refers to both concrete and theoretical liberation from dominant (Western) practices and paradigms. Critical writings on decolonization have significant ethical relevance for public relations and development communication scholars and practitioners whose work impacts essentially colonized (e.g., non-Western, Third World, developing) people and places—for example, by entreating scholars and practitioners to embrace (not erase) *difference* across cultures for social justice purposes.

As Santos et al. (2008) pointed out, countless "other" and "different" worldviews exist outside of Western understanding, and a crucial step toward ethical interactions with non-Western "Others" is acknowledging the heterogeneity and autonomy of those cultures and knowledges (e.g., noncapitalist or nondemocratic societies). Echoing their sentiment, Young (2004), in his work on postmodernism and postcolonial studies, asked: "How can we know *and* respect the Other?" (p. 46). The answer to that question, many of the authors referenced in this discussion have argued, begins with candid and informed self-reflexivity on the part of (dominant) knowers—such as public relations and development communication practitioners and scholars. To quote Santos et al., who wrote about the vast constellation of knowledges (ways of knowing, ways of understanding the world) present all of society: "Self-reflexivity ... is the first step towards the recognition of the epistemological diversity of the world" (p. xxi).

This discussion has only begun to imagine the ethical intersections, implications, and potentials of public relations and development communication scholarship and practice, particularly by drawing from critical feminist, postmodern, subaltern, and (post-)colonial discourses. While some of these interventions have already taken hold in public-relations-as-development-communication literature (e.g., Dutta & Pal, 2010; Curtin & Gaither, 2007), the vast canon of critical-cultural, postmodern, feminist, and (post-)colonial studies—as well as related theories not discussed here, such as Marxism (Ahmad, 1992), deconstruction (Spivak, 1993), psychoanalysis (Bhabha, 1993), and human geography and critical cartographies (Alexander & Mohanty, 2010)—are unexplored in the public relations body of knowledge.

Conclusion

There remains much work to be done in building bridges between development communication and public relations theory and praxis. But if we are to lay claim to public relations as a function of development communication, we must recognize that while public relations practices may well make development communication more ethical or participatory, in some instances it may not. Therefore, public relations research examining development communication must consider two vital questions: the ontological assumptions behind the meaning of "development," and the axiology of communication to achieve development goals. Herein, we have argued that research should not only rely on traditional Western ethical philosophies like deontology and consequentialism to conduct such inquiries. Although these philosophies have served the discipline well, the expansion of global public relations' research domain into the field of development would benefit from the inclusion of the above feminist and postmodern theories, ethics, and moral philosophies with assumptions more immediately compatible with the subject under consideration.

Note

1. Considering the debate surrounding the term "post-colonial" and its variants (see Chrisman & Williams, 1993, pp. 1–4), we adopt the term "(post-)colonial" to refer to what is generally understood as post-colonial theory and critiques of colonial discourses and imperialism.

References

Ahmad, A. (1992). *In theory: Classes, nations, literatures.* London, UK: Verso.

Alexander, J. M., & Mohanty, C. T. (2010). Cartographies of knowledge and power: Transnational feminism as radical praxis. In R. Nagar & A. L. Swarr (Eds.), *Critical transnational feminist praxis* (pp. 23–45). Albany, NY: State University of New York.

Bardhan, N. (2003). Rupturing public relations metanarratives: The example of India. *Journal of Public Relations Research, 15*(3), 225–248.

Bardhan, N., & Weaver, C. K. (2011). Public relations in global cultural contexts. In N. Bardhan & C. K. Weaver (Eds.), *Public relations in global cultural contexts: Multi-paradigmatic perspectives* (pp. 1–28). New York, NY: Routledge.

Bauman, Z. (1993). *Postmodern ethics.* Malden, MA: Blackwell.

Beltran, L. R. (2006). A farewell to Aristotle: "Horizontal" communication. In A. Gumucio-Dragon & T. Tufte (Eds.), *Communication for social change anthology: Historical and contemporary readings* (pp. 76–87). South Orange, NJ: Communication for Social Change Consortium.

Benn, S., Todd, L. R., & Pendleton, J. (2010). Public relations leadership in corporate social responsibility. *Journal of Business Ethics, 96*(3), 403–423. doi:10.1007/s10551-010-0474-5.

Bhabha, H. (1993). Remembering Fanon: Self, psyche and the colonial condition. In P. Williams & L. Chrisman (Eds.), *Colonial discourse and post-colonial theory: A reader* (pp. 112–124). Essex, England: Prentice Hall.

Bowen, S. A. (2004). Expansion of ethics as the tenth generic principle of public relations excellence: A Kantian theory and model for managing ethical issues. *Journal of Public Relations Research, 16*(1), 65–92. doi:10.1207/s1532754xjprr1601_3.

Bowen, S. A., & Heath, R. L. (2005). Issues management, systems and rhetoric: Exploring the distinction between ethical and legal guidelines at Enron. *Journal of Public Affairs, 5,* 84–98. doi:10.1002/pa.13.

Chrisman, L., & Williams, P. (1993). Colonial discourse and post-colonial theory: An introduction. In P. Williams & L. Chrisman (Eds.), *Colonial discourse and post-colonial theory: A reader* (pp. 1–20). Essex, England: Prentice Hall.

Communication Initiative. (2007). World Congress on Communication for Development: lessons, challenges, and the way forward. Washington, DC: World Bank Publications.

Coombs, W. T., & Holladay, S. J. (2013). *It's not just PR: Public relations in society* (2nd ed.). West Sussex, UK: Wiley.

Curtin, P. A., & Gaither, T. K. (2007). *International public relations: Negotiating culture, identity, and power.* Thousand Oaks, CA: Sage.

Deneulin, S. (2014). *Wellbeing, justice and development ethics.* New York, NY: Routledge.

Dower, N. (2010). Development and the ethics of the means. In C. K. Wilber, A. K. Dutt, & T. M. Hesburgh (Eds.), *New directions in development ethics: Essays in honor of Denis Goulet* (pp. 29–37). Notre Dame, IN: University of Notre Dame Press.

Dutta, M. J., Ban, Z., & Pal, M. (2012). Engaging worldviews, cultures, and structures through dialogue: The culture-centred approach to public relations. *PRism, 9*(2). Retrieved from http://www.prismjournal.org/homepage.html.

Dutta, M. J., & Pal, M. (2010). Dialog theory in marginalized settings: A subaltern studies approach. *Communication Theory, 20*(4), 363–386. doi:10.1111/j.1468-2885.2010.01367.x.

Dutta, M. J., & Pal, M. (2011). Public relations and marginalization in a global context: A postcolonial critique. In N. Bardhan & C. K. Weaver (Eds.), *Public relations in global cultural contexts: Multi-paradigmatic perspectives* (pp. 195–225). New York, NY: Routledge.

Dutta-Bergman, M. J. (2005). Civil society and public relations: Not so civil after all. *Journal of Public Relations Research, 17*(3), 267–289. doi:10.1207/s1532754xjprr1703_3.

Edwards, L. (2011). Critical perspectives in global public relations: Theorizing power. In N. Bardhan & C. K. Weaver (Eds.), *Public relations in global cultural contexts: Multi-paradigmatic perspectives* (pp. 29–49). New York, NY: Routledge.

Fanon, F. (2004). *The wretched of the Earth.* (P. Wilcox, Trans.). New York, NY: Grove Press. (Original work published 1963).

Gilligan, C. (1982). *In a different voice: Psychological theory and women's development.* Cambridge, MA: Harvard University Press.

Goulet, D. (1995). *Development ethics: A guide to theory and practice.* New York, NY: Apex.

Grunig, J. E. (2006). Furnishing the edifice: Ongoing research on public relations as a strategic management function. *Journal of Public Relations Research, 18*(2), 151–176. doi:10.1207/s1532754xjprr1802_5.

Gumucio-Dagron, A. (2008). Vertical minds versus horizontal cultures: An overview of participatory processes and experiences. In J. Servaes (Ed.), *Communication for development and social change* (pp. 68–81). New Delhi, India: SAGE.

Haraway, D. (1991). Situated knowledges: The science question in feminism and the privilege of partial perspectives. *Feminist Studies, 14*(3), 579–599. doi:10.2307/3178066.

Harding, S. (1987). Introduction: Is there a feminist method? In *Feminism and methodology* (pp. 1–14). Boston, MA: Hall.

Harding, S. (Ed.). (2004). *The feminist standpoint theory reader: Intellectual & political controversies.* New York, NY: Routledge.

Hartstock, N. (1987). The feminist standpoint: Developing the ground for a specifically feminist historical materialism. In S. G. Harding (Ed.), *Feminism and methodology* (pp. 157–180). Boston, MA: Hall.

Heath, R. L. (2006). Onward into more fog: Thoughts on public relations' research directions. *Journal of Public Relations Research, 18*(2), 93–114. doi:10.1207/s1532754xjprr1802_2.

Herzog, W. (1991). Issues for development communication ethics. *Journal of Mass Media Ethics, 6*(4), 210–221. doi:10.1207/s15327728jmme0604_2.

Holtzhausen, D. R. (2011). The need for a postmodern turn in global public relations. In N. Bardhan & C. K. Weaver (Eds.), *Public relations in global cultural contexts: Multi-paradigmatic perspectives* (pp. 140–166). New York, NY: Routledge.

Holtzhausen, D. R. (2012). *Public relations as activism: Postmodern approaches to theory and practice.* New York, NY: Routledge.

Huang, Y-H. (2001). Should a public relations code of ethics be enforced? *Journal of Business Ethics, 31,* 259–270. doi:10.1023/A:1010719118448.

Hunt, T. (1993). Universal ethics code: An idea whose time has come. *Public Relations Review, 19*(1), 1–11. doi:10.1016/0363-8111(93)90025-8.

Kent, M. L., & Taylor, M. (2002). Toward a dialogic theory of public relations. *Public Relations Review, 28,* 21–37. doi:10.1023/A:1010719118448.

Kim, S.-Y., & Ki, E.-J. (2014). An exploratory study of ethics codes of professional public relations associations: Proposing modified universal codes of ethics in public relations. *Journal of Mass Media Ethics, 29*(4), 238–257. doi:10.1080/08900 523.2014.946602.

L'Etang, J. (1994). Public relations and corporate social responsibility: Some issues arising. *Journal of Business Ethics, 13*(2), 111–123. doi:10.1007/BF00881580.

Lim, S. L. (2010). Global integration or local responsiveness? Multinational corporation's public relations strategies and cases. In G. J. Golan T. J. Johnson & W. Wanta (Eds.), *International media communication in a global age* (pp. 299–318). New York, NY: Routledge.

Messina, A. (2007). Public relations, the public interest and persuasion: An ethical approach. *Journal of Communication Management, 11*(1), 29–52. doi:10.1108/13632540710725978.

Mohanty, C. T. (2003). *Feminism without borders: Decolonizing theory, practicing solidarity.* Durham, NC: Duke University Press.

Motion, J., Haar, J., & Leitch, S. (2012). A public relations framework for indigenous engagement. In K. Sriramesh & D. Verčič (Eds.), *Culture and public relations: Links and implications* (pp. 54–66). New York, NY: Routledge.

Olasky, M. N. (1985). Ministers or panderers: Issues raised by the Public Relations Society code of standards. *Journal of Mass Media Ethics, 1*(1), 43–49. doi:10.1080/08900528509358254.

Paquette, M., Sommerfeldt, E. J., & Kent, M. L. (2015). Do the ends justify the means? Dialogue, development communication, and deontological ethics. *Public Relations Review, 41*(1), 30–39. doi:10.1080/08900528509358254.

Place, K. R. (2010). A qualitative examination of public relations practitioner ethical decision making and the deontological theory of issues management. *Journal of Mass Media Ethics, 25,* 226–245. doi:10.1080/08900523.2010.497405.

Quebral, N. C. (1975). Development communication [in the Philippines; its theories and principles]: Where does it stand today? Media Asia (Singapore). Retrieved from http://agris.fao.org/agris-search/search.do?recordID=XB7601584.

Rogers, E. M. (1976). *Communication and development: Critical perspectives.* Beverly Hills, CA: Sage.

Ryan, M., & Martinson, D. L. (1983). The PR officer as corporate conscience. *Public Relations.Quarterly, 28*(2), 20–23.

Said, E. (1978). *Orientalism.* New York: Pantheon.

Santos, B. S., Nunes, J. A., & Meneses, M. P. (2008). Introduction: Opening up the canon of knowledge and recognition of difference. In B. S. Santos (Ed.), *Another knowledge is possible: Beyond northern epistemologies* (pp. ixx–lxxi). London, UK: Verso.

Servaes, J. (2008). *Communication for development and social change.* New Delhi, India: SAGE.

Servaes, J., & Lie, R. (2013). Sustainable social change and communication. *Communication Research Trends, 32*(4), 4–30.

Smith, L. T. (2012). *Decolonizing methodologies: Research and indigenous peoples* (2nd ed.). New York, NY: Zed.

Sommerfeldt, E. J. (2013a). Networks of social capital: Extending a public relations model of civil society in Peru. *Public Relations Review, 39*(1), 1–12. doi:10.1016/j.pubrev.2012.08.005.

Sommerfeldt, E. J. (2013b). The civility of social capital: Public relations in the public sphere, civil society, and democracy. *Public Relations Review, 39*(4), 280–289. doi:10.1016/j.pubrev.2012.12.004.

Sommerfeldt, E. J., & Taylor, M. (2011). A social capital approach to improving public relations' efficacy: Diagnosing internal constraints on external communication. *Public Relations Review, 37*(3), 197–206. doi:10.1016/j.pubrev.2011.03.007.

Spivak, G. C. (1990). *The post-colonial critic: Interviews, strategies, dialogues.* New York, NY: Routledge.

Spivak, G. C. (1993). Can the subaltern speak? In P. Williams & L. Chrisman (Eds.), *Colonial discourse and post-colonial theory: A reader* (pp. 66–111). Essex, England: Prentice Hall.

Sriramesh, K. (2009). Globalisation and public relations: The past, present, and the future. *PRism, 6*(2), 1–11. Retrieved from http://www.prismjournal.org/fileadmin/Praxis/Files/globalPR/SRIRAMESH.pdf.

Sriramesh, K. (2012). Culture and public relations: Formulating the relationship and its relevance to the practice. In K. Sriramesh, & D. Verčič (Eds.), *Culture and public relations: Links and implications* (pp. 9–24). New York, NY: Routledge.

Starck, K., & Kruckeberg, D. (2001). Public relations and community: A reconstructed theory revisited. In R. L. Heath, & G. M. Vasquez (Eds.), *Handbook of public relations* (pp. 41–60). Thousand Oaks, CA: SAGE.

Surma, A., & Daymon, C. (2014). Caring about public relations and the gendered cultural intermediary role. In C. Daymon & K. Demetrius (Eds.), *Gender and public relations: Critical perspectives on voice, image, and identity* (pp. 46–66). New York, NY: Routledge.

Taylor, M. (2000). Toward a public relations approach to nation building. *Journal of Public Relations Research,12*(2),179–210.doi:10.1207/S1532754XJPRR1202_3.

Taylor, M. (2010). Public relations in the enactment of civil society. In R. L. Heath (Ed.), *The SAGE handbook of public relations* (pp. 5–15). Thousand Oaks, CA: Sage.

Taylor, M. (2011). Building social capital through rhetoric and public relations. *Management Communication Quarterly, 25*(3). 436–454. doi:10.1177/0893318911410286.

Taylor, M., & Doerfel, M. L. (2003). Building interorganizational relationships that build nations. *Human Communication Research, 29*(2), 153–181. doi:10.1111/j.1468-2958.2003.tb00835.x.

Taylor, M., & Kent, M. L. (2006). Public relations theory and practice in nation building. In C. H. Botan & V. Hazleton (Eds.), *Public relations theory II* (pp. 341–359). Mahwah, NJ: Lawrence Erlbaum Associates.

Verčič, D., Grunig, L. A., & Grunig, J. E. (1996). Global and specific principles of public relations: Evidence from Slovenia. In H. M. Culbertson & N. Chen (Eds.), *International public relations: A comparative analysis* (pp. 31–65). Mahwah NJ: Lawrence Erlbaum.

Vujnovic, M., & Kruckeberg, C. (2010). The local, national, and global challenges of public relations. In R. L. Heath (Ed.), *The SAGE handbook of public relations* (pp. 671–678). Thousand Oaks, CA: Sage.

Wilkins, K. G. (1999). Development discourse on gender and communication in strategies for social change. *Journal of Communication, 49*(1), 46–68. doi:10.1111/j.1460-2466.1999.tb02781.x.

Young, R. (2004). *White mythologies: Writing history and the west* (2nd ed.). New York, NY: Routledge.

8 The Impact of Organizations' Ethical Approaches in Times of Crisis

Sora Kim, Jooyun Hwang, and
Xiaochen (Angela) Zhang

Despite the importance of ethics in organizational decision making, businesses often face dilemmas in making ethical decisions that might conflict with market-driven behaviors (Gilbert, 2001). Organizations therefore often overlook the role of ethics in nurturing stakeholder relationships. In times of crisis, when the viability and sustainability of organizations are highly threatened, ethical decisions are especially crucial because stakeholders' trust is often at its lowest. Previous studies in the literature have noted that ethical decisions made during crises are important because they help allocate and utilize resources for the sake of various stakeholders rather than only one (e.g., shareholders) (Donaldson & Preston, 1995; Hill & Jones, 1992).

Scholars have suggested that ethics should be at the heart of strategic decision making because a moral or ethical choice could benefit both the organization and its stakeholders (Gilbert, 2001; Hosmer, 1994). However, relatively little attention has been paid to providing empirical evidence of the effectiveness of the ethical approaches applied during times of crisis. This study attempts to fill the gap in the literature on the effectiveness of ethics by applying two strategic approaches in the context of crisis management: the ethics of justice and the ethics of care. By exploring the relative effects of the ethics of justice and the ethics of care in organizational crises, this study attempts to enhance the understanding of how ethical response strategies can be incorporated into crisis communication.

Literature Review

Ethical Responsibility of Public Relations

Ethics in public relations has been often discussed in terms of the normative responsibility to build and enhance civil society and the public sphere (e.g., Sommerfeldt, 2013) or in terms of a "code of ethics" in public relations practice (e.g., Fitzpatrick & Bronstein, 2006). Scholars in the field have increasingly called for greater emphasis on the ethical role of public relations in community engagement and civic professionalism (Brunner, 2015; Sommerfeldt, 2013). For instance, Brunner (2015) argued for adopting the concept of civic professionalism in public relations because it enables the profession to focus on the public interest and the ethical responsibility of public relations. Civic professionalism in public relations holds that professionals should work for the public good and fulfill their ethical responsibilities to build mutually beneficial relationships between the organization and the public (Brunner, 2015). In addition, by applying the concepts of civil society, public sphere, and social capital in public relations, Sommerfeldt (2013) stressed that community building is the primary role of public relations because it serves to improve democracy in society.

Although these normative approaches to ethics regarding the role of public relations in society are useful in providing directions for the profession, they are not sufficient to move it toward adopting ethics in practice. Without the demonstrated effectiveness of ethical approaches in eliciting the positive responses of stakeholders, it would be hard to persuade organizations to include ethics in their managerial decision-making processes. Thus, by examining the effectiveness of ethical approaches in times of crisis, this study intends to demonstrate that embracing ethical responsibilities would result in positive outcomes for organizations.

Societal needs and pressures to communicate public interests are particularly manifested in crises because they often generate strong stakeholder distrust and discomfort. Proposed by Simola (2003), the ethics of justice and the ethics of care represent two possible ethical approaches to meet the social pressures raised by stakeholders in crisis communication. The ethics of justice approach is characterized by the adherence to "absolute standards of judgment" in making ethical decisions and the use of logic and objectivity to "evaluate conflicting rights and claims" for the purpose of protecting public rights in a crisis (Simola, 2003, p. 354). In contrast, the ethics of care approach emphasizes the "creation or strengthening of relationships among people" (Simola, 2003, p. 354). Despite the differing emphases of these approaches, both tend to stress the importance of maintaining community bonds, protecting public rights, and embracing social needs in crisis communication (Ciulla, 2009; Simola, 2003).

Both the ethics of justice and the ethics of care originated in ethical theories. The ethics of justice stems from Rawls' (1971) research on the theory of justice and Kohlberg's (1973) development of moral reasoning. Rawls (1971) posited that when people "walk in other people's shoes," they are motivated to be impartial and to ensure fairness in their judgments. Building on Rawls' (1971) initial proposition, Kohlberg (1973) further elaborated that morally mature individuals should be capable of fairness and impartiality in making decisions. An ethics of care was proposed by Gilligan (1977) as a complement to the ethics of justice. However, although the ethics of justice can be applied to all people, it was initially developed solely from male perspectives (Simola, 2003). Gilligan (1977) developed an ethics of care based on women's moral reasoning processes. In making a moral decision, women rely more on situational and interpersonal factors than on justice or fairness. Women's moral reasoning processes focus on the care of both self and others. An ethics of care approach was later refined as a concept that was broader than the moral reasoning process of women (Chamberlain & Houston, 1999; Walker, 1998). The ethics of care approach encompasses the importance of caring in relationships, empathy, and sensitivity in responding to the emotions of others.

Ethics of Justice and Care as Crisis Communication Strategies

Because of the high relevancy and implications of these approaches for crisis management, scholars have recognized the ethics of justice and the ethics of care as crisis communication strategies (Bauman, 2011; Simola, 2005; Stein & Ahmad, 2008). Crisis communication that focuses on the ethics of care emphasizes the traits of social virtues, such as sympathy, compassion, and friendship. In contrast, crisis communication based on the ethics of justice emphasizes objective standards and impartial judgement in protecting individual rights involved in crises (Bauman, 2011; French & Weis, 2000). Simola (2003) suggested that the application of the ethics of justice involves the use of scientific evidence derived from scientific method, logic, and impartial evaluations by a third party in crafting crisis communication. Conversely, the ethics of care approach to crisis management emphasizes the nurturing of stakeholder relationships and incorporates organizational responsiveness and attentiveness to stakeholder needs and feelings. Adapting Simola's (2003) definition, this study conceptualizes an ethics of justice approach to crisis communication as a communication strategy that involves fairness, logic, and unbiased scientific judgments with the aim of providing publics with a sense of assurance that the organization is in control of the crisis situation and is resolving it with confidence. Conversely, the ethics of care approach to crisis communication focuses on emotional caring and responsiveness to public needs, which serve to nurture relationships between the organization and its publics.

A majority of scholars have endorsed the ethics of care (Bauman, 2011; Linsley & Slack, 2013; Simola, 2005) rather than the ethics of justice as the strategic approach to crisis management. Because crises always involve public harm and possible responsibilities (i.e., perceived intentionality) on the side of organizations, the ethics of care approach may better show that the organization cares about its stakeholders (Bauman, 2011). However, because this proposition is based mainly on the findings of case studies, it lacks empirical validity. Because stakeholders' perceived intentionality for the organization in crisis is a factor that could influence the relative effectiveness of ethical approaches (Bauman, 2011; Linsley & Slack, 2013), the type of crisis should be considered in the selection of one crisis communication strategy over the other. Bauman (2011) recommended the ethics of care as a primary strategy in crises involving unintentional harm (e.g., victim crisis type). He provided two rationales to support his argument. First, the perceptions of stakeholders matter during a crisis; they tend to perceive that the organization's lack of care caused the crisis even in the context of unintentional harm. Thus, the ethics of care approach better accommodates stakeholders' expectations of care. Second, in an unintentional harm crisis, managing complex relationships with stakeholders is often more important than making impartial judgments or resolving problems.

The severity of the crisis should also be considered in the selection of ethical approaches because it affects stakeholders' perceptions of the organizations' responsibility (Coombs & Holladay, 2002). Crisis severity can be defined as the magnitude of the consequences and the nature of harm caused by the crisis (Collins, 1989; Stein & Ahmad, 2008). It serves to intensify public perceptions of the organization in crisis. As crisis severity increases, publics' attribution of crisis responsibility to the organization may increase. When the impact of a crisis is high, and its consequences are deemed severe, the crisis-affected publics tend to be more emotional and in greater need of emotional support (Kim & Cameron, 2011). In a case study of a shooting at a McDonald's restaurant, Simola (2003) suggested that when a crisis involves a high casualty rate (i.e., high crisis severity), it is better for the organization to be more sensitive and responsive to its stakeholders' needs by adopting an ethics of care approach. Based on the previous literature on ethical approaches, the following hypotheses are proposed.

> H1: An ethics of care approach will be more effective than an ethics of justice approach in a victim crisis in terms of preserving positive public perception of corporate reputation.
> H2: An ethics of care approach will be more effective than an ethics of justice when crisis severity is high in terms of preserving positive public perception of corporate reputation.

This study also proposes the following research question to better understand the consequences of ethical approaches because the previous crisis literature on ethical approaches is still exploratory and lacks theoretical grounds for predicting all relationships among ethical approaches, crisis type, and crisis severity:

> RQ: How do "ethics of justice" versus "ethics of care" in crisis communication strategies affect public perceptions of corporate reputation in different crisis types and crisis severities?

Methods

Design and Procedure

To explore the effects of strategies using the ethics of care and the ethics of justice on public perceptions of corporate reputation, this experiment employed a 2 (crisis type: victim vs. preventable) × 2 (crisis severity: high vs. low) × 2 (crisis response strategy: ethics of justice vs. ethics of care) between-subjects design. A total of 225 students at a large university in the

Southeastern United States participated in this experiment (female: 72.9% vs. male: 27.1%). The crises stimuli involved food infection and poisoning that occurred in a local restaurant. A fictitious company (i.e., Pierre & Schmitt) was used to prevent any preconceptions about the company.

The participants were randomly assigned to one of the eight experimental conditions (on average 28 per condition). All participants were first asked to read a news article about the company's recent crisis. In a victim crisis scenario, respondents read that the crisis (i.e., soup poisoning) was linked to malicious food tampering by outsiders, whereas the restaurant's unsanitary production and distribution system caused the crisis in a preventable crisis scenario (i.e., the cause of the crisis was internal and preventable). The severity of the crisis was manipulated by the extent of crisis damages on customers (low severity: five people got ill but soon recovered, high severity: 17 people died and 56 got ill). Next, the participants were asked to read the company's crisis response messages in response to the crisis. In the ethics of care strategy, the company's responses were empathetic, emphasizing caring relationships with customers (e.g., creating personnel teams to assist victims, their families, and the community by providing transportation, hospital, and funeral arrangements). In the ethics of justice strategy, the company's responses highlighted its independent and objective investigations of the crisis by credible third parties (e.g., the company contacted the Federal Bureau of Investigation [FBI] and the Food and Drug Administration [FDA] to obtain impartial investigations and to ensure timely and accurate decision making). After reading the company's responses to the crisis, the participants completed a survey questionnaire that measured their perceptions of the company's corporate reputation. On average, the experiment took 15 minutes to complete.

Measures and Pre-Test

Corporate reputation was measured by people's cognitive and affective evaluations of the corporation: I think the restaurant is (1) attractive, (2) reliable, and (3) trustworthy; (4) I like the restaurant (1: strongly disagree, 7: strongly agree); and (5) "What is your overall impression of the restaurant?" (1: very unfavorable, 7: very favorable) (Brown & Dacin, 1997; Kim, 2011). To confirm a similar level of message strength and clarity across conditions, 32 undergraduate students participated in a pretest. No significant differences were found among message stimuli reporting the crisis and the company's responses in terms of the readability, flow, and logic of the messages.

Results

Manipulation Checks

As expected, the manipulation checks were successful. The participants in victim crisis conditions ($M = 3.69$, $SD = 1.23$) considered the company a victim of the crisis more than those who were exposed to preventable conditions (M = 6.39, SD = .70) (t (178) = –20.24, p < .0001). In terms of crisis severity, participants in the low condition (M = 5.65, SD = 1.12) saw the crisis as less severe than in the high condition (M = 6.79, SD = .56) (t (165) = –9.71, p < .0001). Regarding the strategy, the participants exposed to the ethics of justice strategy (M = 5.5, SD = 1.1) perceived it to be a more scientific approach than the ethics of care strategy (M = 3.7, SD = 1.5) (t (205) = 9.95, p < .0001). The participants who were exposed to the ethics of care strategy (M = 6.1, SD = 1.2) perceived it to be more compassion-ate and sympathetic than the ethics of justice strategy (M = 2.9, SD = 1.7) (t (199) = –16.72, p < .0001).

Examination of Hypotheses and Research Question

A three-way analysis of variance (ANOVA) was conducted to investigate the degrees to which the ethics of justice and ethics of care approaches influenced the participants' perceptions of corporate reputation in differ-ent types and severities of crisis (RQ1). The results revealed that the crisis response strategy had a significant main effect on publics' perception of corporate reputation (F (1, 217) = 5.97, p = .015, η^2 = .03), which indicated that the ethics of care approach (M = 3.29, SD = 1.4) was more effective than the ethics of justice approach in increasing public perceptions of rep-utation (M = 2.87, SD = 1.2). (See Table 8.1 for the means and standard deviations.) No significant two-way interaction effects were found between crisis type and strategies or between crisis severity and strategies on repu-tation perception (F (1, 217) =1.68, p = .19 and F (1, 217) = .08, p = .78, respectively). Since the gender ratio of our sample was disproportionate, an analysis of covariance (ANCOVA) was conducted while controlling for the gender factor. The ANCOVA revealed the same results as the ANOVA, suggesting no significant impact of gender on the outcome (F (1, 216) = .76, p = .38).

In addition, to determine whether the ethics of care approach was more effective than the ethics of justice approach in the victim crisis (H1) and high crisis severity (H2), pairwise comparisons were further examined. The results suggested that in a victim crisis, the ethics of care approach resulted in higher public perceptions of corporate reputation than the ethics of justice approach (M *(diff)* = .65, SE = .24, p = .008). Thus, H1 was sup-ported. However, no statistically significant difference was found between the effects of the two approaches in the high crisis severity condition (M *(diff)* = .37, SE = .24, p = .12), although the ethics of care strategy revealed a higher mean score for corporate reputation than the ethics of justice strat-egy revealed (see Table 8.1). Instead, a significant difference was identified in the direction opposite to that posited in H2. The ethics of care strategy was more effective when crisis severity is low, resulting in higher public perceptions of corporate reputation (M *(diff)* = .47, SE = .24, p = .05) than the ethics of justice strategy (see Figure 8.1 for two-way interaction effects).

Table 8.1 Means and Standard Deviations of Corporate Reputation

Crisis Response Strategy	Crisis Type	Crisis Severity	Corporate Reputation
			M(SD)
Ethics of Justice	Victim	Low	3.40 (1.4)
		High	2.95 (1.2)
		Total	3.18 (1.3)
	Preventable	Low	2.54 (1.0)
		High	2.58 (1.1)
		Total	2.56 (1.1)
	Total	Low	2.97 (1.3)
		High	2.77 (1.2)
		Total	2.87 (1.2)
Ethics of Care	Victim	Low	3.82 (1.1)
		High	3.82 (1.5)
		Total	3.82 (1.3)
	Preventable	Low	3.06 (1.3)
		High	2.46 (1.3)
		Total	2.76 (1.3)
	Total	Low	3.44 (1.2)
		High	3.14 (1.5)
		Total	3.29 (1.4)

Discussion

The findings of this study yielded valuable insights. When it was adopted as the strategy to respond to the crisis, the ethics of care approach was superior to the ethics of justice approach in providing empirical evidence of its relative effectiveness on public perceptions of a corporate reputation in crisis. The finding further indicates that compared to the impartial and rational approach emphasized in the ethics of justice strategy, people tend to respond positively to an ethics of care. Thus, a more interpersonal approach with care would be effective in maintaining and nurturing stakeholder relationships. This finding is in line with previous studies that claimed that an ethics of care approach should be considered in crisis management because it tends to enhance the relationship between the organization in crisis and its stakeholders (Bauman, 2011; Linsley & Slack, 2013).

Specifically, the ethics of care approach was found to be more efficient than the ethics of justice strategy in a victim crisis (i.e., unintentional crisis). The reason why the ethics of care can be more efficient in a victim crisis than the ethics of justice could be explained by how people attribute blame to the organization in an unintentional crisis. Although the crisis was

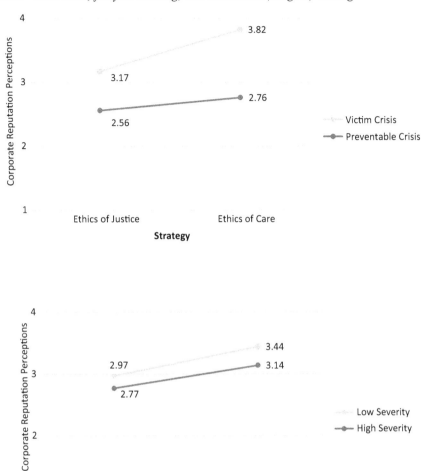

Figure 8.1 Interaction Effects of Ethical Approaches in Different Crisis Types and
Severities.

not created by the organization in a victim crisis (i.e., unintentional and
victim crisis), people tended to attribute less intentionality to the organization when they perceived that it cares in its responses to the crisis, whereas
they seemed to attribute greater intentionality to the organization when they
did not particularly perceive that it cares. This preference of the ethics of
care in a victim crisis indicates that what determines the intentionality of
the organization in a crisis is not the reality of the crisis (i.e., actual crisis
type) but public perceptions of the crisis, and the public perceptions of the

crisis is often affected by how the organization responds to the crisis. This finding provides an important insight into managing victim crises. One can easily observe how often victim crises such as rumors and product tampering by outsiders can damage the organization despite the fact that the organization itself is the victim of the crisis (i.e., unintentional). Our finding emphasizes the importance of managing public perceptions of the crisis even in victim crises through proper crisis communication messages. This finding also confirms Bauman's (2011) recommendation that the ethics of care is a better approach in crises involving unintentional harm. However, Bauman's recommendation was based on case studies conducted without empirical support. Therefore, the empirical evidence found in the present study makes an important contribution to the current knowledge about ethical approaches.

An interesting finding was that the ethics of care approach seemed to be more effective than the ethics of justice approach when crisis severity was low. This finding does not align with recommendations based on previous studies (Linsley & Slack, 2013; Simola, 2003, 2005). Previous research has suggested that an ethics of care approach would be better in a severe crisis because it requires greater intensive emotional support for stakeholders than a less severe crisis requires. This unexpected finding could imply that the positive effects of the ethics of care tend to occur more often when the organization exceeds public expectations than when it meets them. People might consider that the organization's care for stakeholders' interpersonal needs and feelings even in crises with low severity exceeds their expectations and therefore show positive responses to the organization. In addition, the previous literature on consumer behavior has well documented that when a company's performance is beyond consumer expectations, consumers tend to be more satisfied with the company (Kim, 2011; Matzler, Hinterhuber, Bailom, & Sauerwein, 1996). However, this is only one possible explanation. Further investigations should be made in future research.

Finally, the findings of this study make several contributions to the growing discussion in the literature on ethics, civic professionalism, and the role of public relations (Brunner, 2015; Sommerfeldt, 2013; Sullivan, 2004). Because the current discussion on ethics in public relations has been largely limited to providing normative directions based on case studies, practitioner interviews, and extensive literature reviews, scholars should focus more on providing empirical evidence by testing positive outcomes of ethical approaches in public relations, which would serve to ensure substantial changes in the public relations practices of organizations. For instance, it is relatively easy to argue that ethics should be incorporated into an organization's decision making process or that practitioners should focus on building mutually beneficial relationships with stakeholders by adopting civic professionalism because these concepts are normatively correct and thus appeal to many scholars. However, in reality, they are not often applied in practice. Obtaining beneficial relationships for both parties is never easy in the strategic decision-making processes of organizations (Pfau & Wan, 2006). Organizations would hardly apply ethical approaches or civic professionalism in practice without aligning the adoption of ethics or civic professionalism with corporate self-interest in a concrete and tangible way.

In this regard, this study provides a potential positive link between the pursuit of an ethics of care (or even civic professionalism) and corporate reputation (i.e., part of corporate self-interest). The positive link identified in this study could serve to help organizations better acknowledge the importance of an ethics of care in nurturing beneficial organization-public relationships, which is closely related to the notion of civic professionalism. Scholars in ethics and civic professionalism often emphasize that a practitioner's ethical, engaged, and social responsibility and morality issues are the key to better serve the public good (e.g., Sullivan, 2004). However, practitioners often face a dilemma between personal morality/responsibility (e.g., public-serving motives) and organizations' institutional pressure (e.g., firm-serving motives) in decision-making processes. The positive link found between ethics of care approaches and corporate reputation could provide practitioners a justification why they should embrace social virtues of sympathy, compassion, morality, and responsibility when communicating with publics especially in times of crisis. Adopting ethics of care approaches can be linked to achieving organizational goals. The current study thus recommends that better serving the public good could result in better serving corporate interests as people in the study seemed to appreciate organizations' ethics of care for the public good, and as a result, they tended to reveal more positive perceptions of corporate reputation. In addition, given that most public relations professionals identify reputation management as one of the most important tasks they perform at work (Hutton, Goodman, Alexander, & Genest, 2001), the positive corporate reputation identified in this study provides a compelling reason for public relations practitioners to put concepts of civic professionalism and ethics into practice by adopting an ethics of care approach in crisis.

Future Research and Conclusion

Although this research has meaningful implications, several limitations should be identified. The findings of this study are based on a student sample. Although previous studies have confirmed that a student sample can be effective in investigating multivariate relationships (Basil, Brown, & Bocarnea, 2002), future studies are encouraged to use consumer panels to determine what consumers expect from a corporation in crisis communication. In addition, the study considered only victim and preventable types of crises. Future research should focus on an accidental crisis because it tends to generate mid-levels of intentionality in public perceptions.

Despite these limitations, the study provides important insights into the strategic adoption of an ethical approach in times of crisis. Most importantly, this study's findings provide several compelling insights for organizations that attempt to use the ethics of care not only as a strategy in crisis communication but also as a way to nurture relationships with publics.

References

Basil, M. D., Brown, W. J., & Bocarnea, M. C. (2002). Differences in univariate values versus multivariate relationships. *Human Communication Research*, 28, 501–514.

Bauman, D. C. (2011). Evaluating ethical approaches to crisis leadership: Insights from unintentional harm research. *Journal of Business Ethics*, 98(2), 281–295.

Brown, T. J., & Dacin, P. A. (1997). The company and the product: Corporate associations and consumer product responses. *Journal of Marketing*, 61(January), 68–84.

Brunner, B. R. (2015). What is civic professionalism in public relations? Practitioner perspectives—A pilot study. *Public Relations Review*, doi:10.1016/j.pubrev.2015.07.010.

Chamberlain, E., & Houston, B. (1999). School sexual harassment policies: The need for both justice and care. In M. S. Katz, N. Noddings, & K. A. Strike (Eds.), *Justice and caring: The search for common ground in education* (pp. 146–166). New York, NY: Columbia University Teachers College Press.

Ciulla, J. B. (2009). Leadership and the ethics of care. *Journal of Business Ethics*, 88, 3–4.

Collins, D. (1989). Organizational harm, legal condemnation and stakeholder retaliation. *Journal of Business Ethics*, 8(1), 1–13.

Coombs, W. T., & Holladay, S. J. (2002). Helping the crisis managing protect reputational assets: Initial test of the situational crisis communication theory. *Management Communication Quarterly*, 16(2), 165–186.

Donaldson, T., & Preston, L. E. (1995). The stakeholder theory of the corporation: Concepts, evidence, and implications. *Academy of Management Review*, 20(1), 65–91.

Fitzpatrick, K., & Bronstein, C. (Eds.). (2006). *Ethics in public relations: Responsible advocacy*. Thousand Oaks, CA: Sage.

French, W., & Weis, A. (2000). An ethics of care or an ethics of justice. *Journal of Business Ethics*, 27(1), 125–136.

Gilbert, D. R., Jr. (2001). Corporate strategy and ethics, as corporate strategy comes of age. In M. A. Hitt, R. E. Freeman, & J. S. Harrison (Eds.), *The Blackwell handbook of strategic management* (pp. 564–582). Malden, MA: Blackwell.

Gilligan, C. (1977). In a different voice: Women's conceptions of self and morality. *Harvard Educational Review*, 47(4), 481–517.

Hill, C. W. L., & Jones, T. M. (1992). Stakeholder-agency. *Journal of Management Studies*, 29(2), 131–154.

Hosmer, L. T. (1994). Strategic planning as if ethics mattered. *Strategic Management Journal*, 15, 17–34.

Hutton, J. G., Goodman, M. B., Alexander, J. B., & Genest, C. M. (2001). Reputation management: The new face of corporate public relations? *Public Relations Review*, 27(3), 247.

Kim, H. J., & Cameron, G. T. (2011). Emotions matter in crisis: The role of anger and sadness in the publics' response to crisis news framing and corporate crisis response. *Communication Research*, 38(6), 826–855.

Kim, S. (2011). Transferring effects of CSR strategy on consumer responses: The synergistic model of corporate communication strategy. *Journal of Public Relations Research*, *23*(2), 218–241.

Kohlberg, L. (1973). The claim to moral adequacy of a highest stage of moral judgment. *Journal of Psychology*, *70*, 630–646.

Linsley, P. M., & Slack, R. E. (2013). Crisis management and an ethic of care: The case of Northern Rock Bank. *Journal of Business Ethics, 113*(2), 285–295.

Matzler, K., Hinterhuber, H. H., Bailom, F., & Sauerwein, E. (1996). How to delight your customers. *Journal of Product and Brand Management*, *5*(2), 6–18.

Pfau, M., & Wan, H-H. (2006). Persuasion: An intrinsic function of public relations. In C. H. Botan and V. Hazleton (Eds.), *Public relations theory II* (pp. 101–136). Mahwah, NJ: Lawrence Erlbaum.

Rawls, J. (1971). *A theory of justice*. Cambridge, MA: Harvard University Press.

Simola, S. (2003). Ethics of justice and care in corporate crisis management. *Journal of Business Ethics*, *46*(4), 351–361.

Simola, S. (2005). Concepts of care in organizational crisis prevention. *Journal of Business Ethics*, *62*, 341–353.

Sommerfeldt, E. J. (2013). The civility of social capital: Public relations in the public sphere, civil society, and democracy. *Public Relations Review, 39*(4), 280–289.

Stein, E. W., & Ahmad, N. (2008). Using the analytical hierarchy process (AHP) to construct a measure of the magnitude of consequences component of moral intensity. *Journal of Business Ethics*, *89*(3), 391–407.

Sullivan, W. M. (2004). Can professionalism still be a viable ethic? *Good Society*, *13*(1), 15–20.

Walker, M. U. (1998). Moral understandings: Alternative epistemology for a feminist ethics. *Feminist Ethics and Medicine*, *4*(2), 15–28.

9 In the Bind Between Theory and Practice

Public Relations and Ethics of Neoliberal Global Capitalism

Marina Vujnovic and Dean Kruckeberg

Nearly 30 years have passed since the first publication of Kruckeberg and Starck's (1988) book, *Public Relations and Community: A Reconstructed Theory*. In that volume and in later works, these authors with others (e.g., Kruckeberg, 2007; Kruckeberg & Starck, 2004; Kruckeberg, Starck, & Vujnovic, 2006; Kruckeberg & Vujnovic, 2006, March; Kruckeberg & Vujnovic, 2006, August; Vujnovic & Kruckeberg, 2010a; Starck & Kruckeberg, 2001; Vujnovic, Kumar, & Kruckeberg, 2007) have helped to establish and to maintain the argument that the primary goal of public relations as a professionalized occupation, if not a profession, is to serve the community and society-at-large. This idea seems to have opened a floodgate of socially responsible approaches in public relations that span from corporate social responsibility to organizational justice, public communication, civic professionalism, and ethics. All of these approaches maintain that public relations, regardless of variations in its definition, should be a practice that leads to the public good. But this definition begs a question, primarily, has the practice or practices followed suit? If not, what must be done to achieve this goal that may appear—certainly to employing organizations and to clients—to be secondary at most to primary goals that demonstrate financial and other tangible returns on investment (ROIs) to benefit the self-interest of those paying for public relations counsel and services?

Representing a dominant paradigm in public relations theory and research, J. E. Grunig (1992) argues from an organization-centric perspective that public relations should serve the public interest, developing mutual understanding between organizations and their publics, while contributing to informed debate about societal issues. J. E. Grunig and L. A. Grunig (1992) emphasize that public relations is not an outcome, but rather is a process that provides a forum for dialogue, discussion, and discourse. Books such as Tilson and Alozie's (2004), *Toward the Common Good: Perspectives in International Public Relations*, consider the role through which public relations can help to resolve globally significant issues and problems, for example, in addressing the effects of privatization and globalization, emerging public opinion, and democratic movements, as well as of the problems of corruption and professional ethics. Observing that the traditional understanding of public relations appears to have originated from a functionalist and organization-centric perspective that is managerial, strategic, and highly structuralized, Vujnovic and Kruckeberg (2010a) conclude that practitioners have not been fully aware—nor particularly appreciative—of public relations' greater potential and, arguably, of its professional responsibility in serving society-at-large.

Nevertheless, less dominant paradigms have focused on this greater role. For example, Vujnovic (2004, 2005) argues that an organization's responsibility extends beyond "strategic publics," advocating that organizations—guided by their public relations practitioners—should view society, not as a web of strategic publics of primary concern to these organizations, but as a larger social system within which organizations can co-exist and proactively seek harmony. Indeed, Kruckeberg and Vujnovic (2010, Spring) and Valentini and Kruckeberg (2012a) warn that we must question the continuing utility of the concept of segmented publics (plural) in an era of globalization, easy and immediate re-segmentation into multiple worldwide publics, and amidst the dangers of what was once private becoming globally public. Stated more emphatically, Vujnovic and Kruckeberg (2010a, 2010b) argue that, in today's global milieu, the only truly "strategic" public that can be identified with any certainty is the "general public," which has no predetermined "rules of behaviors" and which may have no organization-specific concerns to address, but rather acts—often with immediacy and volatility—on a case-by-case basis upon different circumstances and situations. Certainly, well-educated, insightful, and morally grounded practitioners are among those having pre-eminent—if not unique—professional credentials and encompassing worldviews and, we argue, a professional responsibility to help resolve societal problems that affect all of humankind. Such problems are detrimental, not only to practitioners' organizations and their stakeholders, but also to what J. E. Grunig (1997) and J. E. Grunig and Hunt (1984) refer as "nonpublics"—as well as to the ostensibly nonexistent "general public," the latter which remains unrecognized by many public relations scholars (e.g., Newsom, Turk, & Kruckeberg, 2013). As a professionalized occupation that aspires to be a profession, public relations, as practiced by a professional community, has a responsibility to proactively serve society, a vocational calling that is consistent with the traditional definition of a profession.

Contemporary Public Relations

Ledingham (2008) traces the evolution of public relations from its historic grounding that has been characterized primarily by the application of principles of media relations, which he calls a "production model" (p. 225). He observes that the practice has evolved into its present role to help organizations to achieve mutual goals with stakeholders—an approach that is based on organization-public relationships. Vercic, van Ruler, Butschi, and Flodin (2001) describe a European view, in which public relations is perceived to exist also within and for a public sphere, while Holtzhausen (2000) advocates application of postmodern values, in which public relations practitioners are activists within their organizations. She argues that dissensus and dissymmetry are more appropriate than are current public relations approaches that seek consensus and symmetry. Vujnovic and Kruckeberg with others (e.g., Kruckeberg, 2007; Kruckeberg & Vujnovic, 2006, August; Kruckeberg & Vujnovic, 2006, March; Kruckeberg & Vujnovic, 2010, June; Vujnovic et al., 2007, March) have written extensively about a three-dimensional "organic model" of public relations, in which each organization is only a part of the whole social system that public relations practitioners must consider. In their view, an organization has a responsibility to *all* members of society; thus, they argue that public relations practitioners should view their organizations—whether these are corporations, civil society organizations, or governments—not as hubs having satellites of stakeholders, but rather as one part of a three-dimensional social system in which organizations cooperate with one another in their support of society.

Kruckeberg and Vujnovic (2010, Spring) emphasize that this sharing can only occur when community-building efforts are directed, not just toward *strategic* publics, but also toward "nonpublics" and to the "general public," i.e., all of society. Tsetsura and Kruckeberg (2009, Summer) contend that measurement of ROI for public relations in such contexts is not only impossible, but ultimately is unfair and meaningless, noting Kruckeberg et al.'s (2006) contention that social harmony between the practitioner's organization and society benefits the organization and its stakeholders in financially immeasurable and oftentimes intangible ways. Importantly, all of these approaches implicitly endorse Kruckeberg's (2000, Fall) admonition that practitioners must not blindly take orders or accept their organizations' worldviews without question or challenge when addressing organization-public relations.

Although predominant models may vary in their perspectives on advocacy, mutual understanding, and relationship management, they do not seem to vary in their organization-centric frame of reference and orientation, in which public relations is practiced on behalf of an organization, whether corporation, civil society organization, or government. Although J. E. Grunig and Hunt's (1984) two-way symmetrical model, Holtzhausen's (2000) activist role for public relations practitioners, and Vujnovic's (2004) conceptualization of an ombudsman role might suggest practitioners' greater detachment and autonomy from their organizations, thereby implicitly suggesting practitioners' independence and perhaps impartiality, their frames of reference nevertheless remain relationships *between* organizations and their identified stakeholders. Thus, public relations practitioners' primary responsibility is presumed to be to their organizations or clients, albeit ostensibly for the mutual benefit of these organizations or clients' stakeholders. Primary goals most often are restricted to and are measured by financial and other tangible ROIs that benefit the self-interest of those paying for public relations counsel and services.

This is both easy to understand and, in fact, to accept; however, we argue that public relations practitioners are capable of—and must assume—a greater role and more encompassing responsibilities, not only in building and maintaining mutually beneficial relationships with their organizations' primary stakeholders, but also in their organizations and professional community's contributions to society-at-large.

21st-Century Problems

Certainly, public relations will continue to evolve, not only as it matures as a professional practice amidst dialogue and debate among its scholars and practitioners in their attempts to determine best practices, but also in response to the critical social, political, economic, and cultural phenomena and issues that are emerging in an increasingly complex contemporary global environment. Kruckeberg and others (e.g., Kruckeberg & Tsetsura, 2008; Kruckeberg & Vujnovic, 2007; Valentini & Kruckeberg, 2012a, 2011, Spring) have written about communication technology as the major intervening variable that has created globalism as well as its obverse, multiculturalism, together with the latter's accompanying tensions in a global environment that is replete with a host of issues and problems that beg resolution. Kruckeberg (2002) and Kruckeberg and Vujnovic (2007) identify 21st-century social problems that are so overwhelming and so critical that all available resources must be allocated to them, including the knowledge, skills, and abilities of the public relations professional community. These include environmental challenges, population growth, poverty, hunger, and war; the management of change; tensions resulting from the confluence of technology, globalism, and multiculturalism; fundamental changes in the relationships among governments, corporations, and private citizens; nationalism versus globalism; tensions between modern and traditional societies, as well as within traditional societies themselves, particularly when the latter face overwhelming pressures to modernize; tensions among what were once labeled first, second, and third worlds; global class stratification; and control and direction of technology. Kruckeberg and Vujnovic (2003, May) further identify the challenges of a wide range of complex ideas and events, including free trade, emerging democracies, transnational corporations, public distrust, a rapidly changing media environment, megamergers, and globalization. Such challenges are symptomatic of immense changes that are occurring throughout global society because of communication technology and the resultant globalization and increasing tensions of multiculturalism. Further, Valentini and Kruckeberg (2011, Spring) observe that we live in an era in which communication barriers are more ideological than physical, that is, in which space and time have surrendered to the World Wide Web, creating dramatically changing social relationships. Indeed, Kruckeberg and Tsetsura (2008) identify "tribalism" as today's most threatening form of dysfunctional communities as extremists use demagoguery to form communities of the disenfranchised through modern means of communication and transportation.

Neoliberalism and Globalization

These massive social, political, economic, and cultural changes are occurring within a global environment of increasing neoliberalism and a neoliberal global economy, which must be fully understood by public relations scholars and practitioners in their consideration of the role of public relations and of their organizations, together with an appreciation of the changes in the dynamics and relativity of power and influence in global society that are brought about by communication technology. While Gane (2015, January) defines *liberalism* as a defensive form of political thought that centers on the protection of individual liberty against different types of threat or coercion, Kearey-Moreland (2015, January 23) says that *neoliberal* economics preaches the privatization of public services at all costs, the closure of both ecological and democratic commons, and the commodification of everything—with a vision of progress that is defined solely by the accumulation of private property. Giroux (2002, Winter) describes neoliberalism as the policies and processes whereby private interests are permitted to control as much as possible of social life maximize their personal profit, noting that "neoliberalism has been the dominant global political economic trend adopted by political parties of the center and much of the traditional left as well as the right. These parties and the policies they enact represent the immediate interests of extremely wealthy investors and less than one thousand large corporations" (p. 425).

We argue that contemporary public relations theory and practice are given no choice other than to be situated within the context of neoliberalism and a neoliberal global economy, but that scholars must more actively examine and practitioners must be more cognizant of the implications of, and possible outcomes of, neoliberalism and a neoliberal global economy. Our ambitious goal is to begin a conversation to theorize the interrelationships among neoliberal ideology, economic instability, new technology, democratic capitalism, and public relations practice. Importantly in this discussion, we are not taking issue with capitalism in some of its forms, nor do we wish to engage in diatribes about the powerful role of corporations and other social actors in global society. We agree with Starck and Kruckeberg (2001), who opine that corporations are neither inherently good nor evil, and we recognize that they serve an important societal role, as well as an economic function. We also agree that they undoubtedly are requisite at some level in contemporary global society. Furthermore, we essentially concur with Starck and Kruckeberg (2001), who make no blanket assumptions that increased regulation and containment represent desirable means to ensure corporate responsibility and accountability; thus, in this conversation, we make no specific recommendations related to regulation and containment. Rather, we argue that the public relations professional community has immense, perhaps unique, knowledge, skills, and abilities, as well as a moral responsibility, to help ensure that conditions and changes in the global environment are not deleterious, either to practitioners' organizations, nor—equally important, we argue—to society-at-large.

We contend that public relations practitioners must be particularly cognizant of conditions and changes in the global environment that are brought by and related to neoliberalism, which Martinez and Garcia (n.d.) describe as a set of economic policies that frees private enterprise from government imposition, cuts public expenditures for social services, reduces government regulation, sells state-owned enterprises to private investors, and eliminates the concept of the public good or community—replacing the concept with individual responsibility.

Changes in the Dynamics and Reality of Power and Influence

Communication technology, globalism, multiculturalism, and neoliberalism, both as discrete phenomena as well as dynamically and synergistically in common, are having an immense impact on public relations and its practice as well as on practitioners' organizations, whether these organizations are corporations, governments, or civil society organizations. Valentini and Kruckeberg (2012b) note that, when thinking about 21st-century public relations, one cannot avoid the need to discuss the increasing use and influence of information and communication technologies in the life of organizations, people, and social systems in general. Kruckeberg, Creedon, Gorpe, & Al-Khajha (2014, October) warn that communication technology and its resulting globalism and multiculturalism have greatly diminished and, in some cases, have marginalized traditional stabilizing forces of power and influence because—for better or for worse—digital communication technology provides unprecedented opportunities to challenge and to defeat institutions and loci of power and influence. In an earlier era, the American government needed not to contend with Viet Cong propaganda directed toward American draft-age youth through social media, as Western political powers must contend today with ISIS's attempts to radicalize youth worldwide. Kruckeberg et al. (2014, October) observe that control and authority by nation-states, whether by rule-of-law or by tradition, are being challenged and threatened from beyond these nation-states' increasingly porous borders, while dramatic changes are occurring in the dynamics and relativity of power and influence among corporations, civil society organizations, and governments worldwide.

However, Kruckeberg et al. (2014, October) emphasize that the most significant juxtaposition of power is the empowerment of private citizens worldwide, who can easily and immediately form transnational—if not global—alliances through inexpensive and ubiquitous communication technology that creates unprecedented opportunities for democracy, however, defined, but also increases the threat of totalitarianism or of the anarchy of chaos and disorder. Nevertheless in some ways, this increased citizen power may be illusory.

Kruckeberg et al. (2014, October) warn that communication technology upon which people are becoming increasingly dependent consumers is neither fully understood nor controlled by them and its withdrawal and/ or failure would result in mass helplessness because of the social, political, economic, and cultural infrastructures that have been built around this communication technology. Vujnovic and Kruckeberg (2014, March) describe as social enslavement an environment in which people cannot live their lives without adopting ubiquitous communication technology, whether they cannot (an economic dimension, as well as a social dimension), or whether they choose not. Not so long ago, it would have been preposterous for a Charlotte, NC, television newsperson to urge homeless individuals who are seeking respite from harsh winter weather to send a text message to learn the location of the nearest shelter—obviously making the assumption that the homeless population has televisions and smartphones. Politically, communication technology can make us subject to influence by "dysfunctional communities" that Kruckeberg and Tsetsura (2008) note have a global reach. Vujnovic and Kruckeberg (2014, March) observe that, economically, communication technology that empowers consumers with informed purchasing decisions nevertheless enslaves them with the additional expense of possessing the communication technology that has become essential to function in modernity. Culturally, global assimilation and enculturation that may be beguiling ultimately may not prove desirable to many.

Recommendations

As a professionalized occupation that aspires to be a profession, public relations has a responsibility to proactively serve society, a vocational calling that is consistent with the traditional definition of a profession. The public relations professional community, that is, its scholars and practitioners, must broaden its organization-centric frame of reference and orientation and expand its functionalist perspective, which is managerial, strategic, and highly structuralized, to embrace Vujnovic's (2004, 2005) contention that an organization's responsibility extends beyond "strategic publics" to include a proactive concern with the larger social system, while accepting Kruckeberg's (2000, Fall) admonition that practitioners must not accept their organizations' worldviews without question or challenge—neither in addressing organization-public relationships, but also as a professional community in which well-educated, insightful, and morally grounded practitioners have a professional responsibility to help resolve societal problems that affect all of humankind.

Kruckeberg (1993, Spring) reminds us that practitioners are free to define themselves within meaningful and specific parameters and could do so because of the plentitude of shared professional values worldwide. Public relations scholars and practitioners must broaden their investigation and discussions about public relations' role and responsibilities that lead to the public good, not solely focusing on organization-public relationships. However, this requires more than well-intended and oftentimes sanctimonious altruism, not only in complex social, political, economic, and cultural environments in which communication technology is the major intervening variable that has created globalism and multiculturalism, but also within the context of increasing neoliberalism worldwide and a neoliberal global economy. Bhanji (2008) observes that world politics seem to favor the increasing power of the market at the expense of social needs, despite an increasing number of poor and disenfranchised people in the developing world, further noting that less-developed countries have not been supported by a social safety net and that there has been a misallocation of resources between private goods and public goods.

Bhanji (2008) observes that global financial markets are crises prone and tend to hit developing economies harder. Giroux (2002, Winter) adds that neoliberalism and market fundamentalism have posed a historic challenge to democracy, citizenship, social justice, and civic education. Such contentions provide further credence to Kruckeberg's (2000, Fall) observation concerning the continuing juxtaposition of the power of nation-states and corporations and the implications of this juxtaposition. Communication technology and its resulting globalism and multiculturalism have greatly diminished and, in some cases, have marginalized traditional stabilizing forces of power and influence, sometimes for the better and undoubtedly sometimes for the worse. In light of Kruckeberg's (1989, Summer) depiction of the scope, power, and actions of transnational corporations, which he (1996) argued were morally accountable, the public relations professional community must further view the implications of increasing neoliberalism and a neoliberal global economy from a perspective that extends beyond organization-public relationships. This goal suggests that public relations practitioners are capable of—and must assume—a greater role and more encompassing responsibilities, not only in managing mutually beneficial organization-centric relationships with their organizations' primary stakeholders, but also in their organizations and professional community's contributions to society-at-large in response to critical social, political, economic, and cultural issues that are emerging in an increasingly complex contemporary global environment.

Identification and deliberation of contemporary issues demand, not only public intellectuals among an informed citizenry, but—we argue—requires also "organizational intellectuals" and "professional community intellectuals," who are equipped to ponder these emergent issues and problems that affect everyone and to make—and, as able, to execute—their recommendations accordingly. No shortage exists of issues and problems that demand resolution, for example, inequities in education and as well as the question of corporatization and corporate influence in education (e.g., Giroux, 2002, Winter; Murphy, 2014, August); privacy concerns, in particular for students, as well as other vulnerabilities brought about by ubiquitous communication technology (e.g., Corbin, 2015, February 16; Brown, 2015,

January 19; Chandler and Tsukayama, 2014, May 17); threats to freedom of expression and other human right violations, in particular to minority and oppressed groups, for example, the Charlie Hebdo massacre and increasing anti-Semitism and islamophobia; a fragile and volatile global economy and the implications of this global economy that is based on technology; and the economic sustainability of nation-states and the employment and welfare of their citizens, for example, Greece, and overwhelming mass migrations to Europe.

Of course, this is merely a short list of critical issues in a complex world that beg resolution by public intellectuals, organizational intellectuals, and professional community intellectuals, certainly including the public relations professional community worldwide. Professional contributions to the resolution of these societal problems that are global in scope extend beyond the concept of corporate social responsibility, which motives are oftentimes criticized, particularly as it is practiced by powerful transnational corporations. Calvano (2008), for example, complains that multinational corporations can manipulate their relationships with communities, using philanthropy to buy-off or silence communities, as a form of greenwashing to divert attention from or cover up misdeeds. Of course, the goals of many corporate social responsibility initiatives are far more altruistic and deserve, not cynicism, but endorsement and support. Certainly, well-educated, insightful, and morally grounded practitioners are among those having pre-eminent—if not unique—professional credentials and encompassing worldviews and, we argue, a professional responsibility to help resolve societal problems that affect all of humankind.

Note

Special thanks to UNC Charlotte graduate research assistant Alicia Emmons.

References

Bhanji, Z. (2008). Transnational corporations in education: Filling the governance gap through new social norms and market multilateralism? *Globalisation, Societies and Education, 6*(1), 55–73.

Brown, E. (2015, January 19). *Obama to propose new student privacy legislation.* Retrieved from http://www.washingtonpost.com/local/education/obama-to-propose-new-student-privacy-legislation/2015/01/18/2ad6a8ae-9d92-11e4-bcfb-059ec7a93ddc_story.html.

Calvano, L. (2008). Multinational corporations and local communities: A critical analysis of conflict. *Journal of Business Ethics, 82,* 793–805.

Chandler, M. A., & Tsukayama, H. (2014, May 17). *Tablets proliferate in nation's classroom, taking a swipe at the status quo.* Retrieved from http://www.washingtonpost.com/local/education/tablets-proliferate-in-nations-classrooms-and-take-a-swipe-at-the-status-quo/2014/05/17/faa27ba4-dbbd-11e3-8009-71de85b9c527_story.html.

Corbin, K. (2015, February 16). *Is student data at risk due to out-of-date privacy laws.* Retrieved from http://www.cio.com/article/2884211/education/is-student-data-at-risk-due-to-out-of-date-privacy-laws.html.

Gane, N. (2015, January). Trajectories of liberalism and neoliberalism. *Theory, Culture and Society, (32)*1, 133–144.

Giroux, H. A. (2002, Winter). Neoliberalism, corporate culture, and the promise of higher education: The university as a democratic public sphere. *Harvard Educational Review, (2)*4, 425–463.

Grunig, J. E. (1992). Communication, public relations, and effective organizations: An overview of the book. In J. E. Grunig (Ed.), *Excellence in public relations and communication management* (pp. 1–28). Hillsdale, NJ: Lawrence Erlbaum Associates.

Grunig, J. E. (1997). A situational theory of publics: Conceptual history, recent challenges and new research. In D. Moss, T. MacManus, & D. Vercic (Eds.), *Public relations research: An international perspective*. London, UK: International Thomson Business Press.

Grunig, J. E., & Grunig, L. A. (1992). Models of public relations and communication. In J. E. Grunig (Ed.), *Excellence in public relations and communication management* (pp. 285–325). Hillsdale, NJ: Lawrence Erlbaum Associates.

Grunig, J. E., & Hunt, T. (1984). *Managing public relations*. New York, NY: Holt, Rinehart and Winston.

Holtzhausen, D. R. (2000). Postmodern values in public relations. *Journal of Public Relations Research, 12*(1), 93–114.

Kearey-Moreland, J. (2015, January 23). Reverse the crisis of modernity. *Orilla Packet and Times*, A4.

Kruckebcrg, D. (1989, Summer). The need for an international code of ethics. *Public Relations Review, 15*(2), 6–18.

Kruckeberg, D. (1993, Spring). Universal ethics code: Both possible and feasible. *Public Relations Review, 19*(1), 21–31.

Kruckeberg, D. (1996). Transnational corporate ethical responsibilities. In H. M. Culbertson & N. Chen (Eds.), *International public relations: A comparative analysis* (pp. 81–92). Hillsdale, NJ: Lawrence Erlbaum.

Kruckeberg, D. (2000, Fall). The public relations practitioner's role in practicing strategic ethics. *Public Relations Quarterly, 45*(3), 35–39.

Kruckeberg, D. (2002). Global advertising and public relations. In Y. R. Kamalipour (Ed.), *Global communication* (pp. 88–206). Belmont, CA: Wadsworth/Thompson Learning.

Kruckeberg, D. (2007). An "organic model" of public relations: The role of public relations for governments, civil society organizations (CSOs) and corporations in developing and guiding social and cultural policy to build and maintain community in 21st-century civil society. In the Administration of Ulan-Ude Committee of Social Politics (Ed.), *Municipal social politics and the publics: Realities and perspectives: Materials of the International/Scientific Conference*, (pp. 17–25). Ulan-Ude, Buryatia: Publishing House of Buryatia Scientific Center of Russian Academy of Science.

Kruckeberg, D., Creedon, P., Gorpe, S., & Al-Khajha, M. (2014, October). *The dynamics of power and influence among corporations, civil society organizations and governments: Ramifications of the changing social, political, economic and cultural dimensions of global society in an era of transparency through digital communication.* Paper presented at the Fourth Conference of the Yarmouk University Faculty of Communication in cooperation with the Arab-U.S. Association for Communication Educators, Irbid, Jordan.

Kruckeberg, D., & Starck, K. (1988). *Public relations and community: A reconstructed theory*. New York, NY: Praeger.

Kruckeberg, D., & Starck, K. (2004). The role and ethics of community building for consumer products and services. In M. L. Galician (Ed.), *Handbook of product placement in the mass media: New strategies in marketing theory, practice, trends and ethics* (pp. 133–146). New York, NY: Best Business Books. Russian Edition published October 2004.

Kruckeberg, D., Starck, K., & Vujnovic, M. (2006). The role and ethics of community-building for consumer products and services: With some recommendations for new-marketplace economies in emerging democracies. In C. H. Botan & V. Hazleton (Eds.), *Public relations theory II* (pp. 485–497). Mahwah, NJ: Lawrence Erlbaum.

Kruckeberg, D., & Tsetsura, K. (2008). The "Chicago School" in the global community: Concept explication for communication theories and practices. *Asian Communication Research*, 3, 9–30.

Kruckeberg, D., & Vujnovic, M. (2003, May). *Linking global capitalism with new forms of democracy: Opportunities in community building.* Paper presented in the program, "Is Free Enterprise a Prerequisite for Public Relations: Reflection on the Writings of Hernando DeSoto," at the 53rd Annual Conference of the International Communication Association, San Diego, CA.

Kruckeberg, D., & Vujnovic, M. (2006, August). *Corporate social responsibility within an organic model of public relations: A normative theory of transparency.* Paper presented at the 89th annual conference of the Association for Education in Journalism and Mass Communication, San Francisco, CA.

Kruckeberg, D., & Vujnovic, M. (2006, March). *Toward an "organic model" of public relations in public diplomacy.* Paper presented at the 9th Annual International Public Relations Research Conference, Miami, FL.

Kruckeberg, D., & Vujnovic, M. (2006). The imperative for an Arab model of public relations as a foundation and framework for Arab diplomatic, corporate and nongovernmental organization relationships: Challenges and opportunities. In M. Kirat & W. I. A. Barry (Eds.), *Current realities and future prospects* (pp. 36–41). Sharjah, United Arab Emirates: University of Sharjah.

Kruckeberg, D., & Vujnovic, M. (2007). Global advertising and public relations. In Y. R. Kamalipour (Ed.), *Global communication* (pp. 271–292). Belmont, CA: Thomson Wadsworth.

Kruckeberg, D., & Vujnovic, M. (2010, June). *An "organic model" of public relations.* Paper presented at the International Communication Association pre-conference session, "Global Strategic Thinking—Managing public Relations in a 21st Century global Society," Singapore.

Kruckeberg, D., & Vujnovic, M. (2010, Spring). The death of the concept of "publics" (plural) in 21st century public relations. *International Journal of Strategic Communication.* (Special issue on publics and the public sphere.)

Ledingham, J. A. (2008). Cross-cultural public relations: A review of existing models with suggestions for a post-industrial public relations pyramid. *Journal of Promotion Management*, 14, 225–241.

Martinez, E., & Garcia, A. (n.d.). What is neoliberalism? A brief definition for activists. *CorpWatch*. Retrieved from http://www.corpwatch.org/article.php?id=376.

Murphy, M. E. (2014, August 5). *Why some schools are selling all their iPads.* Retrieved from http://www.theatlantic.com/education/archive/2014/08/whats-the-best-device-for-interactive-learning/375567/.

Newsom, D., Turk, J. V., & Kruckeberg, D. (2013). *This Is PR: The realities of public relations.* Boston, MA: Wadsworth Cengage Learning.

Shear, M. D., & Singer, N. (2015, January 11). *Obama to call for laws covering data. hacking and student privacy*. Retrieved from http://www.nytimes.com/2015/01/12/us/politics/obama-to-call-for-laws-covering-data-hacking-and-student-privacy.html?_r=0.

Starck, K., & Kruckeberg, D. (2001). Public relations and community: A reconstructed theory revisited. In R. L. Heath (Ed.) & G. Vasquez (contributing Ed.), *Handbook of public relations* (pp. 51–59). Thousand Oaks, CA: Sage.

Tilson, D. J., & Alozie, E. C. (Eds.). (2004). *Toward the common good: Perspectives in international public relations*. Boston, MA: Allyn & Bacon.

Tsetsura, K., & Kruckeberg, D. (2009, Summer). Corporate reputation: Beyond measurement. *Public Relations Journal, 3*(3), 1–8.

Valentini, C., & Kruckeberg, D. (2011, Spring). Public relations and trust in contemporary global society: A Luhmannian perspective of the role of public relations enhancing trust among social systems. *Central European Journal of Communication, 4*(1), 91–107.

Valentini, C., & Kruckeberg, D. (2012a). "Iran's Twitter Revolution" from a publics (sic) relations standpoint. In A. M. George & C. B. Pratt (Eds.), *Case studies in crisis communication: International perspectives on hits and misses* (pp. 383–402). London, UK: Routledge.

Valentini, C., & Kruckeberg, D. (2012b). New media versus social media: A conceptualization of their meanings, uses, and implications for public relations. In S. Duhe (Ed.), *New media and public relations* (pp. 3–12). New York, NY: Peter Lang.

Vercic, D., van Ruler, B., Butschi, G., & Flodin, B. (2001). On the definition of public relations: A European view. *Public Relations Review, 27*. 373–387.

Vujnovic, M. (2004). *The public relations practitioner as ombudsman—A reconstructed model*. Unpublished master's thesis, University of Northern Iowa, Cedar Falls, IA.

Vujnovic, M. (2005). *The public relations practitioner as ombudsman—A reconstructed model*. Paper presented at the 8th International Public Relations Research Conference, Miami, FL.

Vujnovic, M., & Kruckeberg, D. (2010a). The local, national, and global challenges of public relations: A call for an anthropological approach to practicing public relations. In R. L. Heath (Ed.), *Handbook of public relations* (pp. 671–678). Thousand Oaks, CA: Sage.

Vujnovic, M., & Kruckeberg, D. (2010b). Managing global public relations in the new media environment. In M. Deuze (Ed.), *Managing media work* (pp. 217–223). London, UK: Sage.

Vujnovic, M. & Kruckeberg, D. (2014, March). *A PR "meta-strategy" based on an examination of "transparency," "Pseudo-Transparency," "Authenticity" and "Trust"*. Paper presented at the 17th Annual International Public Relations Research Conference, Miami, FL.

Vujnovic, M., Kumar, A., & Kruckeberg, D. (2007, March). *An "organic theory" as a social theory of public relations: A case study from India*. Paper presented at the 10th Annual International Public Relations Research Conference, Miami, FL.

10 Public Relations Ethics, Corporate Social Responsibility, and the Private Sector

The Case for Corporate Community Resilience Support for Disaster Preparedness

Natalie T. J. Tindall, Jan Uhrick, and Jennifer Vardeman-Winter

Since the September 11th terrorist attacks, Hurricane Katrina, and other environmental and human-caused disasters in the early 2000s, the state of community disaster preparedness and infrastructure resilience in the United States has become an exigency for local, state, and federal governments, public health agencies, and nonprofits. The private sector, which has not been considered a formal partner in emergency management traditionally, has been excluded from disaster preparedness and disaster recovery efforts except for unofficial, informal measures. One such private sector–community resilience relationship is the informal Waffle House Index. Dillow (2013) summed up the creation of the index:

> Nearly a decade ago, Florida's [former] emergency management chief, W. Craig Fugate, noticed that when information was scarce after a disaster, the status of a 24-hour Waffle House restaurant often indicated whether an area had electricity, gas, and passable roads. So he created a three-color rating: green (fully open), yellow (limited menu), and red (closed). (p. 1)

The Federal Emergency Management Agency (FEMA) uses this informal metric to gauge a community's preparedness and security after a disaster (Arce & Gentile, 2014; Demiroz & Kapucu, 2015). Brubaker (2015) noted that the informal index is an unofficial FEMA resource "to judge the extent of damage to a community following a disaster. … Businesses that are quick to reopen can help provide a sense of normalcy to residents affected by a disaster" (p. 113).

However, research suggests that infrastructures and communities remain fragmented, disconnected, and out-of-date. Khan (2011), writing as the director of the Centers for Disease Control and Prevention (CDC's) Office of Public Health Preparedness and Response, considered the "improved coordination of public health, health care, emergency medical services, and the private sector" was a preparedness issue that must be addressed within the next decade. From a public health and security standpoint, disaster preparedness and resilience building should not be siloed within one area of the community. As Hoog (2011) wrote:

> When it comes to emergency response in the United States, we as a nation possess groups of extremely dedicated and oftentimes very experienced personnel, both in volunteer positions and at various levels of government. The key to moving forward and continuously improving our abilities is to push for a greater sense of cooperation and coordination between the public and private sectors, including the sharing of expertise and resources. (para. 31)

Yet, there are constraints and issues with corporations engaging in community preparedness and resilience beyond the fundamental exchange of goods for money. Corporations are hesitant to conduct such work because it requires activities that destabilize a company's position in a competitive market. Activities that seemingly run counter to corporate interests include freely sharing proprietary information and patented technologies and tools with otherwise paying customers (e.g., local governments); collaborating with competitors in order to establish a common protocol to accomplish a task; opening its doors to external parties such as governments may expose operational or regulatory issues; and exposing internal organizational processes to outsiders, thereby making the organization vulnerable to external threats (DHS, 2009). In short, for-profit companies operating in the critical infrastructure sectors are constrained as to how invested they can be in helping maximize the resilience of a community.

Disaster preparedness is becoming a community issue, and the community includes business leaders and commercial products. In this chapter, we dissect Jennings and Arras' (2008) goal of community resiliency through the prism of public relations ethics and corporate social responsibility. In this multi-year research project, which encompasses this book chapter, forthcoming conference papers, and journal articles, the guiding questions for our research include but are not limited to

- How is preparedness a public relations issue?
- How do corporations perceive this link between preparedness, civic responsibility, and ethics?
- How might corporate community resilience support (CCRS) bridge the gap between community preparedness and the private sector?
- To what extent would corporations consider being incentivized in the form of corporate social responsibility (CSR) programming?

In this chapter, we will not address or have answers for all of those questions. Instead, we are laying out the theoretical linkages for our work, dissecting how public relations ethics, organizational consciousness, and civic professionalism provide clear ethical linkages and mandates for the private sectors' responses to community disasters.

Theoretical Foundations

Ethical Mandate of Public Relations

The concept of civic professionalism was generated among humanities scholars in the early 2000s as a response to understanding the connections between career opportunities and civic engagement. According to Peters (2003), civic professionalism "casts professionals identities, roles, and expertise around a public mission. … inside civic life rather than apart from or above it, working alongside their fellow citizens on questions and issues of public importance." The idea of a profession having a mutually beneficial relationship with the public "that requires ethical responsibility on the part of the professional to better serve the public good" (Brunner & Summerfield, 2015, p. 145) has been a guiding ethical principle for public relations professionals and academics. Accountability and transparency have been the goals of public relations practice, codified in the ethical codes from national and international public relations associations.

The intent of civic professionalism is to offer "a bridge between intellectual and practical learning, and between individual goals and the common good" (Imagining America, 2010). Public relations theorists have long claimed that public relations practitioners act in bridging and spanning capacities. White and Dozier (1992), in describing the function of public relations as a shaper of organizational decision making and opinions: "The dominant coalition needs information to help make decisions. That information frequently is provided by *boundary spanners*, individuals within the organization who frequently interact with the organization's environment and who gather, select, and relay information from the environment to decision makers in the dominant coalition" (p. 93). The public relations practitioner straddles multiple environments—both internal and external to the organization—to provide keen insights and information to those with decision-making authority. This position carries much weight and responsibility. Not only does the practitioner have to negotiate and act as the institutional advocate, the practitioner must also have a "responsibility to community over [raw] self-interest, profit, or careerism" (Baker, 1999, p. 75) and serve as the public conscience (Fitzpatrick & Gauthier, 2000; Neill & Drumwright, 2012; Sision, 2010). In our estimation, the duty of social responsibility and the role of public conscience intertwine to provide guidance on all matters relating to the common public good (Baker & Martinson, 2001), and that includes issues relating to public health that affect a company's internal and external stakeholders.

Fitzpatrick and Gauthier (2000) wrote that "social responsibility means first that one recognizes, accepts, and acts on a general responsibility to one's society. More specifically, and more realistically, it requires responsibility to persons and interests who will be impacted by one's actions" (p. 198). This idea of a socially responsible public relations function has been raised by Baker (1999), who proposed a "social responsibility model" for persuasive strategic communication efforts; by Kruckeberg and Starck (1980), who espoused the practice of restoring and maintaining community; and by Leeper (1996), who coined the idea of "communitarianism" within public relations. One cannot divorce social responsibility from a need to provide ethical counsel, and other scholars such as Bowen (2008, 2009), Goodpaster and Matthews (1982), and Bivins (1992) have championed the idea of the organizational conscience emanating from the public relations department. Neill and Drumwright (2012) defined this position as "a professional who raises concerns when his or her organization's actions might bring about potential ethical problems leading to troubling consequences for various parties, who may be individuals, groups, organizations, or other entities … both within and outside the organization" (p. 221). This professional acknowledges that "all stakeholders have intrinsic value" (p. 221) and is concerned about issues that involve the law as well as issues that involve the spirit of the law. The practitioner, according to Bowen (2010), Bowen and Zheng (2015), L. A. Grunig, Toth, and Hon (2001), and Marsh (2014), is concerned with balancing justice and equity among other considerations.

CSR and Ethics

Understanding CSR. Strauss (2015) noted that "public relations practitioners figure prominently in the CSR debate because of their important role in communicating the corporation's prosocial deeds to a wider audience" (p. 9). CSR has become an integral part of public relations because it is the responsibility of practitioners to understand the environment around the organization, and according to J. E. Grunig and Hunt (1984), "public, or social, responsibility has become a major reason for an organization to have a public relations function" (p. 84). In the past, organizations practiced less CSR and primarily focused on philanthropy, but now, companies need to continue public opinion "as well as the harsh reaction of collective judgment when a company is involved in a publicized affair" (Tixier, 2003, p. 74). Some public relations scholars argue that CSR extends a corporation's view of symmetry with its stakeholders and other publics (Kim, 2011). Businesses have stewardship responsibilities to shareholders, but also stakeholders, which include employees, customers, competitors, suppliers, distributors, and the community (Lantos, 2001).

Weber (2008) notes five reasons that CSR can be beneficial for organizations: (1) CSR has positive effects on company image and reputation which is influenced by communication messages; (2) CSR has "positive effects on employee motivation, retention, and recruitment" which can lead to an improved reputation; (3) CSR will help organizations save money and become more sustainable; (4) revenue will increase from higher shares, and CSR will lead to increased revenue; and (5) CSR can reduce risk and be "used as a means to reduce or manage CSR-related risks such as the avoidance of negative press or customer/NGO boycotts" (pp. 248–249).

The benefits for an organization through these reasons have led to CSR becoming a "leverage point for activists because of its link to reputation," which leads to an ethical dilemma (Coombs & Holladay, 2012, p. 885). This ethical dilemma can be used to build reputation, but it can also create a reputational risk if CSR is practiced unethically (Fombrom, 2005). Public relations ethics must be diligently monitored and balanced by practitioners who utilize CSR due to the potential of unethical use, which can cause permanent damage to an organization.

A major aspect of CSR is a "publics' perceived attributions about the sincerity of CSR purposes" (Kim, 2011, p. 86). An employee can have a great influence on gaining the trust of the public and maintaining an organization's reputation. If employees know about CSR activities and initiatives, their perceptions of the organization may change, and they may become more emotionally attached to the organization (ter Hoeven & Verhoeven, 2013, p. 265). Employees can empower organizations, and when they believe in what the organization is doing for the community, they can contribute to the goals of the organization and help the organization succeed. Organizations have found that internal stakeholders such as employees play a large influence in helping the organization succeed, and some CSR initiatives are directed toward employees. Organizations that help employees develop in the organization and provide training to better their careers as well as creating a good work-life balance have shown that employees will give better service to customers, but they will also be more loyal to the organization and help the organization during potential crises (ter Hoeven & Verhoeven, 2013, p. 266).

Linking CSR and ethics. Burke and Logsdon (1996) believed that "corporate social responsibility 'pays off' for the firm as well as for the firm's stakeholders and society in general" (p. 495). The challenge for CSR is few organizations have good reputations with CSR initiatives, and when these organizations encounter financial problems, there can be a decline in their competitive environments and business decisions. Levitt (1985) and other scholars have argued that some businesses should not become socially involved and engage in CSR. This argument has been perpetuated by the idea that publics and stakeholders should stop businesses from becoming involved with the community because of the concern that organizations engage in CSR only to maximize profit which "becomes the impetus for corporate conduct—or misconduct" (Pratt, 2006, p. 254).

Pratt (2006) addressed the connection between CSR and ethics through the use of the Enron crisis (p. 256). The early 2000s were filled with corporate scandals with Enron being one of these major scandals. Although CSR initiatives were used by the organizations, the scandals impacted the organization to the extent that the general public and stakeholders no longer trusted these organizations, thus creating problems for organizations without scandals and crises (Pratt, 2006). One of these problems comes from organizations abusing CSR for financial purposes. Pratt (2006) noted that Enron "swore by its core values of respect, integrity, communication, and excellence even as it wantonly acted in ways that undermined those values" (p. 257). Cases like Enron led to distrust between publics and organizations which had to be resolved using other methods of CSR. Philanthropy is still a portion of CSR, but organizations have broadened their horizons to better help communities and publics.

Upon further investigation, there are more legal and ethical responsibilities in regard to CSR. Organizations must comply with laws set forth by the federal government, but Lantos (2001) and Smith and Quelch (1993) noted that ethical duties stretch beyond legalities. According to Lantos (2001), "ethical duties overcome the limitations of legal duties. They entail being moral, doing what is right, just, and fair; respecting people's' moral rights" (p. 597). In respect to moral behavior, organizations need to build trust which will in turn enhance the organizations' reputations. By enhancing reputations and serving publics in an ethical manner, organizations can "attract customers, employees, suppliers and distributors, not to mention earning the public's goodwill" (Lantos, 2001, p. 606). A second feature of organizations which practice CSR in an ethical manner is the potential to "minimize the cost of fines and litigation" as well as eliminating the bad publicity which comes with unethical actions (Lantos, 2001, p. 606).

Organizations may have special moral obligations to the community, or they have "causal responsibility" which means "someone caused something to happen and is, therefore morally responsible or accountable for its consequences" (Lantos, 2001, p. 607). In these cases, "causal responsibility" is directly related to ethical CSR, and the organization is then responsible for correcting the harm done as well as preventing future damage. Business for Social Responsibility (BSR) explains that CSR is designed to "achieve commercial success in ways that honor ethical values and respect people, communities, and the natural environment" (Rowe, 2006, p. 442). Rowe (2006) described the connections "rooted in ethical principles concerned with respect for individuals, communities, and the natural environment, the duty to do no harm and responsibility for the consequences of actions" (p. 449). The foundations of CSR and business ethics acknowledge different approaches to the practical focus and applications of CSR, but arguments exist that business ethics and CSR initiatives are artificial because if initiatives are practiced without sincerity, commitment, and vision, then there is no ethical value to CSR.

Skepticism toward CSR. When practicing CSR, organizations need to effectively communicate CSR initiatives in order to remain transparent with publics. Tixier (2003) noted that organizations which are discreet about CSR initiatives may be suspected of commercial manipulation which can lead to "great embarrassment when faced with an issue that exposes the company to criticism of public opinion; or skepticism regarding the employer's good intentions" (p. 76). Organizations who remain transparent with stakeholders reduce skepticism and will create a more credible image with their stakeholders. Organizations who lack transparency are viewed as having something to hide, which decreases their level of credibility.

In addition to the potential skepticism of stakeholders and publics, "the media has traditionally always been ambiguous when it comes to patronage"; therefore, corporate responsibility has been "unanimously approved by the media" (Tixier, 2003, p. 76). The media has traditionally pushed information that can damage an organization's reputation or make them seem less credible; however, CSR has changed this perception. Media representatives have come to respect organizations that are transparent and keep an open line of dialogue with them; therefore, CSR initiatives are communicated. An organization that is forced to communicate its commitments to the public essentially forces those publics to respect them, and, in turn, publics "must communicate to bring on a change of mentalities" (p. 85). This change in mentality can permit an organization to change its reputation in the eyes of stakeholders. The communication of CSR is essential in changing an organization's reputation. Organizations with a bad reputation can change the perception of their publics by effectively communicating CSR initiatives. In order to bring a "change of mentalities," studies have revealed that "responsible activities are increasingly valued and demanded by stakeholders and they in turn, influence corporate reputation and have a significant positive effect on evaluation of the company," which also influences purchase intent (Amaladoss & Manohar, 2013, p. 67).

Incentivizing and Linking to CSR: The PS-Prep Program

In the event of a crisis, including, but not limited to ethical scandals, stakeholders and the general public will have less confidence and trust in the organization. Because of potential crises, organizations have to continually evaluate their governance structures, which places more responsibility on premium conduct (Rowe, 2006). Before a crisis occurs, publics and stakeholders want to see that an organization can be held accountable for its actions, and for reasons like this, CSR has become more prominent (Rowe, 2006). In the private sector, a shift in power has occurred that has pushed the "balance of power away from governments in favor of corporations," and this has been perpetuated by the "influence of globalization, deregulation, privatization, and technological innovation" (Rowe, 2006, p. 445). These nonmonetary influences of CSR are further discussed in Weber (2003), because nonmonetary benefits can still continue to influence the company's competitiveness and financial success (p. 250). Nonmonetary benefits of

CSR have "been seen as an investment into human capital, the environment, and stakeholder relations" (Weber, 2008, p. 251). Therefore, private organizations must be incentivized to participate in community preparedness and resilience. In its recommendations to the U.S. Department of Homeland Security on critical infrastructure resilience, the National Infrastructure Advisory Council (2009) argued that incentives will require government involvement as well as "norming" of resilience among corporate culture:

> In sectors where the economic cost may exceed the perceived benefit, the government may use its own leverage in the marketplace to provide incentives for the adoption of more resilient best practices. For public infrastructure sectors where well-defined market mechanisms do not exist, surrogate approaches will be required. Much like the way "green" practices and reporting of an industry's carbon footprint has increasingly become the norm, government has the leverage to create a similar market differentiator on resilience for investing and doing business. (p. 26)

The PS-Prep Program provides information on how to build resiliency against catastrophes that can cause "operational disruptions, such as unanticipated costs, data loss, impaired facilities, impacted business relationships and even fatalities among employees" (http://www.fema.gov/voluntary-private-sector-preparedness-program-ps-preptm-small-business-preparedness). The PS-Prep Program is a program specifically designed for private sector preparedness. The Department of Homeland Security established PS-Prep in 2007 to implement voluntary private sector preparedness, which will improve the preparedness of the private sector and nonprofit organizations (http://www.fema.gov/about-ps-preptm). PS-Prep helps organizations identify and implement steps to institute and maintain management systems that address "business continuity, organizational resilience, emergency and disaster management (http://www.fema.gov/about-ps-preptm)."

> The Tsogo Sun Group which is a hotel and entertainment group, located in Southern Africa utilized the PS-Prep Program in order to establish programs to enhance its preparedness for natural or man-made disasters (Berrong, 2010). In order to audit the success of the program and implementation, the company selected a team of six members. Tsogo Sun Group set up an internal system. By doing so, the organization has been able to utilize employees and build trust amongst employees while maintaining transparency with the public because of the appearance that the audit has been conducted externally.

In Tsogo Sun case study produced by PS-Prep, Gert Cruywagen, the director of risk, noted that the process of enhancing preparedness highlighted the achievements that his staff had done with regard to resiliency and management. Cruywagen said, "this organizational standard ... and recognition as a result of that shows everybody what there is already" (Berrong, 2010).

Propositions and Recommendations

This chapter has provided conceptual linkages to support the idea that corporations can contribute to public safety beyond expectations, and in return, corporations are incentivized *by* and *through* communication efforts. Five major tenets support the proposed practice of corporate community resilience support (CCRP). They are:

For-profit organizations should invest in making communities more resilient. Corporations have both a financial and an ethical stake in contributing to communities' resilience. In short, the physical well-being of the neighboring community contributes directly to the economic well-being of a for-profit organization: When a corporation's livelihood depends on the goodwill and support of neighboring communities—and the corporation's/industry's processes/wastes/materials increase environmental and public health risk to a surrounding community (e.g., metals and mining industries)—the corporation and industry have an increased moral obligation to contribute to the sustainability and health of communities (Emery, 2005). Preparedness planning—and the processes and discussions that comprise planning—in itself forms the social foundation for such a symbiotic economic relationship:

> Public health professionals and other leaders should use the preparedness planning process to empower communities by strengthening their social capital and to make them more resilient, so that they can weather all hazards and emergencies—which are now inevitable throughout the globe and no community is immune from them—with as little damage as possible, recover from disasters effectively, and return to civic health (55–59).
>
> (Jennings & Arras, 2008, p. 40, citing Adger)

The ethical stakes are equally compelling. The basic nature of disasters calls on ethical decision making, as disasters engender individuals to feel and demonstrate empathy, respect, and professional codes of conduct unto others (Reynolds, 2012). If an organization espouses being a "good neighbor" to surrounding communities, those ethics arise in the event of—and in the planning for—a crisis. Furthermore, in the event of a crisis, individuals— employees of an organization and those residing in areas around the organization—rely on the same physical and social resources to escape harm. Thus, if an organization expects its employees to be treated fairly in the event of a disaster, it must engender such respectful, professional, and equitable policies around preparedness for external constituents like community members.

Governments may need to incentivize companies to conduct CCRP. The National Infrastructure Advisory Council (NIAC) (2009) linked government incentivizing of corporations to greater security during a disaster: "Government incentives to maintain, improve, and prepare [critical infrastructure and key resource sectors] for rapid recovery when faced with potential incidents will provide greater protection of public health and safety during such an incident" (p. 15). To this point, there is precedent for incentivizing professionals among public health/health-care professionals, seen largely in how governments gave special privileges and assurances to doctors and health professionals who aided ill individuals during past epidemics:

> Finally, the notion of professional duty should not be expected to do all the moral heavy lifting in this controversy ... society would be remiss if it concentrated solely on such duties to the exclusion of offering various incentives for altruistic behavior, especially when the level of risk begins to rise beyond the level of duty. In past epidemics, for example, cities have bestowed additional privileges or remuneration on 'plague doctors' who stood their ground instead of fleeing...
> (Jennings & Arras, 2008, pp. 119–120)

CI and public preparedness scholars and professionals have recommended "market-based" incentives like tax incentives, procurement practices, financial disclosure requirements, insurance-based incentives, increased funding for repair and maintenance (NIAC, 2009, pp. 26–27). Although public relations as a function does not routinely interact with the regulatory/operational bodies that grant incentives like tax or insurance reductions, PR communicators are in the unique role to design programs and messages that would position the organization as a "good neighbor" among multiple stakeholders. Specifically, public relations is tasked with establishing and maintaining mutually beneficial relationships between the organization and its various publics, and corporate social responsibility programs are an increasingly important venue through which to do this. To this point, CSR programming demonstrates to publics that by conducting activities that fall outside the mandated, traditional goods-monetary exchange framework, an organization is thereby interested in outcomes that extend beyond financial returns. In this case, an organization could employ a CSR program that falls within the purview of community resilience and be compensated with the traditional CSR benefits.

Incentives can be deployed through the venue of CSR programming to consumer publics. Under the vision and guidance of the public relations function and communicators, CI corporations can promote their operations that help fortify existing CI within a community, operations that exist beyond that of legal requirements or outside of organizational profits. Although communicators should be wary about how overt the promotion about the CCRP activities is (Dhanesh, 2015), the organization that demonstrates ethical behavior will in praxis communicate well in the marketplace of ideas and products (Heath, 2001). Additional incentive for the corporation will emerge in the form of verification/testament/accreditation by a federal agency of the corporation's "extra" CIR operations (something like the Better Business Bureau, but the award is given by the federal government, thereby adding additional credibility among consumers). Subsequently, the public relations communicators of the organization should strategically advertise the accreditation/verification in its marketing and branding efforts (Heath & Palenchar, 2009).

Corporate Community Resilience Support communication conforms with CSR communication tenets and extends to constant dialogue with community partners. Dialogue with publics is a basis for CSR, and dialogue is facilitated through the organizational public relations function, as PR professionals organize, moderate, and analyze strategic business planning based on the discussions at forums like town hall meetings. Through this process, the needs, interests, and perspectives of publics are ingratiated into the fabric of an organization: "Through public dialogue, CSR standards are asserted, contested, and forged. Standards change. So must organizations' strategic management principles" (Heath & Palenchar, 2009, p. 141).

To this point, Lerbinger (2006) proposed a Pyramid of CSR based on five guidelines, two of which are salient in a discussion about CSR and community infrastructure resilience. One tenet—that an organization should minimize any negative effect its operations have on society—is particularly relevant for CI operators, as many involve physical manipulation of the environment and ecology of a community (e.g., gas pipelines, light rail construction, running cable under and over streets, etc.). The other relevant tenet—to make investments regarding the social infrastructure of a community—relates to a corporation's expectation to facilitate dialogue within a community. A corporation should open communication with community members not only about its own operations but also about what the community needs in order to survive and thrive after a disaster. Communicating with publics at both these levels makes a corporation not only a "good neighbor" (Heath & Ni, 2010), but it engenders community publics and the corporation alike to strengthen their own cultures of resilience.

Under the direction of the organizational public relations function, CCRP has the potential to lower costs for public and private CI organizations over time. Communities and infrastructures may not require as much money/time/effort to repair and restore a community after a disaster. Also, through the acts of public dialogue and shared decision making, the communication inherent in CCRP programming and activities establishes and maintains trust-based relationships with community publics. Stronger relationships based on trust and shared goals thereby prevents/mitigates future relationship-based crises (Heath & Ni, 2008).

References

About PS-Prep. (2015, October 6). *What is PS-Prep?* Retrieved from http://www.fema.gov/about-ps-preptm.

Amaladoss, M., & Manohar, H. L. (2013). Communicating corporate social responsibility—A case of CSR communication in emerging economies. *Corporate Social Responsibility and Environmental Management, 20*, 65–80.

Arce, D. G. & Gentile, M. C. (2014). Giving voice to values as a leverage point in business ethics education. *Journal of Business Ethics, 131*, 1–8.

Baker, S. (1999). Five baselines for justification in persuasion. *Journal of Mass Media Ethics, 14*, 69–81.

Baker, S., & Martinson, D. L. (2001). The TARES test: Five principles for ethical persuasion. *Journal of Mass Media Ethics, 16*(2–3), 148–175.

Berrong, S. (2010). *Hotels make room for resilience.* Retrieved from https://docs.google.com/document/d/1F2sD8DvRMG7rP2ZAS9XFgmQ_8NnAMYsu71kfRcnm8jo/edit.

Bivins, T. H. (1992). A systems model for ethical decision making in public relations. *Public Relations Review, 18*, 365–383.

Bowen, S. A. (2008). A state of neglect: Public relations as "corporate conscience" or ethics counsel. *Journal of Public Relations Research, 20*(3), 271–296.

Bowen, S. A. (2009). What communication professionals tell us regarding dominant coalition access and gaining membership. *Journal of Applied Communication Research, 37*(4), 418–443.

Bowen, S. A. (2010). The nature of good in public relations: What should be its normative ethic. In R. L. Heath (Ed.), *Handbook of public relations* (pp. 569–583). Thousand Oaks, CA: Sage.

Bowen, S. A., & Zheng, Y. (2015). Auto recall crisis, framing, and ethical response: Toyota's missteps. *Public Relations Review, 41*(1), 40–49.

Brubaker, J. (2015). Private sector's role in emergency response. *The Private Sector's Role in Disasters: Leveraging the Private Sector in Emergency Management,* 105.

Brunner, B. R., & Summerfield, G. (2015). The academy for civic professionalism: A case study in relationship management and stakeholder engagement. In R. D. Waters (Ed.), *Public Relations in the Nonprofit Sector: Theory and Practice* (pp. 141–153). London: Routledge.

Burke, L., & Logsdon, J. (1996). How corporate social responsibility pays off. *Long Range Planning, 29*, 495–502.

Coombs, T., & Holladay, S. (2012). Fringe public relations: How activism moves critical PR toward the mainstream. *Public Relations Review, 38*, 880–887.

Demiroz, F., & Kapucu, N. (2015). Cross-sector partnerships in managing disasters: Experiences from the United States. In *Disaster Management and Private Sectors* (pp. 169–186). Tokyo, Japan: Springer.

Dhanesh, G. S. (2015). The paradox of communicating CSR in India: Minimalist and strategic approaches. *Journal of Public Relations Research, 27*, 431–451.

Dillow, C. (2013). *How Waffle House became a disaster indicator for FEMA.* Retrieved from http://www.popsci.com/article/science/how-waffle-house-became-disaster-indicator-fema.

Emery, A. C. (2005, September). *Good practice in emergency preparedness and response.* United Nations Environmental Programme and International Council of Mining and Metals. Retrieved from http://www.icmm.com/document/8.

Fitzpatrick, K., & Gauthier, C. (2001). Toward a professional responsibility theory of public relations ethics. *Journal of Mass Media Ethics, 16*(2–3), 193–212.

Fombrom, C. J. (2005). Building corporate reputation through CSR initiatives: Evolving standards. *Corporate Reputation Review, 8*(1), 7–11.

Goodpaster, K. E., & Matthews, J. B. (1982). Can a corporation have a conscience. *Harvard Business Review, 60*(1), 132–141.

Grunig, J. E., & Hunt, T. (1984). *Managing public relations.* New York, NY: Holt, Rinehart and Winston.

Grunig, L. A., Hon, L. C., & Toth, E. L. (2001). *Women in public relations: How gender influences practice.* Mahwah, NJ: Lawrence Erlbaum.

Heath, R. L. (2001). A rhetorical enactment rationale for public relations: The good organization communicating well. In R. L. Heath (Ed.), *Handbook of public relations* (pp. 31–50). Thousand Oaks, CA: Sage.

Heath, R. L., & Ni, L. (2010). Community relations and corporate social responsibility. In R. L. Heath (Ed.), *The Sage handbook of public relations* (2nd ed., pp. 557–568). Thousand Oaks, CA: Sage.

Heath, R. L., & Palenchar, M. J. (2009). *Strategic issues management: Organizations and public policy challenges* (2nd ed.). Thousand Oaks, CA: Sage.

Hoog, R. (2011, Dec. 7). "Public and Private Sector Relationships in Emergency Management." *Disaster Recovery Journal.* Retrieved on September 8, 2016, from http://www.drj.com/articles/online-exclusive/public-and-private-sector-relationships-in-emergency-management.html

Imagining America. (2010). *Civic professionalism: A new paradigm for undergraduate liberal arts education.* Imagining America Paper 9. Retrieved from http://surface.syr.edu/ia/9.

Jennings, B., & Arras, J. (2008, October 30). *Ethical guidance for public health emergency preparedness and response: Highlighting ethics and values in a vital public health service.* Retrieved from http://www.cdc.gov/od/science/integrity/phethics/docs/White_Paper_Final_for_Website_2012_4_6_12_final_for_web_508_compliant.pdf.

Khan, A. S. (2011). Public health preparedness and response in the USA since 9/11: A national health security imperative. *The Lancet, 378*(9794), 953–956.

Kim, H. S. (2011). A reputational approach examining publics' attributions on corporate social responsibility motives. *Asian Journal of Communication, 21*(1), 84–101.

Lantos, G. (2001). The boundaries of strategic corporate social responsibility. *Journal of Consumer Marketing, 18,* 595–632.

Leeper, K. A. (1996). Public relations ethics and communitarianism: A preliminary investigation. *Public Relations Review, 22*(2), 163–179.

Lerbinger, O. (2006). *Corporate public affairs: Interacting with interest groups, media, and government.* Mahwah, NJ: Lawrence Erlbaum.

Marsh, C. (2014). Public relations as a quest for justice: Resource dependency, reputation, and the philosophy of David Hume. *Journal of Mass Media Ethics, 29*(4), 210–224.

Neill, M. S., & Drumwright, M. E. (2012). PR professionals as organizational conscience. *Journal of Mass Media Ethics, 27*(4), 220–234.

Peters, S. J. (2003). Reconstructing civic professionalism in academic life: A response to Mark Wood's paper, "From service to solidarity." *Journal of Higher Education Outreach and Engagement, 8*(2), 183–198.

Pratt, C. (2006). Reformulating the emerging theory of corporate social responsibility as good governance. In C. H. Botan & V. Hazelton (Eds.), *Public relations theory II* (pp. 249–277). New York, NY: Routledge.

Reynolds, P. (2012, August 23). "Ethics and disasters" presentation. Retrieved from https://sis.nlm.nih.gov/dimrc/coursedocs/disastercourse_ethicslegal_day1_508final.pptx.

Rowe, M. (2006). Reputation relationships and risk: A CSR primer for ethics officers. *Business and Society Review, 111,* 441–455.

Sison, M. D. (2010). Recasting public relations roles: Agents of compliance, control or conscience. *Journal of Communication Management, 14*(4), 319–336. doi:10.1108/13632541011090437.

Smith, N. C., & Quelch, J. A. (1993). *Ethics in marketing.* Homewood, IL: Irwin.

Strauss, J. R. (2015). *Challenging corporate social responsibility: Lessons for public relations from the casino industry.* New York, NY: Routledge.

ter Hoeven, C. L., & Verhoeven, J. W. (2013). "Sharing is caring": Corporate social responsibility awareness explaining the relationship of information flow with affective commitment. *Corporate Communications: An International Journal, 18*(2), 264–279.

Tixier, M. (2003). Note: Soft vs. hard approach in communicating on corporate social responsibility. *Thunderbird International Business Review, 45,* 71–91.

U.S. Department of Homeland Security. (2009, September 8). National Infrastructure Advisory Council: Critical infrastructure resilience final report and recommendations. Retrieved from http://www.dhs.gov/xlibrary/assets/niac/niac_critical_infrastructure_resilience.pdf.

U.S. The White House. (2013, February 12). *Executive Order—Improving critical infrastructure cybersecurity.* Retrieved from https://www.whitehouse.gov/the-press-office/2013/02/12/executive-order-improving-critical-infrastructure-cybersecurity.

Voluntary Private Sector Preparedness Program—PS-Prep and Small Business Preparedness. (2015, October 6). The voluntary private sector preparedness program. Retrieved from http://www.fema.gov/voluntary-private-sector-preparedness-program-ps-preptm-small-business-preparedness.

Weber, M. (2008). The business case for corporate social responsibility: A company-level measurement approach for CSR. *European Management Journal, 26,* 247–261.

White, J., & Dozier, D. M. (1992). Public relations and management decision making. In J. E. Grunig (Ed.), *Excellence in public relations and communication management* (pp. 91–108). Hillsdale, NJ: Lawrence Erlbaum.

11 Public Interest Communication and Polarized Issues

More Than a Case of the Measles

Giselle A. Auger

Public interest communication has been defined as "an innovative field that pulls the spheres of media, policy, communities of influence, social marketing and activism to drive change" (University of Florida). Yet the term *public interest* can be difficult to define and complicated by differences of opinion on the issue in question. For example, at times communicating on behalf of organizations for policy change or initiatives designed to provide relief for the greater good can result in very polarized societal conversations regarding the definition of that good.

Ethics covers the gray areas of situational dilemmas where there is no clear right or wrong and no clear indication of good. Recently, rising cases of infectious diseases, particularly measles, spread by those who have elected to forgo immunization for themselves or their children, have illuminated the contentious societal conversations that erupt as the result of polarized views of what constitutes the greater good. For those in public relations, who craft and deliver messages on behalf of organizations, the answer to the ethical conundrum of the greater good can be at times clear, and at others challenging. As such, the following chapter will consider the concept of public interest communication and the greater good, through a case study analysis of the measles outbreak that occurred in early 2015.

The Disneyland Measles Outbreak

A measles outbreak occurred in the United States between December 2014 and March 2015. The first five cases in the outbreak were reported to the California Department of Public Health (CDPH) on the same day—January 5, 2015, where upon the department identified visits to Disneyland and Disney's California Adventure parks in Anaheim, CA, during the preceding December as the common factor in the occurrence of the disease. By August 21, 2015, the Centers for Disease Control and Prevention (CDC) identified 117 cases of measles in the United States associated with the Disneyland outbreak (CDC, 2015).

The Disneyland measles outbreak surprised many who believed the disease to have been eliminated in the United States. In fact, the United States had declared the elimination of measles from the country in 2000 "because of effective vaccination programs and a strong public health system for detecting and responding to measles cases and outbreaks" (Haelle, 2015). Yet measles continues to be common in other parts of the world, "is the most transmissible infectious disease known in humans, and remains one of the top causes of death in children worldwide" (Poland & Jacobson, 2012, p. 103). As such, the disease can be brought into the United States through international travel or from visitors to the country where it poses a risk for outbreaks when it reaches communities where large numbers of people are not vaccinated (CDC, 2015).

The fact that serious infectious disease could so easily reappear in the United States is concerning because in the years between 2000 and the Disneyland outbreak, public opinion toward immunization in the United States moved from one of general acceptance of mass immunization policies to polarized views on the issue. On one side are those with strong anti-vaccination sentiments who have emerged from parts of the population that fear negative physical consequences of immunization and those who have emerged from parts of the population who question the right of government to mandate immunization (Gellin, Maibach, & Marcuse, 2000; Kennedy & Gust, 2008; Lacitis, 2015). On the other side are those who continue to support mass immunization programs and encourage government mandates requiring vaccination for certain diseases such as measles for the protection of the weakest in society (Bailey-Shah, 2015; Dahl, 1986; Poland & Jacobson, 2012). As a result of polarization, many Americans choose not to vaccinate themselves or their children, despite the fact that "[e]ven in highly developed countries, measles kills approximately 3 of every 1,000 persons infected" (Poland & Jacobson, 2012, p. 103). So what happened to polarize public opinion?

Medical Research, Public Health, and the Media

Polarization of public opinion toward vaccination stems from several sources, key among which are a flawed scientific study, the role of the media in disseminating information from the study, and lack of first-hand experience of the disease for most parents who make decisions about immunization for their children.

The most significant of the polarization sources was a fraudulent scientific study authored by Wakefield, Loken, and Hornik and published in one of medicine's most highly reputable journals, *The Lancet* in 1998. Retracted more than a decade after publication (*Lancet*, 2010) the article suggested that immunizations, particularly the measles, mumps, and rubella (MMR) immunization, were connected to the emergence of certain forms of autism (Flaherty, 2011). Alone, an article in a medical journal would not be likely to raise a storm of public debate; it takes media to identify the issue and broadcast it to the public at large. In the MMR vaccine case, the author of the 1998 article appeared in a televised press conference sponsored by a medical charity and "ignited a public health crisis in England" (Flaherty, 2011, p. 1302) as well as a storm of media attention. For example, according to Burgess, Burgess, and Leask (2006), more than 561 articles about the MMR vaccine appeared during an 8-month period and two-thirds of those implied a link between the MMR vaccine and autism.

The relationship between media and public health communication is usually positive and lacking in controversy. Media provides a necessary avenue for the dissemination of information on public health issues and concerns. Such initiatives may be designed to promote changes in public opinion and behaviors that would help both individuals and society at large, for example, the benefits of childhood immunization against infectious disease, benefits of not smoking, or the increased safety associated with wearing seatbelts and using correct child safety restraints in vehicles (Randolph & Viswanath, 2004; Wakefield et al., 2010). Objective coverage of public health initiatives acknowledges concerns of citizens on an individual basis such as the individual right to smoke, as well as societal concerns about the role of government in curtailing individual freedoms such as the right to smoke in public.

In the case of the retracted study by Wakefield et al. (*Lancet*, 2010), however, some argue that media were not an objective outlet for information into the marketplace of ideas, but a polarizing catalyst, providing equal space for both sides in a debate on immunization safety where support for one side—the Wakefield study side—was significantly lacking in population-based medical evidence and general support from medical research scientists at large (Flaherty, 2011; Gerber & Offit, 2009).

Herein lays the ethical conundrum of communicating for the public interest. Public health communication, as a form of public interest communication, is concerned with societal-level change and requires media to disseminate health-related messages. However, ethical issues arise when some individuals within the larger population are at greater risk than others as the result of proposed changes, or when vulnerable members of society stand to gain or lose disproportionately from the changes. Additionally, as in the MMR immunization case, if the information communicated is flawed, then the changes that result could do more harm than good both to society and to individuals within the society. As Holland (2015) explains, "[a]lthough public health is hard to define, its distinctive characteristic is its population perspective" (p. 2). Thus, public health may sometimes promise "benefits, in terms of the health of target populations, at a cost to individuals. This creates dilemmas between the rights and needs of the individual and the rights and needs of the community" (Holland, 2015, p. 4).

Whose Rights Should Prevail?

The question of the right thing to do or the right thing to communicate is not just one faced by individuals but also by organizations. According to the philosophies of consequentialism—the best known of which is that of utilitarianism—"[t]he right thing to do is that which will bring about the best consequences. The wrong thing to do is that which will fail to bring about the best consequences" (Holland, 2015, p. 18). Yet critics argue that this utilitarian perspective does not explain how to determine what the best consequences are, and "it tempts us, in considering what would maximize benefits for the greatest number of people, to assume that what is in the interest of an ideal reasonable being is somehow the same as what would be beneficial for everyone" (Plaisance, 2013, p. 35). Moreover, as Holland (2015) explains, utilitarianism is not about the *greatest number* but rather about the *greatest good* and in some cases the greatest benefit could be to give all of a specific good, for example the entire supply of a medicine to one person to save his/her life, rather than to spread the supply among many people merely to lessen the effects of an illness.

From a societal perspective, one could argue that the greatest good with regard to immunization would be to achieve and maintain herd immunity standards. Defined as "the level of population immunity above which sustained transmission is unlikely" (Burgess et al., 2006, p. 3921) herd immunity protects the overall population by minimizing the spread of infectious diseases to those most vulnerable in the population, namely infants and children too young to be immunized or those with auto-immune disorders.

For many years Americans accepted potential threats to herd immunity, acceptance demonstrated by the varying levels of regulation on immunization requirements established by individual states. The acceptance of more lenient regulations in some states, such as California and Oregon, was based in part on individuals' right to autonomy such as the right for parents to decide whether or not to immunize their children. Perhaps because the Disneyland associated outbreak originated in an iconic and popular theme park, or perhaps because employees at the Disney parks as well as "infants too young to receive the vaccine and children with true medical contraindications to vaccinations became infected" (Halsey & Salmon, 2015, p. 655) public acceptance of the anti-vaccination perspective shifted. What had been a cautious truce between the concepts of public good and autonomy, or the right of individuals to decide whether to immunize either themselves or their children, became a contentious public debate.

Utilitarianism in its search for the greatest good has provision for autonomy. As John Stuart Mill (1975) noted, "the only purpose for which power can be rightfully exercised over any member of a civilized community, against his will, is to prevent harm to others" (p. 15). Thus, if we apply this to the Disney outbreak, as Americans were suddenly made aware of the potential harm found in populations lacking in herd immunity, they began to question policies that allow religious, medical, and philosophical exemptions to immunization. They began to see the value in a different good than autonomy—the need to protect the weaker or less fortunate in society from the potentially fatal harm of infectious diseases like measles. As a result, large segments of the public became vocal in their desire for stricter immunization laws, petitioning their state governments and supporting proposed mandates on mass immunization programs.

The swing in public opinion was surprising considering that in 2014 the United States experienced its highest number of measles cases since 2000, with 668 reported cases (CDC, 2015) and yet there was no public outcry against lenient vaccination requirements at that time. It appears that the Disneyland outbreak provided a pivotal catalyst toward support for immunization not unlike the anti-vaccination catalyst created by the fraudulent Wakefield et al. study 17 years earlier. Whatever the reason, the Disneyland outbreak resulted in headlines such as "Oregon legislator wants to eliminate 'philosophical' vaccine exemption" (Bailey-Shah, 2015), "The good thing about the Disney measles outbreak" (McCarthy, 2015), and "Finally, California lawmakers say vaccination is a social responsibility" (Klein, 2015).

As Holland (2015) indicates, "there has always been concern amongst some medical ethicists and bioethicists that individual rights in general, and the principle of autonomy in particular, have been allowed to overshadow more community-oriented goods and values" (p. 5). And in the Disney case, it appears that public sentiment shifted suddenly from one of a willingness to accept some potential negative effects on the larger population as the result of decreased herd immunity in exchange for individual autonomy and decision making, to one where the greater good would be to tighten requirements for immunization through government mandates.

Yet, one could argue that government mandates that require children to receive certain immunizations before they are allowed to attend day care or public schools interferes with individual autonomy, or the right of an individual as a person of reason to decide the best option for one's self or one's children. According to Immanuel Kant, an 18th-century moral philosopher, it would not be ethical to merely consider an individual as part of the herd needed for herd immunity. Simply, the Kantian perspective is one of deontological philosophy where individuals, as moral agents, have certain duties to themselves and to society.

Key among these theories is the concept of the individual as an end in itself and not merely a "means to an end" (Holland, 2015; Plaisance, 2013). Thus, requiring the immunization of an individual could be seen as unethical because it perceives the individual as part of the herd and the means to the end of developing herd immunity. Holland (2015) explains it as such: "health is a good, but not the only good (i.e., we value things other than health). Nor is health necessarily the main good, the thing we value most highly" (p. 24). In the United States, and elsewhere, individual autonomy is also a highly valued good.

The concept of autonomy is explained thus, by Holland (2015):

> Autonomy "has become established as a major element in Western moral and political culture. It underpins the liberal emphasis on the rights of individuals, specifically the right of the individual to pursue

their own conception of the good. A 'conception of the good' is a view of how to live based on one's beliefs about what makes life valuable or worthwhile." (p. 49)

However, Kantian philosophy also includes the key concept of universality, wherein one's actions, when applied universally, would be acceptable (Holland, 2015; Plaisance, 2013). In the case of immunization refusal, the test of universality points to a failure for individual autonomy. If everyone in a population were to select religious, political, medical, or philosophical exemptions from immunization, the population would be at great risk for mass outbreaks of infectious diseases with high levels of morbidity and mortality. Moreover, even if one did not apply the concept of universality those refusing immunization could be said to be benefiting from free-riding (Holland, 2015).

Because of the continuing high level of immunization in the United States, albeit less so in certain states, those electing to forgo immunization are free riding the protection generated by the majority of individuals who are immunized, whether through free choice or state mandate, and because of whom the herd protection exists. Such behavior, Holland (2015) argues is unacceptable by Kantian logic, noting that "according to Kant's dictum, immunization free-riding is an action that is always morally wrong, by its very nature, and irrespective of consequences" (p. 205).

Communicating in the Public Interest

Given the tension and conflict in considering just two goods in highly polarized societal issues—those of public health and autonomy—it becomes apparent that there is no clear answer to what constitutes the greater good. Moral philosophies can be found to support either side in the controversy. As a result, it can be difficult for those practitioners charged with communicating health initiatives to the public to balance responsibilities to their employer with responsibilities to society, particularly when the subject is contentious and both supporters and opponents of the initiative are equally concerned about the issue.

Yet there are professional tactics those in public interest communication can use to ensure their behaviors do not inadvertently ignite a storm of controversy or provide the pivotal catalyst in polarizing an issue, unless that was the desired outcome. For example, using factual and accurate information that is easily comprehended by the receivers of the information, can educate the public about important health issues, building public opinion, and ultimately influencing policy change. It may take years for public opinion to change, but hopefully in time change will come as it did when society's perceptions of smoking moved from one of acceptance to one of polarization (right to smoke vs. dangers of second-hand smoke) which led in time to policy change.

Such communication contributes to what Ratzan (2001) describes as health literacy in that an individual's cognitive and social skills are used to develop motivation and the ability to find, understand, and use information to promote and maintain good health. Despite the wealth of information available, he argues:

> [O]ur presiding goal should be ethical art and technique for effective delivery of information. The communication we are talking about should not be lost in the technology; it means getting the right message to the right people, at the right time, with the intended effect. It requires both the science and the art of communicating health. (pp. 210–211)

This science and art falls into the category of public relations. Practitioners must, "capture not only the attention of the public amid [a crowded media environment] but also motivate them to change health behaviors that are often entrenched or to initiate habits that may be new or difficult" (Randolph & Viswanath, 2004, p. 419).

It is not an easy task to try to motivate people to change their health behaviors, nor one to be undertaken lightly. Social change is never easy and rarely lacking in controversy and health initiatives are even more difficult, concerning as they do, the rights of individuals to make decisions about their health, or their children's health, without undue constraint by the government. It takes those committed to the importance of such change—those in public interest communication—to clearly communicate the need for such change. In doing so they must acknowledge and carefully consider the concerns of those who oppose the change as well as the potential costs of such change on both the individual and society.

Conclusion

There is no clear answer to the question of what constitutes the greater good on polarized and contentious societal issues. There will always be trade-offs between the rights of individuals and the needs of the larger society. Yet, it is among the ethical duties of media and public interest communicators to ensure that the concerns of individuals are addressed in communicating about the issue in question and that the potential gains for society and individuals within that society are clearly explained.

The case of the measles and public interest communication highlights some of the moral issues faced by public communicators and their responsibilities to themselves, their employers, and to society. For example, Wakefield et al. produced a fraudulent report (*Lancet*, 2010) but it was a press conference sponsored by a nonprofit organization that stimulated media interest and launched a societal debate that continues nearly two decades later. It is unlikely that the organizers of the Wakefield press conference intended to do anything immoral or irresponsible yet the media event ignited societal debate and changed the health behaviors of so many people that herd immunity was lost in some places and dangerously threatened in others. Thus, public communicators should be mindful that the best intentions can have unintended and long-reaching consequences.

Despite the failure of public interest communication in the case of the Wakefield press conference, this case study is also a reminder of the positive impact public interest communication can have on individual behavior and societal norms. As Wakefield, Loken, and Hornik (2010) note, "mass media campaigns can produce positive changes or prevent negative changes in health-related behaviours across large populations" (p. 1). In the case of the Disneyland outbreak, a significant shift in public opinion resulted in a move from acceptance of individual autonomy, or the right of individuals to decide whether to immunize either themselves or their children at a cost to herd immunity, to one where autonomy was no longer socially acceptable because of the dangers to the larger population. Included in the shift was a publicized announcement by Autism Speaks, changing its stance on immunization and encouraging parents to immunize their children (American Speech Language Hearing Association [ASHA], 2015), which states:

> Research has asked whether there is any link between childhood vaccinations and autism. The results of this research are clear: Vaccines do not cause autism. We urge that all children be fully vaccinated. (p. 1)

More significant, as a result of the shift in public opinion, reevaluation of immunization exemptions in several states including California and Oregon have led to the enactment of California Senate Bill 277 and sustained efforts by legislators in other states to implement similar laws. Signed by the state's governor, Jerry Brown, on June 30, 2015, California Senate Bill 277 abolished the personal-belief exemption, which allowed parents to opt out of vaccinating their children for many reasons, though certain medical exemptions will still apply (Willon & Mason, 2015). Despite passage of the new law the polarized debate continues with opponents of the law in California and concerned citizens in other states arguing that such laws interfere with individual freedoms including the right for children to attend school and parents' rights to parent their children in the way they see best (Richardson, 2015).

References

American Speech Language Hearing Association (ASHA). (2015, April). Autism Speaks launches push for adults with ASD, alters vaccination stance. *The ASHA Leader, 20*(4), 14.

Bailey-Shah, S. (2015). *Oregon legislator wants to eliminate "philosophical" vaccine exemption.* Retrieved from http://www.katu.com/news/problemsolver.

Burgess, D. C., Burgess, M. A., & Leask, J. (2006). The MMR vaccination and autism controversy in the United Kingdom 1998–2005: Inevitable community outrage or a failure of risk communication? *Vaccine, 24*, 3921–3928. doi.10.1016/j.vaccine.2006.02.033.

Centers for Disease Control and Prevention. (2015). *2015 Measles cases in the U.S.* Retrieved from http://www.cdc.gov/measles/cases-outbreaks.html.

Flaherty, D. K. (2011). The vaccine-autism connection: A public health crisis caused by unethical medical practices and fraudulent science. *Annals of Pharmacology, 45* (October), 1302–1304.

Gellin, B. G., Maibach, E. W., & Marcuse, E. K. (2000). Do parents understand immunizations? A national telephone survey. *Pediatrics, 106*(5), 1097–1102.

Gerber, J. S., & Offit, P. A. (2009). Vaccines and autism: A tale of shifting hypotheses. *Clinical Infectious Diseases, 48*(4), 456–461.

Haelle, T. (2015, January 21). California measles outbreak shows how quickly disease can resurface in U.S. *U.S. News & World Report*. Retrieved from http://usnews.com.

Halsey, N. A., & Salmon, D. A. (2015). Measles at Disneyland, a problem for all ages. *Annals of Internal Medicine, 162*(9), 655–656.

Holland, S. (2015). *Public health ethics* (2nd ed.). Malden, MA: Polity.

Klein, K. (2015). Finally, California lawmakers say vaccination is a social responsibility. *The Los Angeles Times*. Retrieved from http://www.latimes.com/opinion.

Lacitis, E. (2015). Vashon's parents try to get along despite deep vaccination divide. *The Seattle Times*. Retrieved from http://www.seattletimes.com.

Lancet, The. (2010, February 6). Retraction—Ileal-lymphoid-nodular hyperplasia, non-specific colitis, and pervasive developmental disorder in children. *The Lancet, 375*, 445–445. doi:10.1016/S0140-6736(10)60175-4.

McCarthy, C. (2015, February 2). The good thing about the Disney measles outbreak. *The Huffington Post*. Retrieved from http://www.huffintonpost.com.

Mill, J. S. (1975). On liberty. In *Three Essays: On Liberty, Representative Government, the Subjection of Women*. Oxford: Oxford University Press, 5–141.

Plaisance, P. L. (2013). *Media ethics: Key principles for responsible practice* (2nd ed.). Los Angeles, CA: Sage.

Poland, G. A., & Jacobson, R. M. (2012). The re-emergence of measles in developed countries: Time to develop the next-generation measles vaccines? *Vaccine, 30*(2), 103–104. doi:10.1016/j.vaccine.2011.11.085.

Randolph, W., & Viswanath, K. (2004). Lessons learned from public health mass media campaigns: Marketing health in a crowded media world. *Annual Review of Public Health, 25*, 419–437. doi:10.1146/annurev.publhealth25.101802.123046.

Ratzan, S. C. (2001). Health literacy: Communication for the public good. *Health Promotion International, 16*(2), 207–214.

Richardson, V. (2015, July 2). California vaccine bill battle erupts into all-out political war. *Washington Times*. Retrieved from http://www.washingtontimes.com.

University of Florida. (n.d.). *Public interest communications at the University of Florida*. Retrieved from http://frank.jou.ufl.edu/public-interest-communications-at-the-university-of-florida/.

Wakefield, M. A., Loken, B., & Hornik, R. C. (2010). Use of mass media campaigns to change health behavior. *The Lancet, 376*, 1261–1271. doi:10.1016/S0140-6736(10)60809-4.

Willon, P., & Mason, M. (2015, June 30). California Gov. Jerry Brown signs new vaccination law, one of nation's toughest. *Los Angeles Times*. Retrieved from http://www.latimes.com.

Part III

Moral and Civic Responsibility in the Digital Age

12 Building an Ethic of Responsibility

Dialogue and Communitarianism as Public Relations Archetypes

Michael L. Kent and Maureen Taylor

Public relations communication has traditionally been used in functional ways such as advertising, marketing, publicity, and lobbying to help organizations of all kinds shape their environments. Under a functional orientation, stakeholders, publics, and society at large are often treated as merely the receivers of organizational messages and actions. Organizations use one-way communication to tell publics what they want them to know. Public relations practiced in this functional orientation is rarely ethical and does little to empower the public. This chapter argues that by shifting our frameworks for understanding ethical public relations away from a functional orientation, we can practice more ethical public relations.

The frames through which individuals view life influence what is seen (Burke, 1966, 1968). Anyone who has ever seen an ocean during a storm can appreciate the awesome power of the sea (Osborn, 1977). Most of us have seen media coverage of ships being tossed around in storms, or houses being swept off shore and into the ocean during a storm surge or tsunami. Similarly, many people have a fear of the dark, and celebrate the joy of daylight and the sun. The sea, the sun, and the dark, represent "basic, unchanging patterns of experience" (Osborn 1967, p. 115), or cultural archetypes.

Archetypes are metaphorical concepts that represent nearly universal human experiences and are regularly drawn upon in language and communication. People talk about: "exposing something to the light of day," something "existing in the shadows," or "a dark day" to describe a terrible event. Archetypes can help us to advance our understanding of public relations ethics because they can describe prosocial public relations activities that are instructive of how good people should act.

Public relations practice has also been informed by an assortment of dominant metaphors such as the ideas of "information subsidies" (Gandy, 1982), "symmetry," and "excellence" (J. E. Grunig, 1992). For many years, concepts such as excellence and symmetry were treated as archetypes and assumed to have universal recognition and applicability. Over time, these concepts were criticized for their lack of universal appeal. As the global field of public relations coalesced, public relations practitioners from across the world realized that symmetry and ethics were not synonymous, and were often mutually exclusive, such as when organizations feign interest in stakeholders or publics in order to build brand or organizational loyalty (cf., Kent, Harrison, & Taylor, 2006).

In the last two decades, other theories and models have emerged for talking about the practice of ethical public relations like the idea of OPRs (organization–public relationships) (Ledingham & Bruning, 1998, 2000), and crisis and risk communication. We believe that the time has come for new, genuinely representative archetypes and metaphors guiding ethical public relations practices: community and dialogue. As will be explained next, "community" and "dialogue" will have greater relevance to public relations practitioners around the world because of their nearly universal appeal.

The Value of Public Relations to Community Building

Community is a concept that resonates in every place in the world: neighborhoods, towns, cities, internally within organizations, among members of groups, within and across racial and ethnic boundaries, and in different nations and cultures. Of course, not every community is equally positive, but the ideal of community and its power for creating identification, cohesion, shared norms and values, etc., is a fairly universal concept. Thus, we believe that community is a compelling and useful archetype for describing public relations practice and guiding public relations professionals as they embark on their communication careers.

The metaphorical archetype of community, studied by scholars in an area of theory called communitarianism, shifts the focus away from self-centered individual and organizational interests, lacking both empathy and universal appeal (cf. Kent, 2010), to a focus on multiple stakeholders and publics (cf. Botan & Taylor, 2004; Kent & Taylor, 2002; Kruckeberg & Stark, 1988; Leeper, 1996). This community focus positions organizations within larger networks of individuals and publics.

We believe that an emphasis on relationships and community will enable public relations professionals and scholars to ask new questions and practice public relations in new ways (cf., Heath, 2006; Taylor & Kent, 2014; Weiss, 1993). Changing the way that we think about the world is not an easy task. The terminology, definitions, metaphors, and archetypes from our past limit our ability to see certain things (cf. Reddy, 1979). As Weiss suggests (1993), people need to have models and mentors to help them adjust to a changed environment. The job of communication professionals is to act as that guide, bringing new ideas to their organizations and helping stakeholders and publics realign themselves.

Public relations provides advocacy for organizations as they participate in society. Public relations communication such as crisis, corporate social responsibility (CSR), issues management, lobbying, publicity, risk, and other functions of public relations emerge as strategies that help all types of organizations to shape their environments. Historically, public relations practitioners have been most valued by their organizations when they support larger organizational objectives, such as growing revenue, minimizing regulation, or gaining some form of competitive advantage. Under the functional mindset of public relations, the publics, communities, society, political structures, and the economy are things to be acted upon. When public relations professionals work as content creators and message producers rather than working as strategic thinkers and organizational counselors, then our value to organizations and society is diminished.

The functional mindset of public relations is not only narrow but it is unsustainable in the highly networked society of the 21st century. The remainder of this chapter explores the concepts of communitarianism and dialogue as alternative frameworks that allow us to better practice ethical public relations.

The Principles of Communitarianism

Amitai Etzioni was one of the founders of the modern Communitarian movement. According to Etzioni, communitarianism is an "environmental movement" that seeks to enhance the moral, social, and political environment in which we live. As Etzioni (1993) explained, communitarians work with others "to bring about the changes in values, habits, and public policies that will allow us to do for society what the environmental movement seeks to do for nature: to safeguard and enhance our lives" (pp. 2–3). Communitarianism rejects the liberal notion that humans are isolated individuals with "rights, interests, values, and ends independent of social context" (Weiss, 1993, pp. 125 ff). We are all connected and we are all interdependent. What one person or organization does affects many others.

Duty to others without any expected personal reward is a major tenet of communitarianism. Etzioni noted that we must recognize that "we have some duties that lay moral claim on us for which we derive no immediate benefit or even long-term payoff" (p. 10). This approach may seem odd in an economic and political system that rewards those organizations that make quick profits. But the communitarian movement challenges corporations to engage in corporate social responsibility. CSR challenges citizens and communication professionals to shift their focus away from getting all that they can get for themselves or their organization (individualism) to a more collectivist focus that considers other citizens, civil society groups, ethnic groups, and social classes. Communitarianism asks people to uphold the social contract and enact their responsibilities as good citizens. Instilling communitarian values in communication professionals will encourage them to think about the relationships and well-being of all stakeholders and publics with whom they have contact. Communitarianism can be achieved by focusing on dialogic practices.

The Power of the Dialogic Metaphor to Transform Public Relations

If community is an archetype of how people in society *should* interact with others, then dialogue can be understood as a metaphor for how to help organize those relations. Metaphors are linguistic or rhetorical strategies for explaining one thing in terms of something else. Americans often rely on war or sports analogies to explain something else. The best metaphors are compelling and generative because they allow us to see relationships in new ways. Sometimes common metaphors like sports metaphors are considered dead metaphors because their cliché use of language does not actually lead to a better understanding of the thing the words are describing. Effective metaphors are both evocative and interesting. Metaphors help us see something new through something old.

By introducing public relations practice to the metaphor of dialogue, we make public relations about talking, conversations, discussions, negotiations, discourse, and relationships. Public relations practice benefits from a concept that is more easily understood.

Israeli Theologian Martin Buber (1970/1923) is considered by most to be the father of the modern concept of dialogue. Buber suggested that dialogue involves an effort to recognize the value of the other—to see others as ends and not merely as a means to achieve selfish goals. Buber suggested that individuals should view others not as objects but as equals (pp. 53ff.). Buber's work is based on reciprocity, mutuality, involvement, and openness.

In the field of public relations, Pearson (1989a, 1989b), building on Buber, suggested that "public relations is best conceptualized as the management of interpersonal dialectic" (1989a, p. 177). Pearson suggested that what is important to the practice of ethical public relations is to have a dialogic "system" rather than monologic "policies." Pearson also argued for a focus on community, writing that

> the focus for an organizational ethicist must shift dramatically from not what action or policy is more right than another (a question that is usually posed as a monologue), but what kind of communication system maximizes the chances competing interests can discover some shared ground and be transformed or transcended. (1989a, p. 206)

Almost a decade after Pearson's first articles on dialogue appeared, Botan suggested that "dialogue manifests itself more as a stance, orientation, or bearing in communication rather than as a specific method, technique, or format" (1997, p. 4). Dialogue is an orientation toward others that acknowledges the inherent value and importance of other human beings as they live in a shared society. Dialogue is not simply a two-way communication process; there are actual behaviors and activities that have to happen *before* dialogic communication occurs. For instance, people and organizations need to commit to empathy, patience, risk, sympathy, and trust. Perhaps most importantly, interlocutors must go into a dialogic interaction with a willingness to be changed, or admit when they are wrong.

Important Features of Dialogue

As Kent and Taylor (2002) explained, dialogue includes five features: (1) mutuality, or the recognition of organization–public relationships; (2) propinquity, or the temporality and spontaneity of interactions with publics; (3) empathy, or the supportiveness and confirmation of public goals and interests; (4) risk, or the willingness to interact with individuals and publics on their own terms; and finally, (5) commitment, or the extent to which an organization gives itself over to dialogue, interpretation, and understanding in its interactions with publics (pp. 24–25).

Dialogic communicators struggle to put aside their own personal agendas to create and foster communicative spaces and opportunities where even the weakest or most marginalized have the potential to communicate as equals. For dialogue to happen the prerequisites to dialogue including trust, risk, and empathy have to happen.

Making the claim that a new archetype, community, and a new metaphor, dialogue, are needed to make public relations into a more ethical practice is of course easier than enacting that claim. Both building community and engaging in dialogue are difficult. Communitarianism provides the broad societal background to rethink the role of organizations in society, and dialogue provides the process through which organizations, publics, communities, and others can engage. Community is the archetype that resonates with all groups and cultures, while concepts like excellence, individualism, and functionalism are not universally held.

Today, in our highly networked world, we believe that one context where the principles of community and dialogue can be enacted is in the realm of social media communication. Social media represents an ideal context for professional communicators to start making the mental and cultural changes necessary to become more dialogic. Social media are valuable because they have become so ubiquitous in the business and professional world. We are at an important time in their development because the norms of social media engagement are not yet as fixed as the norms are in other mass media. Professional communicators still have the ability to do and try new things in social media spaces.

Applications of Communitarianism and Dialogue to Social Media Communication

For decades, technology critics warned people about the dangers of networked technologies and databases of information (Brand, 1988; Burnham, 1984; Vallee, 1982). They were not wrong. Today, communication technologies are transforming how organizations, individuals, and groups see the world, and engage other people and organizations. Since the late 1990s, organizations, new and old, large and small, public and private, now have the ability to instantly communicate with others via the Internet. The first wave of mediated communication occurred via the Internet and websites, but now, social media platforms have emerged as "spaces" for conversations. The defining features of social media are that they are relational, involve feedback, and have the potential to take place in real time—unlike the broadcast media.

However, as Kent (2008) suggested of blogs, there are different types of blogs: news blogs, political blogs, personal blogs, but there is no single defining type of blog. The same is true of social media. Although most social media research and mass media stories only focus on a few well-known sites such as Facebook, Twitter, YouTube, and LinkedIn, there are literally thousands of social media sites that revolve around everything from images of people's favorite things, to news, pets, politics, sports, religion, various industries, and others. The many kinds of social media also vary by membership characteristics: age, group affiliation, educational level, cultural background, languages spoken, hobbies, interests, and so on.

Social media are both media and medium: content and channel, and their features and uses vary widely. Social media are also valuable communication tools because they allow organizations to control content and access to people. However, social media are often treated as marketing and advertising tools rather than tools to create community or dialogue. The current one-way, sender-to-receiver, "public forum" use of social media engenders only the most facile interactions. Social media have enormous untapped potential for enacting community.

However, there is an inherent inconsistency between the structure and potential of social media and the evolving role of public relations in organizations (cf., Duhé, 2012; Kent & Saffer, 2014). Social media can provide a special communicative place that goes beyond marketing and advertising to facilitate what Etzioni and Buber may have hoped for in their theorizing about ethical relationships. Through social media, we can re-envision how organizations orientate their actions to the larger society and also reconsider the goal of communication.

Building Community: Adjusting Organizations to People and People to Organizations

Bryant (1953), writing about rhetorical theory more than half a century ago, argued that rhetoric was the process of "adjusting ideas to people and people to ideas" (p. 407). Bryant was speaking about persuasion, but he could just have easily have been speaking about dialogue. Both involve a process of adjustment, adaptation to an audience, efforts to empathize with others, and the ability to take new positions as events emerge.

Before the Internet, few genuinely rhetorical venues ever existed where organizations could speak to stakeholders and public directly. Indeed, the idea of organizational dialogue was something only possible *within* organizations relatively recently, with the advent of social media. Social media provide organizations and individuals direct access to thousands, tens of thousands, and sometime millions of people without the need for a mass media gatekeeper. And social media are a unique organizational phenomenon that can be used for more than simply marketing and advertising.

We believe that a communitarianism orientation provides organizations with a way of serving the broader social/societal interests of the organization and steering organizations away from self-serving goals and activities. Currently, social media are primarily used by organizations unidirectionally, as communication tools for marketing and advertising. In a communitarian orientation, organizations would situate their interests in a much broader environment and look for ways to bring as many different groups together in their activities. Public relations would follow a bridging approach (called *Tertius Iungens*) where organizations see their communicative functions to build and foster relationships, rather than promote selfish, individualistic, activities designed only to serve elites (shareholders, CEOs, etc.) (cf., Kent, Sommerfeldt, & Saffer, 2015).

Dialogic social media are not focused on reaching the most people but on providing genuinely valuable information to stakeholders and publics (by "genuinely valuable" we mean not about sales, products, or services). The most enduring organizations are open to new information, adapt, and change, admitting when they have been wrong and taking steps to solve the problem (deGeus, 1997). The enduring organization's orientation is on the broader community, not itself. In order to have that kind of external focus, organizations use public relations to listen to others.

Listening

Many organizations use social media primarily for marketing and advertising because they give organizations the ability to control the communication channel and messages. In a reconfigured dialogic/community orientation, organizations would spend more time and resources asking questions and listening to the community's answers. Social media would be used to locate those with different perspectives or who disagree with organizational positions, not to act as cheerleaders for the advertising and marketing departments. A primary function of public relations would be to aggregate, synthesize, articulate, and then counsel organizational leaders on courses of action based on this listening.

Basically, many of the skills taught in courses such as Group Communication, Interpersonal Communication, Organizational Communication, and so on, apply here. Social media are a special medium in terms of their ability to give access to so many people heretofore unavailable to organizations. But social media are still just a communication channel that are subject to the principles of effective rhetoric and group and interpersonal communication. Professional communicators need to learn to use social media dialogically so that knowledge gained about other communities can be used to improve organizational communities.

Amplification of community needs

Social media can also be used as a mouthpiece to amplify messages from the community. Instead of privileging one-way communication from organizations to stakeholders and publics, or the community, organizations can help individuals and groups come together via their social media tools. Imagine a communication model much like crowd funding, where prosocial groups are brought together to work with corporations and organizations on socially responsible causes via social media (or CSR).

One such organization might be The Long Now (TLN), a nonprofit, activist, organization founded in 1993 (Brand, 1999) by a group of artists, intellectuals, scientists, inventors, and business professionals to raise awareness about "technology, capitalism, democracy, and long-term responsibility." TLN's principles, or "Guidelines for a long-lived, long-valuable institution," include the following: "serving the long view, fostering responsibility, rewarding patience, minding mythic depth, allying with competition, taking no sides, and leveraging longevity" (http://longnow.org/about).

To achieve their goals, TLN has focused on symbolic activities designed to raise awareness and uphold their principles of long-term thinking. Their focus has not been on the founders' individual interests, but on their stakeholders and publics. TLN uses social media to listen, connect members, crowd source ideas and projects, share ideas, and collaborate. TLN has raised millions of dollars and used its funds on an extraordinary range of projects that include purchasing a "two-mile-long swath of mountain land … covered by a forest of ancient bristlecone pine trees (considered among the world's oldest living things with some as old as 4,900 years)" (http://longnow.org/clock/nevada); the Rosetta Project, "a global collaboration of language specialists and native speakers working to build a publicly accessible digital library of human languages" (http://rosettaproject. org); PanLex, an effort to make every word of every language of the world's 7,000 languages accessible to everyone; the Long Bets, an effort to improve long-term thinking by encouraging people to find solutions to problems far into the future; and sponsoring more than 150 talks by leaders in dozens of fields: Art, Climate Change, Education, Energy, the Environment, the Internet, Journalism, Law, Music, Public Policy, Religion, and Terrorism.

TLN serves as a model for amplifying community needs and dialogic thinking. It always makes its decisions based on long-term thought, sound science and research, dialogue, trust in their stakeholders and publics', and advancing the interests of their members and the world. Social media allow it to listen and speak. Although organizations like TLN are rare, the presence of even one demonstrates that organizations can succeed by placing the interests of stakeholders first, and always focusing on the good of the community.

Conclusion

This chapter argues that public relations communication has traditionally been used in functional ways such as advertising, marketing, and publicity. Public relations as an ethical communication profession can be so much more. Public relations builds relationships. Public relations builds communities. We believe that by adopting new metaphors such as communitarianism and dialogue, the field of public relations can better perform its role in society. A change in the way that we think about public relations will create a change in the way that we practice it.

References

Botan, C. (1997). Ethics in strategic communication campaigns: The case for a new approach to public relations. *Journal of Business Communication, 34*, 188–202.

Botan, C. H., & Taylor, M. (2004). Public relations: State of the field. *Journal of Communication 54*(4), 645–661.

Brand, S. (1988). *The media lab: Inventing the future at M.I.T.* New York, NY: Penguin Books.

Brand, S. (1999). *The clock of the long now: Time and responsibility.* New York, NY: Basic Books.

Bryant, D. C. (1953). Rhetoric its function and its scope. *Quarterly Journal of Speech, XXXIX*, 407.

Buber, M. (1970). *I and thou* (W. Kaufmann, Trans.). New York, NY: Charles Scribner's Sons.

Burke, K. (1966). *Language as symbolic action: Essays on life, literature, and method.* Berkeley, CA: University of California Press.

Burke, K. (1968). Encyclopedia entry: Dramatism. *International Encyclopedia of the Social Sciences* (pp. 445–452). New York, NY: Macmillan.

Burnham, D. (1984). *The rise of the computer state.* New York, NY: Vintage Books.

deGeus, A. (1997). The living company. Boston, MA: Harvard Business School Press.

Duhé, S. (Ed.). (2012). *New media and public relations.* New York, NY: Peter Lang.

Etzioni, A. (1993). *The spirit of community: The reinvention of American society.* New York, NY: Simon and Schuster.

Gandy, O. H. (1982). *Beyond agenda setting: Information subsidies and public policy.* Norwood, NJ: Ablex.

Grunig, J. E. (1992). *Excellence in public relations and communication management.* Hillsdale, NJ: Lawrence Erlbaum.

Heath, R. L. (2006). Onward into more fog. *Journal of Public Relations Research, 18*, 93–114.

Kent, M. L. (2008). Critical analysis of Blogging in public relations. *Public Relations Review, 34*(1), 32–40.

Kent, M. L. (2010). What is a public relations "Crisis?" Refocusing crisis research. In W. T. Coombs & S. J. Holladay (Eds.), *Handbook of crisis communication* (pp. 705–712). Oxford, England: Wiley/Blackwell.

Kent, M. L., Harrison, T. R., & Taylor, M. (2006). A critique of Internet polls as symbolic representation and pseudo-events. *Communication Studies, 57*(3), 299–315.

Kent, M. L. & Saffer, A. J. (2014). A Delphi study of the future of new technology research in public relations. *Public Relations Review, 40*(4), 568–576.

Kent, M. L., Sommerfeldt, E. J., & Saffer, A. J. (2015, in press corrected proof). Social network analysis, power, and public relations: Tertius iungens as a path to organizational trust and relationship building. *Public Relation Review.*

Kent, M. L., & Taylor, M. (2002). Toward a dialogic theory of public relations. *Public Relations Review, 28*, 21–37.

Kruckeberg, D., & Stark, K. (1988). *Public relations and community: A reconstructed theory*. New York, NY: Praeger.

Ledingham, J. A., & Bruning, S. D. (1998). Relationship management and public relations: Dimensions of an organization–public relationship. *Public Relations Review, 24*, 55–65.

Ledingham, J. A., & Bruning, D. S. (2000). *Public relations as relationship management: A relational approach to the study and practice of public relations*. New York, NY: Taylor and Francis.

Leeper, K. (1996). Public relations: Ethics and communitarianism. *Public Relations Review, 22*, 163–179.

Osborn, M. (1967). Archetypal metaphor in rhetoric: The light-dark family. *Quarterly Journal of Speech, LIII*(2), 115–126.

Osborn, M. (1977). The evolution of the archetypal sea in rhetoric and poetic. *Quarterly Journal of Speech, 63*(4), 347–363.

Pearson, R. (1989a). *A theory of public relations ethics*. Unpublished Doctoral dissertation, Ohio University, Athens, Ohio.

Pearson, R. (1989b). Business ethics as communication ethics: Public relations practice and the idea of dialogue. In C. H. Botan & V. Hazleton Jr. (Eds.), *Public relations theory* (pp. 111–131). Hillsdale, NJ: Lawrence Erlbaum.

Reddy, M. (1979). The conduit metaphor: A case of frame conflict in our language about language. In A. Ortony (Ed.), *Metaphor and thought* (2nd ed., pp. 164–201). Cambridge, MA: Cambridge University Press.

Taylor, M., & Kent, M. L. (2014). Dialogic engagement: Clarifying foundational concepts. *Journal of Public Relations Research, 26*, 384–398.

Vallee, J. (1982). *The network revolution: Confessions of a computer scientist*. Berkeley, CA: And/Or Press.

Weiss, P. (1993). Feminism and communitarianism: Exploring the relationship. In P. Weiss (Ed.), *Gendered community: Rousseau, sex, and politics*. New York, NY: New York University Press.

13 Interplay in the Digital Media Environment

Putting Focus on the Blurring Line Between Advertising and Public Relations in South Korea

Samsup Jo

In a narrowed definition of public relations comparing it to advertising, it has been noted that public relations can be distinguished from advertising largely through the third-party endorsement theory. The theoretical framework of third-party endorsement values the credibility of a public relations message over advertising content. However, this long-lasting belief has been increasingly threatened by the market-driven media environment and rapid penetration of social media.

One role of public relations is to provide media with information subsidies in order to gain media coverage while given credible endorsement by a third party. Gandy (1982) coined the term *information subsidies* to refer to this kind of provision that helps journalists gather news more readily. In fact, Gandy (1982) cautioned practitioners about the negative side effects of information subsidies, most notably that organizations with more public relations resources will have more access to the media, yielding more news content that can serve as advertising.

Given the radical shift to digital communication, it is conceivable that newspaper journalists will become more dependent on information subsidies. Facing cutbacks in advertising revenue for the newspaper largely due to a reduction in print subscriptions, journalists must compensate for the loss of revenue in some way. Thus, newspaper companies are increasingly dependent on advertisers, and news editorials are affected by clients or advertisers who can provide economic benefits. Therefore, journalists feel more economic pressure when they choose news stories or frame news content (Jo & Pae, 2013).

Furthermore, the public's substantial dependence on digital media platforms increasingly pushes organizations to amplify the use of information subsidies to online portals and social media platforms. In sum, the transformation of media platforms is rapidly changing the way the public gathers information from traditional media to online and digitalized media. In other words, the traditional public relations process is undergoing a change from offline media to digital media, which is operationalized largely by big IT companies such as Google.

In the past, the media has had its own role in screening the information subsidies to select objective news as editorial content. However, under the current digital media environment, traditional media has yielded this role to online portals or search engines, which now play the agenda-setting function and decide the rank and order of news content to be displayed. For example, many online news companies use clickbait to entice readers to expose advertising content disguised as news content, this impairing journalism value and public good. New digital news companies are largely gaining their income from advertising revenues that stem from the number of clicks, provided to advertisers. Moreover, the newspaper industry is increasingly facing revenue cutbacks and the pressure of reduction of staff reporters due to the digital-driven media transformation. Decline of advertising revenue for newspapers and online news media raises a number of ethical and management issues from the perspective of sustainable management in a different cultural context.

Toth (2009) argued that incorporating a systematic, rhetorical, and critical approach to public relations would advance public relations knowledge and theory building. She states that the rhetorical approach to public relations is to examine the authentic meaning of the messages and evaluate the message by the criteria of ethical values to the public interest. In addition, the critical perspective of public relations encourages resistance to messages that are distributed by a largely powerful institution in society such as Google. For decades, the separate function of media and sources has played a key role in maintaining a mutual beneficial relationship to illustrate its respective value. In this vein, it is worthwhile to examine the changing picture of public relations through the lens of an ethical paradigm rooted in rhetorical and critical approaches in different cultural contexts.

In this chapter, I explore how the public relations landscape is presented in a different cultural context compared to the traditional public relations paradigm. Rather, the chapter approaches public relations through an ethical lens.

Information Subsidies, Market-Driven Journalism in Digital Environment

The mutually beneficial relationship between media and information sources has consisted of routine practices that have explained the role of public relations for decades (Gandy, 1982). The media gain information easily with the aid of the public relations sector, while public relations benefits through credible news content and a third-party endorsement largely by media. Thus, these relationships are symbiotic since both parties gain from the relationship.

However, a combination of the traditional media's financial crisis and the acceleration of digital content and platforms clouds the role of third-party endorsement and raises a number of pros and cons to public relations.

With the decline of traditional media, more traditional media such as newspapers and TV networks are likely to depend on information subsides provided by social institutions. Sallot and Johnson (2006) found that journalists benefit from information subsidies, especially during times of news-editorial staff cutbacks. What Rubel (2008) referred to as "media catching" has gained momentum among public relations practitioners and journalists. Namely, the pitching direction from public relations practitioners to journalists has shifted so that journalists depend more on information sources placed on the web and other social media. In other words, media are becoming more dependent on resources from the corporate and government sector that own financial resources to subsidize; media seem to seek news stories that are helpful in generating advertising revenue and financial income.

In this vein, the traditional relationship between journalists and public relations practitioners has changed dramatically (Waters, Tindall, & Morton, 2010). McManus (1994) coined the term of market-driven journalism which is journalism operated to gain profit rather than raise public interest or civic community. The acceleration of digital communication has possibly exacerbated the financial crisis of newspapers and resulted in more frequent reliance on information subsidies. Based on in-depth interviews with public relations officers, Curtin (1999) cautioned that the increased use of public relations materials would not necessarily support the agenda-building goals of sponsoring organizations that send out public relations materials to the media. Thus economic constraints seem to push media to maximize financial profit rather than pursue public interest which the public expects (Curtin, 1999).

Davis (2000) explored the use of information subsidies in British corporations and government extensively. He argued that the efficacy of public relations is determined by a combination of four factors: (a) economic capital, (b) cultural capital, (c) human resources, and (d) strategic application. He found that the vast majority of public relations resources are used by those organizations with greater economic and political resources. His findings suggest that big corporations and government have more economic resources that can influence media agendas. The implication of his findings suggest that the media seem to value economic profit rather than journalism values that seek public good.

Another new issue facing the fields of journalism and public relations is native advertising. According to journalism ethics, publishers and editors should not mislead readers or viewers by showing advertising content in editorial content. However, these lines are blurred with the advent of native advertising. The burgeoning array of unprecedented formats and new digital social media provide the public with a range of media choices (Peeler & Guthrie, 2007). However, the content of new media do not yet deliver the credibility old media such as TV networks and newspapers render through their gatekeeping role. According to Carlson (2014), native advertising infringes upon journalism ethics, arguing sponsored contents breach independent editorial autonomy. The case of native advertising encroaches on the role of third-party endorsement that public relations practitioners and journalists have held in common for decades.

Content marketing is another form of native advertising, placing sponsor-funded content alongside editorial content or showing other content you might be interested in which is sponsored by a marketer alongside editorial recommendations. The ethical concern of native advertising is its format, which may mislead consumers.

Digital endorsement is updated quickly to catch consumers' attention; however, the problem is that many posts, blogs, replies, comments, and reviews are generated by fake consumers and bloggers. The problem lies in whether media are really independent from economic profit pressure. Some scholars diagnosed that the current online community is contaminated due to a massive marketing trend and market-driven journalism. From the perspective of the critical approach, the present public relations practice that values clients' interest rather than public interest needs to be assessed by both the theoretical and reflective paradigm.

Botan and Taylor (2004) called for the need of a co-creational perspective in which organizations and the public make meaning together, which aligns with public relations' function in a society. By contrast, current media relations practice is more likely to lean to the client due to economic constraints on the media and the neoliberalism paradigm. Sponsored blogs and editorial content are placed on top of Google searches; thus, objectivity seems to be pushed to a lower position. For example, German freelancer journalists often perform a dual job of journalist and public relations professional to earn more income from public relations writing (Koch & Obermaier, 2014). Koch and Obermaier (2014) raised the ethical concern that journalism value and public relations focus are inherently incompatible. Playing both the gatekeeper role and information supplier at the same time does not seem to be compatible from the point of public interest that journalistic autonomy values.

The value of publicity has long been recognized as superior to advertisement due to the credibility of the media that is not affected by advertisers or clients. However, the long cherished notion of third-party endorsement is lost when there are economic constraints on traditional media and there exists a ubiquity of digital platform among the public. Moreover, what seems like third-party endorsement is often editorial content with an array of digital formatting, blogs, and social media in disguise. Although scholars urge ethical behaviors and strong regulatory actions by the government, the difficulty of monitoring new media and detecting disguised advertising content challenges the clear line between news editorials and advertising content (Peeler & Guthrie, 2007). In a narrowed perspective, the superiority of news placement from many press releases is the core value of publicity compared to advertising coined by message credibility. However, if news contents is increasingly affected by advertisers and clickbait tactics, the value of publicity is equal to that of paid advertisement.

The rapid penetration of online communication with smartphones and digital technology has expanded digitalized strategic communication both in public relations firms and in the client sphere. With new media formats, editorial content is blurred between public relations and advertising, threatening the traditional message credibility of editorial content. Unlike traditional media, digital media enables bloggers to act immediately and publish, endorse, and repost with a single click (Langett, 2013). Langett (2013) argued that independent bloggers and public relations practitioners cultivate beneficial relationships if they abide by the four components: intelligibility, truth, trustworthiness, and legitimacy, based on Habermas' theory of communicative act (1987). The field of public relations expands its theoretical perspective from Excellence theory driven by systematic perspective to civil society based on rhetorical perspective. Taylor (2009) urged that public relations should embrace civil society as a theoretical framework to broaden public relations contribution to society. The civil society framework is closely linked with a democracy that facilitates information exchange and participation of stakeholders in a society. As noted, public relations and media are intertwined and "render each other possible" to foster a fully functioning society (Bentele, 2004) Taylor (2009) argued, civil society assumes a free and independent media system that serves public interest.

Public Relations in South Korea and Blurred Line among Journalism, Advertising, and Public Relations

South Korea has also seen the size of its public relations industry fluctuate with economic conditions, but the activities of PR enterprises and experts in the nation, whose market economy ranks 14th in the world, are nevertheless brisk with some 600 public relations agencies in operation.

Most public relations theories can be traced to American scholarship of the early 20th century. However, many other countries around the world practice public relations without the nomenclature commonly used in academic circles. In South Korea, public relations has been practiced under the term *Hong-Bo*. Roughly the equivalent of "public relations" as practiced and defined in the Western world, this term is close to media relations in the United States and is literally translated as "publicizing widely."

A few scholars explored the meaning and practice of *Hong-Bo*, or the equivalent of public relations in the Western world. In sum, public relations in Korea mainly focuses on media relations which is largely equivalent to managing media coverage, attempting to generate positive news and avoiding negative coverage. Jo and Kim (2004) and Rhee (2002) replicated the four models of public relations to explore public relations practices in South Korea. They found that public relations practitioners are primarily involved with media relations.

According to a study of Korean advertising and editorial news production, Jo (2011) found that public relations professionals perceived the line that traditionally separated advertising and editorial news production has become blurred. Instead of offering information subsidies news releases, public relations practitioners perceive that purchasing advertisement space plays a key role in maintaining favorable relationships with newspapers. In particular, newspapers attempt to secure advertisements as much as possible with the help of business organizations. When a special section is prepared, the newspaper journalist asks for brand information, corporate information, and for the feature story; additionally, they ask for advertising subsidies to fill in the special section spaces. The practice is akin to an exchange of a news story and advertisement. The power of market-driven journalism among newspapers suggests that information subsidies were easier to give to newspapers when advertising subsidies were attached. If public relations practitioners subsidize advertising, the placement of news stories would be much easier than in the past. However, the effect of publicity in newspapers appears to be questionable due to the abundance of media outlets such as social media platforms (Jo, 2011; Jo & Pae, 2013). News content is controlled by the power of advertisers and public relations practitioners driven by market-driven journalism and a marketing approach, the public interest is no longer served.

In recent years, government agencies and some clients placed featured stories in newspapers to support their own position favorably on an issue. The government agency would pay the newspapers to place featured stories in daily newspapers. The process of placement of the news stories in the newspapers is similar to advertising placement. For example, a few newspapers are selling editorial space in exchange of placement of feature articles. Planning special editions for new brand and consumer awards are also geared to elicit advertisers' financial donations or placements. This paid editorial content has become a routine public relations program among some public relations firms in South Korea, thus blurring the line between editorial autonomy and advertising. One liberal newspaper criticized these actions, stating paid featured stories clearly manipulate public opinion, breach journalism ethics, and mislead readers (Choi, 2015). In addition, special sections, award events, and sponsored sections are filling up newspapers more than ever. These editions are not meant to provide news contents and cover public issues, but rather they are meant to induce advertising income or financial sponsorship. Thus, the digital media environment shift has forced newspapers to pursue advertising revenue rather than focus on the public good.

While public relations practitioners expressed their concerns about the media's economic environment blurring the line between editorial content and advertising content and thereby reducing the credibility of third-party endorsement, the practice continues. Public relations practitioners have recognized that the purpose of placement of advertisement and sponsored contents to the newspaper is to manage a favorable relationship between the organizations and the newspapers, not to attract readers (Jo, 2011;

Jo & Pae, 2013). Thus, the primary purpose of media relations has been reduced to the role of providing financial support in exchange for favorable news coverage.

Hofstede's (1983) idea of the collectivist culture, in contrast to Western individualism, could help explain the close relationship between sources and the media. In addition, the concept of *Chaemyon* (Kim & Yang, 2011) might explain the unique relationship between public relations officials and the media. *Chaemyon* refers to saving one's face and allows for mutuality in an exchange relationship. In short, if a source provides advertising subsidies, the media feels the pressure to return the favor in the form of favorable news content. The unconventional media-source relationship secedes from the conventional relationship in that a cozy relationship between two parties may harm public good.

Digital Media and Ethics of Public Relations

In this chapter, I raised the controversial issue of the blurred line between editorial content and advertising content in a digital media environment in Korea. Native advertising attempts to mislead readers by disguising editorial content so the public will perceive the content as a news editorial. Power bloggers post their comments and reviews for the sponsored products without disclosing a sponsored brand. In terms of narrowed difference between advertisement and publicity, the superiority of publicity as a third-party endorsement, rendered by the media is disappearing with the rapid growth of the digital media environment. Thus, newspapers are selling editorial content to the public relations practitioners with the most resources due to the economic pressure to compensate for the loss of advertising revenue. In a narrowed sense, the most distinguished advantage of public relations compared to advertising is lost because message credibility by the role of endorsement of credible media. Digital media makes it possible for public relations practitioners to pitch their stories to the public directly, passing the gatekeeper's review, and the media seems to prioritize financial profit. In sum, market-driven journalism and economic constraints hinder the concept of a fully functioning society. Another dilemma is how to teach public relations ethics in a digital media environment. Ham (2012) claimed the online community is contaminated with false reviews, fake postings, and sponsored content. While the new media introduce ubiquitous platforms to communicate with the public effectively, the function of the third-party endorsement is paradoxically losing its value due to the contaminated online sphere. In addition, the ethical picture of public relations is increasingly being challenged for blurring the line between editorial content and advertising, sponsorship, and marketing tactics in Korea.

Public relations cannot forgo third-party endorsement. The field should not give up the value of message credibility endorsed by third parties such as media and experts, and unaffiliated parties, because that quality makes public relations unique. Civil society depends on the active exchange of communication and open discourse on issues in which the public is involved, and scholars must continue to reflect on this concept. If the media does not cover issues or controversies, but instead only covers the wants of corporations the public good does not exist.

Although the digital media environment brings an array of new formats to communicate with the publics, the fundamental value of public relations—credibility—should be taken into account in a public relations discipline. By building credibility and trust with the public, public relations can differentiate itself from other disciplines with its core values. In sum, public relations need to reflect on its core value of mutual beneficial relationships between organizations and their publics and how it contributes to society.

References

Bentele, G. (2004). New perspectives public relations in Europe. In B. van Ruler & D. Vercic (Eds.), *Public relations and communication management in Europe: A nation-by-nation introduction to public relations theory and practice* (pp. 485–496). Berlin, Germany: Walter de Gruyter.

Botan, C. H., & Taylor, M. (2004). Public relations: State of the field. *Journal of Communication, 54*(4), 645–661.

Carlson, M. (2014). When news sites go native: Redefining the advertising-editorial divide in response to native advertising. *Journalism*, 1–17.

Choi, W. (2015). Ministry of Employment and Labor acknowledged that it paid for the editorial content. *Hankyoreh Daily Newspaper*, August 26.

Curtin, P. A. (1999). Reevaluating public relations information subsidies: Market driven journalism and agenda-building theory and practice. *Journal of Public Relations Research, 11*(1), 53–90.

Davis, A. (2000). Public relations, news production, and changing patterns of source access in the British national media. *Media Culture and Society, 22*(1), 39–59.

Gandy, O. H., Jr. (1982). *Beyond agenda setting: Information subsidies and public policies*. Norwood, NJ: Ablex. Habermas, J. (1987). *The theory of communicative action: Volume II: Lifeworld and system: A critique of functionalist reason* (T. McCarthy, Trans.). Boston, MA: Beacon Press.

Ham, S. (2012). *Study on perceptions and responses of public relations professionals regarding corporate crisis on social media*. Doctoral dissertation, Konkuk University, Seoul Korea.

Hofstede, G. (1983). National cultures revisited. *Behavior Science Research, 18*(4), 285–305.

Jo, S., & Kim, Y. (2004). Media relations or personal relations in Korea. *Journalism and Mass Communication Quarterly, 81*(2), 275–289.

Jo, S. (2011). Advertising as payment: Information transactions in the South Korean newspaper market. *Public Relations Review, 37*, 399–404.

Jo, S., & Pae, J. (2013). The study of relationship between advertisers and newspaper. *Korean Journal of Public Relations, 17*(2), 40–75.

Kim, Y., & Yang, J. (2011). The influence of *Chaemyon* on face work and conflict styles: Searching for the Korean face and its impact. *Public Relations Review 37*, 60–67.

Koch, T., & Obermaier, M. (2014). Blurred lines: German freelance journalists with secondary employment in public relations. *Public Relations Review, 40,* 473–482.

Langett, J. (2013). Blogger engagement ethics: Dialogic civility in a digital era. *Journal of Mass Media Ethics, 28,* 79–90.

McManus, J. (1994). *Market-driven journalism: Let the citizen beware?* Thousand Oaks, CA: Sage.

Peeler, L., & Guthrie, J. (2007). Commentary 1: Advertising and editorial content: Laws, ethics, and market forces. *Journal of Mass Media Ethics: Exploring Questions of Media Morality, 22*(4), 350–353.

Rhee, Y. (2002). Confucian culture and excellent public relations: A study of generic principles and specific and applications in South Korean public relations practice. *Journal of Public Relations Research, 5*(3), 190–201.

Rubel, S. (2008). *Does the thrill of the chase make PR obsolete?* Retrieved from http://www.micropersuasion.com/2008/08/does-the-thrill.html.

Sallot, L. M., & Johnson, E. A. (2006). Investigating relationships between journalists and public relations practitioners: Working together to set, frame and build public agenda, 1991-2004. *Public Relations Review, 32,* 151–159.

Taylor, M. (2009). Civil society as a rhetorical public relations process. In R. Heath, E. Toth, & D. Waymer (Eds.), *Rhetorical and critical approaches to public relations II* (pp. 76–91). New York: Routledge.

Toth, E. (2009). The case for pluralistic studies of public relations, rhetorical, critical, and excellence perspective. In R. Heath, E. Toth, & D. Waymer (Eds.), *Rhetorical and critical approaches to public relations II* (pp. 48–60). New York: Routledge.

Waters, R. D., Tindall, N. T. J., & Morton, T. S. (2010). Media catching and the journalist-public relations practitioner relationship: How social media are changing the practice of media relations. *Journal of Public Relations Research, 22*(3), 241–264.

14 Digital Social Advocacy and Public Communication

Linda Hon

This chapter explores digital social advocacy as a form of public communication that is fundamentally different from previous forms of grassroots public relations. The main argument is that digital technologies have expanded the public sphere by increasing the ability of citizens and organizations to directly communicate, collaborate, and express support or dissent in ways that were not possible before the advent of these tools.

Literature Review

J. E. Grunig (1976) was the first public relations scholar to theorize about why organizations practice public relations as they do. His four models of public relations (J. E. Grunig, 1984) laid the groundwork for understanding that most public relations was organization-centric with the goal of creating public opinion, attitudes, and behavior in line with the organization's interests. In contrast, he suggested a more ethical and effective approach would be one that considered both the organization's and public's interests (i.e., symmetrical).

J. E. Grunig (2000) later argued collaboration should be the core value of public relations, and symmetry should be characterized by collaborative advocacy, a term suggested by Spicer (1997), or cooperative antagonism, a term offered by Raiffa (1982). Addressing activist publics in particular, J. E. Grunig (2000) rejected the position that communication could not be practiced collaboratively around activist issues because, as other scholars (Dozier & Lauzen, 2000; L'Etang, 1996a, 1996b; Rodino & DeLuca, 1999) have argued, activist groups have too little power compared to the organizations they oppose. Further, J. E. Grunig (2000) rejected the assumption put forth by Rodino and DeLuca (1999) that activists who collaborate with corporate and government interests are eventually co-opted by these organizations and ultimately sacrifice the interests of the activist publics (J. E. Grunig, 2000).

Digital technologies offer great promise for helping public relations practice the normative model of collaborative advocacy. In ways not possible before the digital era, activist publics can communicate with authentic voice. No longer are formal organizations or media gatekeepers exclusively in control of the messages in public discourse. Instead, as Castells (2001) described, an electronic grass-rooting of civil society is occurring and manifests itself through a more horizontal infrastructure of connectivity (Carty, 2015). Further, because of the lower transaction costs of many digital technologies, the organizations activist publics need to engage with for meaningful long-term structural change (typically corporate and government entities) have more opportunity for the meaningful two-way communication with publics that often was avoided during the heyday of mass media.

If the purpose of this book is to posit a vision for public relations that leads to a more professional and ethical practice as well as a more just society, then evaluating what responsible digital social advocacy looks like is necessary. Edgett (2002) defined advocacy as "the act of publicly representing an individual, organization, or idea with the object of persuading targeted audiences to look favorably on—or accept the point of view of—the individual, the organization, or the idea" (p. 1). Edgett noted Martinson's (1994) argument that parties to communication share basic needs and "meeting these needs honors their humanity" (p. 9). For Edgett, ethical public relations is the "process for ensuring that the communication needs of all parties are met" (p. 9). This chapter seeks to illustrate how digital technologies allow the communication needs of activist publics to be met in ways that were previously not possible. In doing so, the ideal of a democratic civil society in which citizens and organizations can openly dialogue, debate, and collaborate is furthered.

Perspectives for thinking about digital technologies tend to fall into three camps. The first is the optimist who sees a utopian ideal emerging from the empowerment of people through digital tools. Clay Shirky (2008) is the archetype of this point of view. His popular book, *Here Comes Everybody*, described the changes brought by the digital revolution whereby people could communicate, collaborate, and organize without the institutional constraints of the era of mass media. Anyone now can publish content and/or advocate for a cause. Critics of digital media fall into the pessimist camp. Notable here is Malcom Gladwell (2010) who described much digital behavior as slacktivism, or a short-term fix of civic engagement that fails to create meaningful long-term social change. This chapter rejects both of these points of view as too extreme. Instead, a realist perspective is proposed that suggests digital media are neutral. Digital media can give voice to groups that would otherwise be marginalized and, in doing so, serve the greater good (Demetrious, 2013). However, digital media also can be used to suppress voices through increased opportunity for surveillance and retaliation (Glaisyer, 2010). In addition, digital media can be used to mobilize supporters around a cause most people believe is not in the public interest such as terrorism (Murdoch, 2010).

The concept of public interest has been one of great importance to public relations. Yet, who defines what the public interest is? Perspectives for thinking about this term were offered by White in J. E. Grunig and White (1992). According to White (J. E. Grunig & White, 1992), practitioners define the public interest according to how they see the role of public relations in society. Those who view their work similar to that of a lawyer embrace a *pragmatic social role* for public relations. They believe every client deserves representation and practice public relations asymmetrically to serve their client's interests alone. Practitioners who take a *conservative social role* see themselves as defenders of established capitalistic institutions against threats such as activism. Activists often practice public relations by taking a *radical social role*. They represent social change organizations or causes that asymmetrically communicate on behalf of their cause and build resources by aligning themselves with other groups geared toward solutions to social problems.

Holtzhausen (2000) was the public relations scholar who provided one of the first perspectives on public relations as activism. She rejected the meta-narrative of public relations as organizational communication management implicit in public relations practice and scholarship (particularly in Western countries). She went on to suggest that democracy, rather than capitalism, offers a better explanation for the existence of public relations. Therefore, "public relations can contribute to grassroots democracy through activism and radical politics" (Holtzhausen, 2000, p. 93). Holtzhausen's ideas are directly relevant to digital social advocacy because of their focus on "power and how it subjects people at both the macro and micro levels of society" (Holtzhausen, 2012, p. 13). This political struggle is the nexus where digital media and grassroots public relations meet.

White's (J. E. Grunig & White, 1992) final social role for public relations is *idealistic* and takes a symmetrical approach. Summarizing what this role means for public relations, J. E. Grunig (2000) explained:

> It presupposes that public relations serves the public interest, develops mutual understanding between organizations and their publics, contributes to informed debate about issues in society, and facilitates a dialogue and collaboration between organizations and their publics. Whereas the radical social role sees public relations as a way of directing social change in ways its client organizations prefer, the idealistic world view sees society as emerging from collaboration and from the management of conflict between groups in society. (p. 30)

With these perspectives in mind, the focus here is how digital media have lowered "the barrier to entry for civic engagement," especially among people who never considered themselves activist communicators (Demby, 2013, para. 2). One of the strongest arguments for the unique opportunities for communicators presented by digital technologies was provided by Earl and Kimport (2011). They classified the effects of digital media on public communication as either supersizing or leveraged affordances. Supersizing refers to the increased reach and speed as well as the lower transaction costs of digital media. Reach has to do with the networked (i.e., spider web) aspects of digital media compared to the one-to-many model of mass communication and the one-to-one nature of interpersonal communication (Shirky, 2008). An example of increased speed is when an online petition is shared through social media compared to the conventional technique of door-to-door canvassing. Lower transaction costs of digital media are especially critical since, traditionally, the costs of social participation tended to be high (i.e., time away from work or family) as well as more extreme costs such as retaliation and/or incarceration (Murdoch, 2010).

In addition to the supersizing benefits of digital technologies, Earl and Kimport (2011) argued that the real advantages lie in what digital media make possible that previous technologies could not, or what they referred to as leveraged affordances. Shirky (2008) and Earl and Kimport (2011) identified several leveraged affordances that Hon (2015) classified as macro (societal), meso (organizational), and micro (individual).

At the macro level, digital media have created what Shirky (2008) called mass amateurization whereby anyone can publish content and/or advocate for a cause. Since the means of production have been shifted to the masses, so too has the power to disrupt the status quo. So, latent groups without formal authority or resources can form. These groups no longer need to rely on mainstream media or organizational gatekeepers to spread their messages, and activists can be impervious to a hostile climate for their cause. As Carty (2015, p. 9) explained: "Almost anyone and anything can be recorded and disseminated without the permission of the elites (be they the professional mainstream press, corporate gatekeepers, the police, the military, or campaign managers)."

Meso-level affordances have to do with new forms of organizing and leadership. In the digital era, the need for formal organizations with centralized leadership and a standing membership has eroded. Nor do activists have to physically meet—what Earl and Kimport (2011) referred to as co-presence—to plan strategy and tactics. Instead, organizing tends to be flat, horizontal, and ad hoc. However, online organizing does not completely replace offline activist events such rallies, marches, and vigils. Rather, digital social advocacy tends to create a spillover effect (Jenkins, 2006), whereby "organizing in cyberspace often facilitates contentious engagement on the streets" (Carty, 2015, p. 20; see also Gerbaudo, 2012).

Micro-level affordances include the reduced need for cultivating and sustaining collective identity and long-term allegiance among supporters for an activist cause (Tarrow, 1998; Tilly, 2004). Traditional social movement theory has highlighted the importance of identity and allegiance as critical for building the worthiness, unity, numbers, and commitment needed to turn an activist campaign into an enduring social movement (Tilly, 2004). However, digital tools have provided the opportunity for even "clicktivism" (Carty, 2015, p. 32) to have meaningful effects such as the widespread increases in levels of awareness about amyotrophic lateral sclerosis (ALS) and the millions of dollars raised when the Ice Bucket Challenge went viral. And, whereas traditional social movements tended to unite people around issues of race, class, and/or gender (Carty, 2015), digital networks tend to appear as "interstitial locations that consist of the nooks and crannies in and around dominant institutions" (Mann, 2000, p. 142). In these digital spaces, "diverse groups of citizens can operate outside the formal political system and dominant institutions to raise new issues and promote new sets of values" (Carty, 2015, p. 27).

Hon (2015) developed a model of public relations and digital social advocacy that identified how supersizing effects occurred and leveraged affordances were manifested in the Justice for Trayvon campaign. Trayvon Martin was a 17-year-old African-American boy who was fatally shot by neighborhood watchman, George Zimmerman, February 26, 2012, in Sanford, FL. Zimmerman was questioned by police, claimed self-defense, and was released without being charged. Rejecting Zimmerman's recounting of the events to police, family and supporters of Martin used online petitioning and social media to raise awareness about the case, which eventually turned into a news and social media firestorm. Zimmerman ultimately was arrested for second-degree murder but then was acquitted in 2013.

This chapter extends Hon's (2015) model of public relations and social digital advocacy by examining how one organization, Million Hoodies for Justice, illustrates how grassroots public relations unfolds in the digital realm. Million Hoodies was formed by 25-year-old advertising executive Daniel Maree in March 2012, immediately after Martin's death became national news (Wolfson, 2014). Hoodies is a reference to the hooded sweatshirt that Martin was wearing when he was killed. According to current executive director, Dante Barry, Million Hoodies rallied people after the Martin shooting who rejected the traditional narrative in mainstream media about "a law enforcement or vigilante hero and a criminal Black person" (Barry, 2015, para. 9).

Million Hoodies refers to itself as a national racial justice network that now includes over 50,000 members and 15 chapters across the United States (http://www.millionhoodies.net). The Martin case and Million Hoodies have been cited as the precursors to the uprisings in the United States over police brutality toward African-Americans (particularly men) that created the Black Lives Matter movement (Carpentier, 2015; Smith, 2014; Williams, 2013).

Methodology

A case study approach was taken to examine the emergence of Million Hoodies as an example of digital social advocacy. A LexisNexis search was conducted using the search term "Million Hoodies" within the category of all news during the time period from the day the first story appeared—September 6, 2013—to July 1, 2015. Within this time period, 39 articles were located. To explore Million Hoodies' social media communication, content posted on Million Hoodies' Facebook page was selected for analysis. Because the initial period of mobilization is of particular importance (i.e., because digital media allow unprecedented opportunities for grass-roots activists to build a base of support), the time frame examined here is from the day the site was founded—March 20, 2012—until 2 weeks after Zimmerman's July 13, 2013, acquittal, or July 27, 2013. These latter 2 weeks were included to capture sentiment at the turning point when Million Hoodies realized it needed to re-group. The Pew Research Internet Project documented that Facebook is used by 71% of online adults, compared to 28% for LinkedIn, 28% for Pinterest, 26% for Instagram, and 23% for Twitter (Duggan, Ellison, Lampe, Lenhart, & Madden, 2015). Facebook also is better suited for analyzing longer messages than the microblogging site, Twitter, which limits tweets to 140 characters. A total of 662 posts were read or reviewed in reverse chronological order, including supporting content such as links to news stories or videos; promotional material such as fliers and posters; and photos or artwork uploaded by supporters. This base of content was supplemented by several articles that did not emerge from the LexisNexis database but appeared through a search of Google using the term, Million Hoodies. The researcher also examined the Million Hoodies website.

Results

Supersizing Effects

When Million Hoodies first appeared on Facebook, Maree seemed to fit the description of what Earl and Kimport (2011) call a "lone wolf" activist, or someone who takes on the task of organizing himself or herself (p. 15). The first post is a plain sign, declaring the page to be the "Trayvon Martin Official Global Facebook Page," which was liked by 61 people and shared by 17 (March 20, 2012). A post, presumably from Maree, said, "Welcoming all hoodies around the world" (March 20, 2012).[1]

One of the first and most obvious examples of supersizing effects (i.e., increased reach, speed, and lower transaction costs) is touted on the Facebook page March 28, 2012: "Million Hoodies, you should all be proud of this!" Below the post is a graphic that illustrated the timeline from Martin's death to March 26, 2012, when Martin's family delivered two million signatures from Change.org, an online petitioning platform, to Sanford authorities, demanding Zimmerman's arrest.

Leveraged Affordances—Macro

All of the material reviewed suggests that Million Hoodies' digital social advocacy is characterized by mass amateurization, especially during its early formative stage. Million Hoodies began as an organic entity of Martin supporters with no professional staff. At the time of this writing, Million Hoodies has a staff of eight, but it is not clear from the website whether these eight are paid employees or volunteers.

Million Hoodies illustrates how digital social advocacy shifts the means of production and the power that comes with production to the masses. Much of the content on the Facebook page is uploaded personal photos, artwork, and videos created by supporters and then curated and shared by Million Hoodies. For example, a May 29, 2012, post showed a photo of a mural featuring a face looking down and completely obscured by the hood of a hoodie. The post indicated that the mural was composed by Baltimore street artist Justin Nether.

Million Hoodies is easily described as a latent group that formed without formal authority or resources. As Maree recounted about the Martin shooting to CBS News, "I was outraged and wanted to do something about it" (quoted in "Million Hoodies March held in NYC," 2013, para. 10). Million Hoodies also came together without the endorsement of any established institution although posts often refer to allied organizations such as GlobalGrind.com, a site that features news and entertainment reporting about African Americans. Similarly, Million Hoodies was formed without formal resources. Maree has used thousands of dollars of his own for the printing and travel costs associated with protest events organized by Million Hoodies (Demby, 2013). However, in 2013, Maree was selected for a $100,000 Do Something Award for his work with Million Hoodies (Carrasquillo, 2013).

Some of Million Hoodies' posts make explicit that the mainstream news media would not be the gatekeeper for the group's messages and suggest that the group thought some national media were hostile to the activists' grassroots movement. For example, a July 16, 2013, post said, "Hey Fox News we're ready for you! Millionhoodies isn't your daddy's movement. You better buckle up for @danielmaree this Saturday at 10 pm."

This post's reference to Maree's Twitter account is just one example of the networked aspect of Million Hoodies' digital social advocacy. The many-to-many principle is obvious throughout many of the Facebook posts as supporters share content across the web and other social media platforms, particularly Twitter and YouTube.

Leveraged Affordances—Meso

Million Hoodies provides many examples of leveraged affordances at the meso level. The activist network has no need for a brick and mortar formal organization since it can communicate, collaborate, and organize offline protests online.

Neither does the group need formal, centralized leadership. Maree's passion and commitment seem to be the main catalyst for the group's visibility and clout and are a powerful example of digital social advocacy's potential for creating new ways of enacting leadership that is more horizontal than vertical. Maree's guidance to supporters is obvious in a post a day after the verdict was announced: "Please bring your kids with you to the protest in

Union Square today … it's going to be a historic event and we need to keep it peaceful" (July 14, 2013).

Million Hoodies' Facebook posts also suggest the novel distribution of labor found in digital social advocacy. Throughout the entire time period examined for this study, Million Hoodies frequently reached out to its volunteer workforce to spread its messages. For example, on the 1-year anniversary of Martin's death, a post urged supporters to join the fight against gun violence: "We will be tweeting and Facebooking the names of kids killed by gun violence in the last year ….We must stop the violence. Please follow us @millionhoodies or watch this page to join in" (February 26, 2013).

Co-presence is unnecessary for Million Hoodies. Although the group planned and executed numerous offline events, interactions among supporters are largely online. For example, on November 30, 2012, Million Hoodies posted, "Make your voices (and radios) heard today at 5pm in honor of Jordan Davis!" (Davis was another African-American teenage male fatally shot in 2012 after an encounter with a white adult male who was angry about the loud music coming from the car Davis was in.)

Another characteristic of digital social advocacy—a power law distribution—appears within the Million Hoodies network. Power laws suggest that 20% of the people in a group do 80% of the work (Shirky, 2008). This suggestion of small teams that carry most of the weight can be seen in all of Million Hoodies' communication. Most of the posts appear to come from Maree. Yet, a July 21, 2013, post suggested behind-the-scenes organizing by a small group of others: "Not many people know the three amazing women who have been essential to the Million Hoodies from the very beginning. They are as brilliant as they are gracious."

Leveraged Affordances—Micro

Million Hoodies illustrates how digital media can unite a large base of supporters even in the absence of the strong collective identity and organizational allegiance associated with long-term membership in traditional social movement organizations. None of the Facebook posts suggests that supporters previously had been members of established activist organizations. Yet, at the same time, Million Hoodies' Facebook communication demonstrates the power of social media platforms for building and sustaining a sense of togetherness and commitment to a cause. Many of the posts include numerous photos of people—individuals, groups of friends, parents with their children—wearing hoodies or clothing with the symbolic "I am Trayvon" message. All of these posts allude to a seemingly powerful desire among supporters to make a statement about their being part of a larger movement against racial injustice.

Despite the fluidity of the Million Hoodies' Facebook community, many of the posts also indicated a sense of solidarity among supporters that is characteristic of collective identity. For example, one of the last posts during the time period examined here came from a supporter who had uploaded 43 photos from a vigil in Los Angeles that was part of the post-verdict 100 City National Rally July 20, 2013. The post read, "Joined 1000s taking to the street today in a national rally of solidarity in prayer and support. ... A coming together of all ages and backgrounds. It was great to meet up with our friends" (July 21, 2013).

Conclusion

The purpose of this chapter was to illustrate how a novel form of grassroots public relations—digital social advocacy—has expanded "the contours within which groups and individuals can voice concerns" (Carty, 2015, p. 32). This expansion means that citizens outside of formal structures can communicate, collaborate, and agitate for social change among themselves and with the organizations they oppose.

The activist network, Million Hoodies, was chosen as an example to illustrate how digital social advocacy is characterized by supersizing effects and leveraged affordances at the macro, meso, and micro levels. Million Hoodies, particularly the group's social media communication, demonstrates how the soft power of volunteer activists can effectively challenge the entrenched power of mainstream media and government institutions such as law enforcement. As Million Hoodies current executive director, Dante Barry, said, "It's not a coincidence that most people of color are found on social media ... because it gives voice to the voiceless and allows us to tell our stories in a way that is authentic, in a way that is real" (quoted in Wolfson, 2014, para. 21).

Digital social advocacy is not offered here as a panacea. Demetrious (2013) provided a sobering critique of some "digital publics" (p. 149). She conceded that many online activists have "achieved worthy ends and reached vast numbers of people who perhaps would not have been otherwise engaged" (p. 155). Yet, she pointed out that digital social advocacy runs the risk of falling into the same asymmetrical public relations strategy and techniques that public relations in other forms has been criticized for. When it does, digital social advocacy becomes superficial and individualistic rather than an example of genuine civic communitarianism.

Demetrious's warning leads to questions of ethics, morals, and values in public relations practice. Velasquez (1991) argued that these terms can be used interchangeably but noted there are differences in their exact meaning. Ethics are used to develop rules or principles that help solve problems involving moral or values. Morals have to do with long-held beliefs about right or wrong. Values are beliefs about what is important.

Pearson is considered one of the first scholars to address ethics in public relations (see Pearson, 1989b). However, Pearson (1989a, 1989b) credited Sullivan (1965) for being the seminal scholar who articulated a philosophy of public relations ethics. Sullivan (1965) suggested three types of values in public relations. According to Sullivan (1965), technical values do not involve ethical problems because they are impersonal and amoral (e.g., what kind of evaluation research to conduct). By contrast, partisan and mutual values are the basis for ethical problems. Partisan beliefs, such as loyalty to the client, have caused ethical dilemmas in public relations when they have led to too much commitment and obedience at the expense of mutual values. Sullivan defined mutual values as basic human rights that no one can take away. These include a person's "right to true information in matters which affect him" and the "right to participate in decisions which affect him" (p. 428). At this point, the implications of digital social advocacy's potential for advancing mutual goals should be obvious.

This chapter closes on an optimistic note. Digital strategy and tools offer public communicators an unprecedented opportunity and key resource for mobilizing, collaborating, and helping sustain the momentum needed for long-term and systemic social change. To the extent this opportunity and resource serve the normative ideal of collaborative advocacy among the greatest number of people and institutions, then digital social advocacy's benefits will outweigh its limitations and imperfections.

Note

1. Direct quotes from posts reflect the original wording and punctuation.

References

Barry, D. (2015, February 26). 3 years and a million hoodies later, the death of Trayvon Martin still represents injustice. *MTV News*. Retrieved from http://www.mtv.com/news/2090957/dante-barry-trayvon-martin-million-hoodies/.

Carpentier, M. (2015, August 13). 'Things will never be the same': The oral history of the new.civil rights movement. *The Guardian*. Retrieved from http://www.theguardian.com/commentisfree/2015/aug/09/oral-history-civil-rights-movement-ferguson.

Carrasquillo, A. (2013, August 23). Million Hoodies virtual march on Washington aims to be a rally for the social age. *BuzzFeed*. http://www.buzzfeed.com/adriancarrasquillo/million-hoodies-virtual-march-on-washington-aims-to-be-a-ral#.krmJ9XpD16.

Carty, V. (2015). *Social movements and new technology*. Boulder, CO: Westview.

Castells, M. (2001). *The internet galaxy: Reflections on the internet, business and society*. Malden, MA: Blackwell.

Demby, G. (2013, July 25). After Zimmerman verdict, activists face a new, tougher fight. *NPR*. Retrieved from http://www.npr.org/sections/codeswitch/2013/07/24/205119191/after-zimmerman-verdict-activists-face-a-new-tougher-fight.

Demetrious, K. (2013). *Public relations, activism, and social change. Speaking up*. New York, NY: Routledge.

Dozier, D. M., & Lauzen, M. M. (2000). Liberating the intellectual domain from the practice: Public relations, activism, and the role of the scholar. *Journal of Public Relations Research, 12*(1), 3–22.

Duggan, M., Ellison, N. B., Lampe, C., Lenhart, A., & Madden, M. (2015). *Social media update 2014*. Retrieved from http://www.pewinternet.org/2015/01/09/social-media-update-2014/.

Earl, J., & Kimport, K. (2011). *Digitally enabled social change. Activism in the Internet age.* Cambridge, MA: Massachusetts Institute of Technology.

Edgett, R. (2002). Toward an ethical framework for advocacy in public relations. *Journal of Public Relations Research, 14*(1), 1–26. doi:10.1207/S1532754X JPRR1401_1.

Gerbaudo, P. (2012). *Tweets and the streets. Social change and contemporary activism.* New York, NY: Pluto.

Gladwell, M. (2010, October 4). Small change. Why the revolution will not be tweeted. *New Yorker.* Retrieved from http://www.newyorker.com/magazine/2010/10/04/ small-change-3.

Glaisyer, T. (2010). Political factors: Digital activism in closed and open societies. In M. Joyce (Ed.), *Digital activism decoded* (pp. 85–98). New York, NY: International Debate Education Association.

Grunig, J. E. (1976). Organizations and public relations: Testing a communication theory. *Journalism Monographs*, No. 46.

Grunig, J. E. (1984). Organizations, environments, and models of public relations. *Public Relations Research and Education, 1*(1), 6–29.

Grunig, J. E. (2000). Collectivism, collaboration, and societal corporatism as core professional values in public relations. *Journal of Public Relations Research, 12*(1), 23–48.

Grunig, J. E., & White, J. (1992). The effects of worldviews on public relations theory and practice. In J. E. Grunig (Ed.), *Excellence in public relations and communication management* (pp. 31–64). Hillsdale, NJ: Erlbaum.

Holtzhausen, D. R. (2000). Postmodern values in public relations. *Journal of Public Relations Research, 12*(1), 93–114. doi:10.1207/S1532754XJPRR1201_6.

Holtzhausen, D. R. (2012). *Public relations as activism: Postmodern approaches to theory and practice.* New York, NY: Routledge.

Hon, L. (2015). Digital social advocacy in the Justice for Trayvon Campaign. *Journal of Public Relations Research*, 27(4), 299–321. doi:10.1080/10627 26X.2015.1027771.

Jenkins, H. (2006). *Convergence culture.* New York, NY: New York University.

L'Etang, J. (1996a). Corporate responsibility and public relations ethics. In J. L'Etang & M. Pieczka (Eds.), *Critical perspectives in public relations* (pp. 82–105). London, UK: International Thomason Business.

L'Etang, J. (1996b). Public relations and rhetoric. In J. L'Etang & M. Pieczka (Eds.), *Critical perspectives in public relations* (pp. 106–123). London, UK: International Thomson Business.

Mann, M. (2000). Has globalization ended the rise of the nation-sate? In D. Held, & A. McGrew (Eds.), *The global transformations reader: An introduction to the globalization debate* (pp. 136–147). Cambridge, MA: Polity.

Martinson, D. L. (1994). Enlightened self-interest fails as an ethical baseline in public relations. *Journal of Mass Media Ethics, 10*(4), 210–222.

Murdoch, S. (2010). Destructive activism: The double-edged sword of digital tactics. In M. Joyce (Ed.), *Digital activism decoded* (pp. 137–149). New York, NY: International Debate Education Association.

Pearson, R. A. (1989a). Albert J. Sullivan's theory of public relations ethics. *Public Relations Review, 15*(2), 52–62.

Pearson, R. A. (1989b). *A theory of public relations ethics.* Unpublished doctoral dissertation, Ohio University, Athens, OH.

Raiffa, H. (1982). *The art and science of negotiation*. Cambridge, MA: Harvard University.

Rodino, V., & DeLuca, K. (1999, June). *Unruly relations: Not managing communication in the construction of the activist model of communication*. Paper presented to the PRSA Educators Academy Second Annual Research Conference, College Park, MD.

Shirky, C. (2008). *Here comes everybody*. New York, NY: Penguin.

Smith, M. D. (2014, August 27). How Trayvon Martin's death launched a new generation of black activism. *The Nation*. Retrieved from http://www.thenation.com/article/how-trayvon-martins-death-launched-new-generation-black-activism/.

Spicer, C. (1997). *Organizational public relations: A political perspective*. Mahwah, NJ: Lawrence Erlbaum.

Tarrow, S. (1998). *Power in movement: Social movements, collective action, and politics*. New York, NY: Cambridge.

Tilly, C. (2004). *Social movements*. Boulder, CO: Paradigm.

Velasquez, M. (1991). *Philosophy: A text with readings* (4th ed.). Belmont, CA: Wadsworth.

Williams, E. W. (2013, September 6). Daniel Maree: A civil rights leader for the 21st century. *San Jose Mercury News*. Retrieved from http://www.mercurynews.com/news/ci_24034270/daniel-maree:-a-civil-rights-leader.

Wolfson, E. (2014, August 15). How lessons from Trayvon helped make Ferguson news. *Newsweek*. Retrieved from http://www.newsweek.com/how-lessons-trayvon-helped-make-ferguson-news-264942.

15 From the Natural World to Artificial Intelligence

Public Relations as Covenantal Stewardship

Donn J. Tilson

Public relations as defined and conceptualized has too often advanced an asymmetrical worldview with presuppositions, values, and models of practice antithetical to the common good. In an increasingly interconnected, fragile world organizationally centric behavior at the expense of society is no longer sustainable much less justifiable. Further, radical anthropocentrism disconnects humankind from its relationships with others and with nature and, ultimately, from its humanity (Crutzen, 2002; Francis, 2015). Even symmetrical worldviews that foster "value-based relationships" (Wilson, 1996, p. 75) do so "[within] an expectation of reciprocity" (Guth & Marsh, 2005, p. 142) to the exclusion of "publics" unable to participate (Hutton, 1999).

What is needed instead is a new interpretation of public relations that reflects a worldview beyond the standard formulations and that values a larger sense of relationships. Within a worldview of *caritas* (charity, benevolence), public relations practice framed as a *covenantal model* of public relations (Baker, 2002; Tilson, 2011) and as *covenantal stewardship* with an expanded definition of "publics" is preferable. Research suggests governments, ancient civilizations, indigenous peoples, and nongovernmental organizations (NGOs) reflect a "naturalistic" worldview (Haviland, 1978) that guides public relations behavior as stewardship-guardianship in a pro-social manner for the benefit of all whether human, nonhuman, living, ancestral, or unborn. Such practice of administrative and communicative authority—a *caritas* approach to relationship-building that seeks the greater good of others without reciprocity—challenges traditional public relations thinking and underscores the imperative to reformulate the discipline's body of knowledge.

Methodology

This study uses a broader interpretation of public relations than traditional perspectives in examining and reformulating its essential definitions, theories, principles, concepts, and worldviews. A combination of qualitative methods was used to obtain data on public relations as conceptualized and practiced including a textual analysis of historical material, media coverage and institutional media, including electronic material, and telephone and e-mail interviews of key individuals to probe the development of strategies and effects.

Origins and Evolution

Over the years organizational public relations behavior has been influenced by "the most widely respected authority on public relations in the world [who] helped set standards for its ethics and approaches for the remainder of the 20th century" (Fry, 1991, p. 31), Edward L. Bernays, who referred to the practice "in a slightly Orwellian coinage, as 'the engineering of consent'" (Chronicles, 1995, p. 23). A nephew of Sigmund Freud, graduate of the U.S. World War II Creel Committee propaganda office, and "deeply influenced by the writings and philosophy of Walter Lippman, who first coined the phrase 'the manufacturing of consent'" (Olsen, 2005, p. 28) and "felt the public is often misinformed, ill-formed, and poor judges of great issues" (Simon, 1984, p. 34), it was not surprising that Bernays "made psychological manipulation a kind of inheritance" (Gabler, 1995, p. 28). His writings reflect a "deep contempt for the average person" (Olsen, op. cit.), and his "utterly frank … praise of propaganda" (Olsen, op. cit.) in a 1935 journal article, "Molding Public Opinion," is unmistakable as he uses "the propagandist" and "the methods of propaganda" interchangeably for "counsel on public relations" and "public relations campaign" contending the "public's interest" is important only "in so far as this coincides with the industry's own private interest" (Bernays, 1935, p. 86). His corporate clients—American Tobacco and General Motors among others—followed his counsel as the "The Public Be Damned" era developed; as railroad tycoon William Henry Vanderbilt bellowed, "'I don't take any stock in this silly nonsense about working for anybody's good but our own'" (Cutlip, 1995, pp. 188–189). Through public concerns over cigarette smoking and cancer, a U.S. government bailout of GM and congressional investigations into its failure to alert consumers about defective ignition switches in millions of vehicles causing scores of injuries and deaths (Tilson, 2015), comments by a GM regional public relations manager during the bailout—"public relations is about business and … a PR strategy … won't be greeted warmly … if it doesn't offer a good return on investment" (Cobb, 2008; cited in Tilson, 2009, p. 379)—and internal GM memos concluding that fixing the switches "would take too long and cost too much" (Durbin, 2014, p. 3a) confirm the Bernays' "doctrine" is alive and well.

Asymmetrical, "exploitative" (Haviland, 1978) worldviews based on assumptions about "morality, ethics, human nature, religion, politics, free enterprise, or gender" (J. E. Grunig & White, 1992, p. 32) find expression in various definitions of public relations. The "most common definitional components" include "management" (Hutton, 1999, p. 201), with variations as a "management function," "managing strategic relationships," and "relationship management." These suggest a Bernaysian universe of propaganda and manipulation as do definitions that argue public relations should be "the strategic management of competition and conflict for the benefit of one's own organization—and when possible—also for the mutual benefit of the organization and its various stakeholders or publics" (Wilcox & Cameron, 2009, p. 116).

Increasingly, there has been "a growing discontent with the managerial, corporation-focused kind of research… that has dominated PR scholarship" and a "unanimous criticism of what is referred to as the 'Grunigian Paradigm'… the form of PR research … that only examine[s] one side of PR—the functional, corporate one" to the exclusion of diverse publics, "long neglected fields and topics like gender, race, culture, colonialism, inequality or ecology," and "the role that PR plays as a discursive force in society" (Dühring, 2015, pp. 7, 12). For example, a review of public relations definitions underscores a framing that excludes a diverse world of "publics" and confirms an organizationally anthropocentric worldview. Bernays refers to the "publics" that need "molding" as "people," "individuals," "contributors," and "customers" (Bernays, 1935). A mid-1970s survey of public relations leaders confirmed their publics included "customers, stockholders, employees, suppliers …" (Harlow, 1977, p. 36). A 1981 Public Relations Society of America (PRSA) task force concluded "public relations is an organization's efforts to win the cooperation of groups of people" (Kendall, Baxter, & Pessolano, 1989, p. 23). Scholarship continues to define "publics" as "the people with which they [practitioners] engage," and "[the goal of PR] to influence the behavior of groups of people" (Cutlip et al., 2000; cited in Edwards, 2012, p. 12). As Guth and Marsh (2012) observed, "one area of agreement among public relations practitioners is the definition of the term *public*: any group of people who share common interests or values in a particular situation" (p. 5).

Some argue public relations should include other "publics" in society. As early as the 1950s organizations began to shift to "open" systems, adapting to their "ecology" through boundary spanning and "eco-systems" or networks of organizational social relationships (McElreath, 1997). If organizations are "living organisms" with "enough feedback … [to] make appropriate adjustments … to keep on living" (ibid., p. 13) then "practitioners must consider… their environmental constituencies, that is, all entities potentially affected by [their efforts]" (Starck & Kruckeberg, 2001; cited in Molleda & Ferguson, 2004, pp. 333–334), a view that stands "in opposition to the… literature that predominantly suggests that only those publics that have direct consequences for the organization are publics with whom … practitioners should deal" (Vujnovic & Kruckeberg, 2005, p. 338) even *inactive publics* "who are impacted by the actions of an organization" and have "importance" (Hallahan, 2000, pp. 499, 501). In particular, as Reeves noted, the "science known as ecology … adds an entirely new dimension to public relations … and will require the consideration of relationships with species of life other than human, and the relationship of all life to its natural environment" (Harlow, 1977, p. 58).

New Worldviews, Models of Practice

As early as the 19th century voices in public relations have recognized the practice must "mean relations for the general good" (Goldman, 1965, p. 3), and definitions—that is, PRSA's "a strategic communication process that builds mutually beneficial relationships between organizations and their publics" (Corbett, 2012)—have underscored the importance of a *social dimension* of behavior in the best interests of all. Nonetheless, a worldview that provides for the common good with a motivation/expectation of symmetry—mutual benefit argues against a key component in assessing the quality of relationships—"the extent to which both parties provide benefits to the other because they are concerned for the welfare of the other—even when they get nothing in return" (Hon & J. E. Grunig, 1999; cited in Guth & Marsh, 2005, p. 197). And, definitions of the practice still characterize "publics" as only people and organizations.

Embracing *caritas* (charity, benevolence) as a worldview argues against symmetry and represents a commitment to the greater good with no obligation demanded from the recipient in return, contending that compassionate social behavior can be its own reward (Tilson, 2014a) and can be considered an "excellent worldview" as "it helps organizations build caring—even loving—*relationships*" (J. E. Grunig & White, 1992, p. 38). In a classification system of dominant values of culture two *instrumental values—Helpful* and *Loving*—are dimensions of *caritas* and "relate to modes of conduct, and represent beliefs that are socially and personally preferable in all situations" (Rokeach, 1973; cited in Mueller, 2004, pp. 132–133). *Caritas* encompasses qualities such as *tolerance* (respect of others, practice of justice, reciprocity), *empathy*, and one of its "fruits," *mercy* or *compassion*, is expressed in works of social responsibility. Studies of communication and institutional culture contend that acting with compassion and fostering a caring environment is essential to building "trust, credibility and respect" (Oestreicher, 2011, p. 17). *Caritas* underlies much of socially responsible behavior both modern and ancient, and, in the worldview of non-Western societies—for example, traditional African cultures—compassion "is greatly admired and to be ... cultivated" (Tutu, 1981; cited in Allen, 2006, p. 347).

Caritas further suggests a *covenantal model* of public relations as a theoretical ground. With a *covenantal model* "professional practices qualify as morally legitimate because, and to the extent that, they are structures to merit the trust of clients" (Koehn, 1994; cited in Baker, 2002, p. 193), and professionals establish their authority "because they are experts ... or service providers" who make "a public promise to serve ... a particular (client) good" and "dedicate their lives" to promoting that interest (Baker, 2002, pp. 194, 196, 197). However, the public promise must be "to furthering an end which is genuinely good" and "desirable in its own right"—"health, salvation, or justice"—inasmuch as "the pledge would not ground authority if the promised good were actually an evil" (ibid., pp. 198, 197, 199). As such, then, public relations not only must foster "real and substantive relationships" (ibid., p. 201) but ensure that it "does not sacrifice the good of others for the good of the client" (ibid., p. 204). In this sense, practitioners exercise a far broader notion of traditional counselor-client relationships—"a kind of 'lawyer' representing… clients in the court of public opinion" (Hutton, 1999, p. 200), as Ivy Lee envisioned himself, or as a "legal-like" *"councillor in* (or *on) public relations"* as coined by Bernays (Bernays, 1944; cited in Mencken, 1945, p. 578). Such practice can be considered *covenantal stewardship*, with practitioner as trustee holding in trust the client's welfare—or the employer's—and the public good much as social responsibility is defined as "stewardship" (Tilson, 2014a, p. 114) with resources distributed wisely and a broader sense of "publics."

Covenantal Stewardship in Practice

In reviewing the practice of *covenantal stewardship* in ancient civilizations, indigenous cultures, and present-day governments and NGOs the historical record can teach much about *caritas* and its centrality to institutional behavior and the importance of the social dimension for public relations practice. Generally, "such behavior has reflected a pro-social, *covenantal* relationship among peoples as counseled by royal officials, administrative staff, and village elders, who remind those in a position of authority of their culturally based sense of obligation to provide for the general welfare" (Tilson, 2014b, p. 68). In such situations, counselors serve as "the corporate conscience" (Gorelick, 2004, p. 8) guiding others to good stewardship with empathy and compassion (For managers, 2015, p. 5), "the essence of an organization's cultural environment" (Pincus, Rayfield, & DeBonis, 1991, p. 25). For example, pre-figuring modern-day public relations counsel, a host of prophets during the Monarchy in Israel (c. 1020 B.C.–586 B.C.) guided by their faith served as "advisors to the king on matters of religion, ethics and politics" (*Facts About Israel*, 2008, p. 10), advocating social justice and care of the environment, exhortations that would become additions to Jewish scripture. Concern for the general welfare reflected a biblical Covenant, "a solemn agreement of fidelity" between God and Israel (Hill, 2013, p. 189), with "the quality of inter-societal relationships … [the] barometer of Israel's relationship with God" (Hoppe, 1985, pp. 5–6), which today is expressed in government social programs and Torah-based stewardship inspiring a "flourishing environmental movement" (Hill, op. cit., p. 196) and an emergent Ministry of Environmental Protection with administrative and public relations staffs that formulate and promote national policy. Similarly, in 16th-century America, Hiawatha, a Mohawk steward extraordinaire, is credited with co-founding the Iroquois League that united warring Native

American nations into an alliance governed by a constitution that embodied the "wisdom and justice... of the Great Spirit" (Hewitt, 1890; cited
in Henry, 1955, p. 274). As spokesperson of Dekanawida, a prophet-like
Huron who envisioned a Great Peace based on Iroquois beliefs that valued
mutual respect and regard for the natural world, Hiawatha counseled tribal
elders, "who agreed to unite ... for the common good" (Bunson & Bunson,
2012, p. 49). A model for the fledging U.S. Republic, the alliance lasted for
300 years. Today, Iroquois culture, gift for communication, and concern
for others thrive through their media (each nation maintains a website) and
social advocacy—the Seneca have led opposition to the use of the name
Washington Redskins in the National Football League—and Hiawatha is
celebrated as a hero.

Such consultancies of conscience reveal the presence of a personal influence model of public relations practice that underscores the importance of
interpersonal communication in relationship building within institutions
and, more important, a personal commitment to social responsibility—
often based on religious beliefs—of the individual (Tilson, 2014b). Guth and
Marsh (2005) noted public relations behavior that takes a "values-driven
approach" "is ... guided by personal ... values" among others (professional,
societal, etc.) which "implies ... ethical activity" (p. 2). History suggests
"religions are the most ancient formulators of culture and values in the
world" (Kaplan, 2010, p. 266), and studies of altruistic behavior indicate
the influence of hero-role models who "have taught ... empathy and social
responsibility" (Oliner, 2007, p. 10) and are religious. Further, advisors considered to have spiritual powers can effectively counsel those in authority toward a greater appreciation of the general welfare particularly when
both share a spiritually based commitment to social justice, exercising the
stewardship essential to creating humane, effective institutions and societies
(Oestreicher, 2011; Oliner & Oliner, 1995).

All Are Kindred Beings

A broader sense of "community" than traditional views and one that speaks
to the importance of diversity in society—as ancient and indigenous cultures reflect—embraces not only those in an "extended family" and on the
margins of humanity but members of the natural world as well. A review
of the historical record across time and civilizations reveals that a more
holistic concept of inclusiveness calls for a re-definition of "publics" in
public relations practice and a worldview guided by *caritas* and *covenantal
stewardship*.

In second-century B.C. India Emperor Asoka, "one of the truly great
leaders of world history, tempering politics with idealism," (Lensen, 1960,
p. 17), modeled himself after his grandfather who "devoted himself to public
business and the public good" (Schulberg, 1968, p. 78). Drawn to "the compassion and nonviolence of Buddhism" (Hill, 2013, p. 126), Asoka sought

to inspire others "not by prescriptions and imperatives" but by his rule and personal practice of faith, representing "two interdependent obligations— to respect others and to perform good deeds" (Nikam & McKeon, 1966, p. xx). Guided by "a sense of kinship of all men and a respect for all living creatures," he appointed officials to care for his subjects, prisoners and their families, peoples of bordering regions, and, in particular, animals, giving them medical assistance (including planting medicinal herbs) and "watering sheds ... shade trees, and rest houses" (ibid., p. 3, 21). His edict, disseminated by scribes and carved on rocks and pillars throughout the empire, are a public declaration of his compassion and *covenantal stewardship*, entreating "abstention from cruelty to living beings" (ibid., p. 31) and "courtesy to slaves... servants... elders, and gentleness to animals" (Gokhale, 1966, p. 118). Today, Bhutan and Nepal, evangelized by Asoka Buddhist monks, are working with World Wildlife Fund to protect the environment (Tilson, 2011); Bhutan's constitution "protects the environment as a core value" of its national identity, fostered by former King Jigme Singye Wangchuck who "worked very hard to keep our culture, and our environment ... intact" (World Wildlife Fund, 2015, p. 14).

In Namibia a naturalistic worldview that extends community to include ancestors and the environment as a sacred whole has shaped the social fabric for millennia (Tilson, 2014b). For the Topnaar the ocean is a "God-given reservoir ... to use wisely" (Mapaure, 2008, p. 157). For them, ancestor spirits inhabit the seas and take "care of the fish so that the community would always have food [which] gave rise to an obligation ... to take care of the environment" (ibid., p. 162). Tribal leaders "entrusted with powers ... hold the core values of the community ...and pronounce ...on what is good for the community's welfare currently and in the future"; discussions "strive to come to a consensus ... inclusive of everyone, including future generations ...in the context of the whole ecosystem" (ibid., pp. 151, 163). A chief "has to serve as well as lead his people, if he wants to hold his job ... because the elders will not permit it" (Gunther, 1955, p. 290).

Following independence in 1990, Namibia confirmed traditional governance in matters of the environment becoming the "first African nation to incorporate environmental protection in its constitution" (Roberts, 2011, p. 2) and empowering communities to manage wildlife resources in a sustainable manner and to benefit from that. With civil and government partners and NGOs like World Wildlife Fund (and public education campaigns) local peoples have protected more than 29 million acres, restored native wildlife, and generated $5.1 million "from tourism, sustainable wildlife uses" (World Wildlife Fund, 2012, Projects section, para. 2), affirming the "strong link between cultural and traditional values of local communities" and encouraging a "sense of being proud custodians of wildlife" (Diggle, 2012; cited in Tilson, 2014b, p. 66).

William Wilberforce is celebrated largely for rallying support to abolish the slave trade in 19th-century England. He introduced resolutions in

Parliament and joined abolitionists "who raised public awareness ... with pamphlets, books, rallies and petitions" (BBC History, 2015, para. 2), "the first successful ... agitation of the modern type ... imitated [throughout] England" (Trevelyan, 1953, p. 130). The "conscience of Parliament" (Who's Who, 2006, p. 4), he championed causes from child labor, orphans, widows, prisoners and the sick (Metaxas, 2007) to one that "had always mattered" to him—the Society for the Prevention of Cruelty to Animals, "the first animal welfare society in the world" (Tomkins, 2007, p. 207), which today cares and advocates for thousands of animals annually. As his letters and diaries confirm, his "compassion for ... slaves and the poor was ... real, heartfelt" (ibid., p. 220) "nor did his concern for the well-being of others end with his own species" (Metaxas, 2007, p. 266). A devout Christian, he felt "we are all our brothers' keepers ... and had a responsibility to help those less fortunate ... a 'social conscience'" (ibid., p. xvi), and to be "good and faithful stewards" of God's gifts.

Toward a New Interpretation

Worldviews and conceptualizations of public relations based on an appreciation of the interconnectedness of the world can sooner guide managers and their public relations counsel toward socially responsible behavior than those that place humans "in a position of inherent superiority over other species" (Jurmain, Kilgore, Trevathan, & Ciochon, 2014, p. 6) and their organizations at the center of a universe that uses communication to manipulate publics. Indigenous peoples have long cherished a community-of-beings worldview with "no separation between nature and cultures" where "plants and animals ... rivers, mountains, and glaciers are alive" and acted as stewards in a "sacred, personal relationship between humans and other living beings" (Berkes, 2008, pp. 11, 115). Humans are a "component of a vast biological continuum... [and] each species is unique" as sentient beings with their own needs (Jurmain et al., 2014, pp. 6, 22), and social relationships place "a high value on the community concern for the well-being of the individual ... and the individual ... for the whole community" (White, 2009, p. 220). According to Pope Francis (2015) an "integral ecology" "has no place for a tyrannical anthropocentrism" but recognizes "the natural environment as a collective good, the patrimony of all humanity... [and a] responsible stewardship" grounded in a covenantal relationship "with God... our neighbor ... and the earth itself" (pp. 93, 44, 62, 78, 42).

Indeed, environmental and animal welfare organizations that care for and represent their "client-publics" reflect a *caritas* worldview and *covenantal stewardship* in their efforts, and such advocacy has a long public relations history often with "traces ... of pure altruism ... initiatives undertaken ... without an apparent agenda" (Lamme & Russell, 2010, p. 341). For such organizations, nonhuman, kindred species of the natural world are "publics" not unlike any others and deserve equal consideration even though they are passive or *inactive publics*. The Royal Society for the Prevention of Cruelty to Animals, for example, represents "animals who have no voice… [each of which] has the right to be counted as an individual" (2015, paras. 3, 7). Stretching the definition of "publics" is not unprecedented. Corporations are considered "public figures" by courts and referred to as "individuals" in public relations literature (Heath, 2001, p. 6; Wilcox, Ault, Agee, & Cameron, 2000, p. 266). In 2013 New Zealand's Whanganui River, sacred to the Maori people, was granted "personhood" with full legal rights (Stone, 2013, p. 24). According species of the natural world dignity and respect as any client or public is right and proper as "the basic moral principle of equal consideration of interests … whatever those interests may be must, according to the principle of equality, be extended to all beings … human or nonhuman … as the capacity for suffering [is] the vital characteristic that gives a being the right to equal consideration" (Singer, 1975, pp. ix, 6, 8). As science confirms animals and even plants are "intelligent life-forms" that solve complex problems, communicate, "act altruistically toward… relatives," and feel pain, an ethos of compassion calls for their inclusion in a *caritas* worldview that maintains all life "should be treated with respect and not as passive resources" (Marinelli, 2015, pp. 36, 40). Efforts "to ensure that all animals can live … free from pain and suffering" (Royal Society for the Prevention of Cruelty to Animals, 2015, para. 1), or to exercise "an urgent responsibility to be its [the Arctic tern] steward" "for the sake of its own environment" (Greenpeace, 2015, p. 5; Leonard, 2015, p. 1) ultimately reflect the work of those "who … cherish the earth and all the creatures in it" (Schweiger, 2014, p. 4).

Developments in artificial intelligence, however, may soon stretch definitions of public relations "publics" even further. Robots (a term coined by Czech playwright Karel Capek in 1921) that walk, converse, think, and learn in a humanoid form with consciousness and feelings will present conceptual, ethical, and legal challenges to public relations and society. If sentient species of the natural world should be included as public relations publics, then sentient entities artificially created should be also. And, if animals, and even natural features such as rivers, have rights and legal status to protect their well-being, then humanoids should have equal privileges and protection under the law. Robots sent into disaster zones to perform dangerous tasks, full autonomy telepresence doctors and robobosses, hotel room service, museum tour guides (currently in London's Tate Museum), and office staff such as the REEM-B (Von Drehle, 2013) will be subject to the same conditions employees face—unfair treatment, harassment, discrimination. As Patrick Stewart of *Star Trek* fame observed, "if we create independent life but keep it under our control … It can … be a form of slavery" (Strauss, 2014, p. 51). Or, if a humanoid acts negligently, unethically, or criminally, should it not be fired, censured, or even prosecuted? Are lethal autonomous weapons systems sent into combat subject to the Geneva Code if they commit war crimes (human rights groups want the United

Nations to ban "killer robots" that act without human input) (Heilprin, 2014, p. 11a)? Can an auto assembly robot, such as the one that grabbed and crushed a contractor at Volkswagen's Baunatal plant be charged with murder—"prosecutors were considering whether to bring charges" (Robot kills, 2015, p. 10a)? And, how do managers handle office romances between androids à la Björk's video *All Is Full of Love*?

Final Observations

British theoretical physicist Stephen Hawking has warned aggression "threatens to destroy us all" and calls for humanity "to replace aggression with empathy, which 'brings us together in a peaceful loving state'" (Mazza, 2015, p. 1). When public relations practitioners use communication "to manipulate publics for the benefit of the organization" they not only steer behavior "toward actions that are unethical ... [and] socially irresponsible," but their organizations "can wreak havoc on their publics ... when their fundamental values and assumptions ... suggest that it is ethical for the organization ... to exercise 'dominion' over that environment" (J. E. Grunig, 1989; J. E. Grunig & White, 1992; cited in Tilson, 1999, p. 69). Should an organization fail through its public relations efforts to manage conflict with key publics it will become increasingly difficult to establish the legitimacy essential to organizational survival. As Simões (1992) noted regarding the proper exercise of organizational authority and public relations in a democracy:

> Its {the organization} actions must be geared toward the common good and never to its own interests ... public relations will not have its existence justified as long as practitioners consider communication as an end in itself ... If there are no open communication channels, or if the organization lacks credibility, each party will be isolated from one another ... If it is not possible to organize a system of negotiation ... the public may rebel with violence. (cited in Tilson, 2004, p. 65)

In an age of mistrust, misunderstanding, conflict, and news coverage of atrocities committed in the name of a particular religion or ideology what is desperately needed are communicators and initiatives that diffuse tensions, foster discussion, understanding, and tolerance, and invite public participation in such efforts. As community power theorists contend, "significant others" in a community (family, friends, and others) can indeed influence public opinion as well as the behavior of individuals in a positive direction (McElreath, 1997; cited in Tilson, 2014a, p. 111). When practitioners play a role as change agents in society, they "illustrate the nobler aspects of public relations when practiced with concern for the common good and in keeping with models that emphasize the social responsibility of the profession" (ibid.). As Kruckeberg and Stark (1988) noted, "public relations is essentially a process of restoring a sense of community. This process of developing 'community' applies to corporations and to various organizations as well as to towns and cities" (cited in Public Relations Society of America, 2003, p. 2). Initiatives built on "interaction to achieve actualization of all members of the community" have been characterized as *strategic cooperative communities* (Wilson, 1996, pp. 75–76), and organizations that proceed in their relationships on the basis of "mutual respect, trust, and human dignity, not on profit or personal gain" are "focused on the good of all rather than being primarily self-interested" (ibid.), an approach that "goes beyond traditional rationalist and number-oriented management thinking by taking a long-term, consensual view of relationships" (Tilson, 2010, p. 5). Reconceptualizing worldviews, definitions, and models of public relations in a more biocentric manner is a further step in that direction given the critical role the discipline plays in society. Inasmuch as studies show biodiversity is important ecologically, culturally, and economically, expanding the theoretical universe of public relations to include nonhuman species of the natural world makes practical as well as moral sense. More important, framing public relations as *covenantal stewardship* within a *caritas* worldview can transform human behavior from dominion to guardianship guided by an ethos of compassion rather than self-centeredness.

Emerging views of public relations as "engendering community, common purpose" (L'Etang, 2008; cited in Galloway, 2013, p. 153) and *dialogic* models that call for finding common ground through "listening, empathy" (Wilcox & Cameron, 2009, p. 59) approximate a *caritas* worldview and a *covenantal model* of public relations and can be considered "aspects of spirituality" with practitioners "clearly involved in work that connects to spiritual practice" (Galloway, op. cit.). Inasmuch as "faith communities have immense potential to provide the value structures to change consciousness and behavior" (Kaplan, 2010, p. 266), it is not surprising the role that spirituality played in guiding Asoka, Wilberforce, and Namibian society toward a practice of *covenantal stewardship*. In nation-states that have experienced civil conflict—i.e., post-apartheid South Africa—organizational studies underscore the importance of changing "the 'hearts and minds' (spiritual essence) of employees" rather than imposing laws and regulations to effect acceptance of affirmative action and other social programs (Leonard & Grobler, 2005, p. 24). Other research (i.e., Edelman Trust Barometer) reveals not only that "relationships are fundamentally about building trust ... [and] the foundation of all trust is integrity" but that "people won't care how much you know until they know how much you care" (Goodwin, 2015, pp. 20–21), a quintessential dimension of *covenantal* public relations.

To fashion a more just, caring, and inclusive society, organizations and their management must begin to do so at work. Oliner and Oliner (1995) envisioned a "caring society" with "caring institutions" that would "encourage autonomy and independence of thought" while building group cohesiveness, "create conditions conducive to trust building," give employees opportunities to engage in "caring routines" such as mentoring and peer counseling, facilitate "employee contacts with diverse groups within the organization and ... outside it for the purpose of mutual understanding ... and [to] appreciate cultural differences" in long-term rather than temporary relationships, promote efforts "to think holistically ... in solving problems," and develop individuals who "see themselves as personally related to and responsible for global welfare ... principles of stewardship ... a deep respect for natural and diverse life forms... [and] a more humane ... future" (pp. 202–204). Oestreicher (2011) echoed such principles of "leadership and communication" in reflecting upon the "Camelot wisdom" in Arthurian literature, suggesting that in their organizations and relationships public relations professionals "exercise empathy, remain ethical, involve others {a Round-Table effect}, and create balance ... think and feel" (p. 19) among other "modern lessons" from King Arthur. Collectively, "caring" organizations can awaken a society's social conscience—one of the dimensions the public relations profession believes is fundamental for democracy (Public Relations Society of America, 1997)—and, in so doing, foster a spirit that values the fundamental dignity of all life inasmuch as a basic moral test of a society is the welfare of its most vulnerable members. With a deeper understanding of the profession, it can be said that, within the context of public relations, communication constitutes an act with moral consequences.

Ultimately, the circles of influence in an organization or in society return to the individual, the epicenter of each sphere. While "the virtuous individual needs a virtuous environment" (Schindler, 1989, p. 162), the will to be virtuous must begin with each person. As public relations practitioners and educators embrace virtue in their professional and personal lives, they will develop the moral character necessary to transform society into communities that are civil, ethical, equitable, and caring for all.

References

Allen, J. (2006). *Rabble-rouser for peace*. New York, NY: Free Press.

Baker, S. (2002). The theoretical ground for public relations practice and ethics: A Koehnian analysis. *Journal of Business Ethics, 35*(3), 191–205.

BBC History. (2015). *William Wilberforce*. Retrieved from http://www.bbc.co.uk/history_figures/wilberforce_william.shtml.

Berkes, F. (2008). *Sacred ecology* (2nd ed.). London, England: Routledge.

Bernays, E. (1935). Molding public opinion. *Annuals of the American Academy of Political and Social Science, 179*, 82–87.

Bunson, M., & Bunson, M. (2012). *Saint Kateri: Lilly of the Mohawks*. Huntington, IN: Our Sunday Visitor.

Chronicles. (1995, March 20). *Time*, 23.

Corbett, G. (2012). [Letter to membership]. New York, NY: Public Relations Society of America.

Crutzen, P. (2002). Geology of mankind. *Nature, 415*, 23.

Cutlip, S. (1995). *Public relations history: From the 17th to the 20th century. The antecedents*. Hillsdale, NJ: Lawrence Erlbaum.

Dühring, L. (2015). Lost in translation? On the disciplinary status of public relations. *Public Relations Inquiry*, 4(1), 5–23.

Durbin, D. (2014, March 31). House: GM refused to fix defect for millions of cars. *The Miami Herald*, p. 3a.

Edwards, L. (2012). Defining the "object" of public relations research: A new starting point. *Public Relations Inquiry*, 1(1), 7–30.

Facts About Israel. (2008). Jerusalem, Israel: Israel Information Center.

For managers, compassion beats anger. (2015, Summer). *The Public Relations Strategist*, 21(2),5.

Francis, Pope. (2015). *On care for our common home: Laudato si'*. Boston, MA: Pauline Books & Media.

Fry, S. (1991). A conversation with Edward L. Bernays, Fellow PRSA. *Public Relations Journal*, 47(11), 31–33.

Gabler, N. (1995, December 31). The fathers of P.R. *The New Times Magazine*, 28–29.

Galloway, C. (2013). Deliver us from definitions: A fresh way of looking at public relations. *Public Relations Inquiry*, 2(2), 147–159.

Gokhale, B. (1966). *Asoka Maurya*. New York, NY: Twayne.

Goldman, E. (1965, November 19). *Public relations and the progressive surge: 1898–1917*. Address to the annual meeting of the assembly of the Public Relations Society of America, New York, NY.

Goodwin, D. (2015). It's about trust: Helping your organization build relationships. *Public Relations Strategist*, 21(3), 20–21.

Gorelick, J. (2004, October 14). *Keepers of the corporate conscience: The role of the board in ethical oversight*. Address to the Center for Business Ethics, Waltham, MA.

Greenpeace. (2015). *Project Arctic Tern: A proposal to Greenpeace supporters*. Washington, DC: Author.

Grunig, J. E., & White, J. (1992). The effects of world views on public relations theory and practice. In J. E. Grunig (Ed.), *Excellence in public relations and communication management* (pp. 31–64). Hillsdale, NJ: Lawrence Erlbaum.

Gunther, J. (1955). *Inside Africa*. New York, NY: Harper & Brothers.

Guth, D., & Marsh, C. (2005). *Adventures in public relations: Case studies and critical thinking.*Boston, MA: Allyn & Bacon.

Guth, D., & Marsh, C. (2012). *Public relations: A values-driven approach* (5th ed.). Boston, MA: Allyn & Bacon.

Hallahan, K. (2000). Inactive publics: The forgotten publics in public relations. *Public Relations Review*, 26(4), 499–515.

Harlow, R. (1977). Public relations definitions through the years. *Public Relations Review*, 3, 49–63.

Haviland, W. (1978). *Cultural anthropology* (2nd ed.). New York, NY: Holt, Rinehart and Winston.

Heath, R. (2001). Defining the discipline. In R. Heath & G. Vasquez (Eds.), *Handbook of public relations* (pp. 1–9). Thousand Oaks, CA: Sage.

Heilprin, J. (2014, May 14). Ban of autonomous killer robots debated. *The Miami Herald*, p. 11a.

Henry, T. (1955). *Wilderness Messiah: The Story of Hiawatha and the Iroquois*. New York, NY: William Sloan Associates.

Hill, B. (2013). *World religions and contemporary issues*. New London, CT: Twenty-Third Publications.

Hoppe, L. (1985). *Deuteronomy*. Collegeville, MN: The Liturgical Press.

Hutton, J. (1999). The definition, dimensions, and domain of public relations. *Public Relations Review*, 25(2), 199–214.

Jurmain, R., Kilgore, L., Trevathan, W., & Ciochon, R. (2014). *Introduction to physical anthropology*. Belmont, CA: Wadsworth.

Kaplan, M. (2010). Will religions guide us on our dangerous journey? In K. Moore & M. Nelson (Eds.), *Moral ground: Ethical action for a planet in peril* (pp. 263–266). San Antonio, TX: Trinity University Press.

Kendall, R., Baxter, B., & Pessolano, F. (1989). *Accreditation primer* (4th ed.). New York, NY:Public Relations Society of America.

Lamme, M., & Russell, K. (2010). Removing the spin: Toward a new theory of public relations history. *Journalism Communication Monographs*, 11(4), 281–362.

Lensen, G. (1960). *The world beyond Europe: An introduction to the history of Africa, India, Southeast Asia, and the Far East*. Boston, MA: Houghton Mifflin.

Leonard, A. (2015, June 15). [Letter to membership]. Washington, DC: Greenpeace.

Leonard, A., & Grobler, A. (2005). Communicating affirmation action in three South African organisations: A comparative case study perspective. *Communicare*, 24(2), 17–46.

Mapaure, C. (2008). Fishing among the Topnaar: An expropriated tradition. In M. Hinz & O. Ruppel (Eds.), *Biodiversity and the ancestors: Challenges to customary and environmental law—Case studies from Namibia* (pp. 151–174). Windhoek, Namibia: University of Namibia.

Marinelli, J. (2015). Smarty plants. *National Wildlife*, 53(3), 36–40.

Mazza, E. (2015, February 23). Stephen Hawking warns that aggression could "destroy us all." *The Huffington Post*. Retrieved from http://www.huffingtonpost.com/2015/02/23/stephen-hawking-aggression_n_6733584.html.

McElreath, M. (1997). *Managing systematic and ethical public relations campaigns* (2nd ed.). Dubuque, IA: Brown & Benchmark.

Mencken, H. (1945). *The American language: An inquiry into the development of English in the United States* (Supplement I). New York, NY: Alfred A. Knopf.

Metaxas, E. (2007). *Amazing grace: William Wilberforce and the heroic campaign to end slavery*. New York, NY: HarperCollins.

Molleda, J., & Ferguson, M. (2004). Public relations roles in Brazil: Hierarchy eclipses gender differences. *Journal of Public Relations Research*, 16(4), 327–351.

Mueller, B. (2004). *Dynamics of international advertising: Theoretical and practical perspectives*. New York, NY: Peter Lang.

Nikam, N., & McKeon, R. (Eds.). (1966). *The edicts of Asoka*. Chicago, IL: University of Chicago Press.

Oestreicher, P. (2011, Winter). Arthur: King, leader, PR professional. *Public Relations Strategist*, 17(4), 17–19.

Olinar, S. (2007, June). What makes a hero? Turns out, nobody knows. *Impulse*, 10, 10.

Oliner, P., & Oliner, S. (1995). *Toward a caring society*. Westport, CT: Praeger.

Olsen, C. (2005, July). Bernays vs. Ellul: Two views of propaganda. *Public Relations Tactics*, p. 28.

Pincus, J., Rayfield, R., & DeBonis, J. (1991, November). Transforming CEOs into chief communications officers. *Public Relations Journal*, 47(11), 23–27.

Public Relations Society of America. (1997). *Accreditation review study course: Coach's manual*. New York, NY: Author.

Public Relations Society of America. (2003). *Accreditation study course*. New York, NY: Author.

Roberts, C. (2011, September/October). Innovation for Africa. *WWF Focus, 33*, 2.

Robot kills man at Volkswagen plant. (2015, July 3). *The Miami Herald*, p. 10a.

Royal Society for the Prevention of Cruelty to Animals. (2015). What we do. Retrieved from http://www.rspca.org.uk/Whatwedo.

Schindler, T. (1989). *Ethics: The social dimension*. Wilmington, DE: Michael Glazier.

Schulberg, L. (1968). *Historic India*. New York, NY: Time-Life Books.

Schweiger, L. (2014). [Letter to membership]. Reston, VA: National Wildlife Federation.

Simon, R. (1984). *Public relations concepts and practices* (3rd ed.). New York, NY: John Wiley & Sons.

Singer, P. (1975). *Animal liberation: A new ethics for our treatment of animals*. New York, NY: The New York Review.

Stone, D. (2013). Rivers are people too. *National Geographic, 223*(5), 24.

Strauss, M. (2014). Command performance. *Smithsonian, 45*(2), 48–51.

Tilson, D. (1999). Against the common good: The commodification of Latin America. *Media Development, 46*(3), 69–73.

Tilson, D. (2004). Privatization and government campaigning in Ecuador: Caudillos, corruption, and chaos. In D. Tilson and E. Alozie (Eds.), *Toward the common good: Perspective in international public relations* (pp. 63–82). Boston, MA: Allyn & Bacon.

Tilson, D. (2009). Current research in public relations: A critique and questioning of global trends. *African Communication Research, 2*(3), 367–396.

Tilson, D. (2010). Corporate social responsibility—A new imperative? A view of the social dimension of public relations through the rearview mirror of time. In T. Watson (Ed.), *Proceedings of the First International History of Public Relations Conference* (pp. 436–450). Bournemouth, England: Bournemouth University.

Tilson, D. (2011). *The promotion of devotion: Saints, celebrities and shrines*. Champaign, IL: Common Ground.

Tilson, D. (2014a). Public relations and religious diversity: Toward the common good. In I. Nahon-Serfaty & R. Ahmed (Eds.), *New media and communication across religions and cultures* (pp. 110–128). Hershey, PA: IGI Global.

Tilson, D. (2014b). An alternative view of social responsibility: The ancient and global footprint of *caritas* and public relations. In B. St. John, M. Lamme, & J. L'Etang (Eds.), *Pathways to public relations: Histories of practice and profession* (pp. 56–73). London, England: Routledge.

Tilson, D. (2015). Public relations and social responsibility: An imperative for the profession. In K. Vaidya (Ed.), *Public relations and social media for the curious: Why study public relations and social media*. Canberra, Australia: Curious Academic.

Tomkins, S. (2007). *William Wilberforce: A biography*. Grand Rapids, MI: Willima B. Eerdmans.

Trevelyan, G. (1953). *History of England* (Vol. 3). Garden City, NY: Doubleday & Company.

Von Drehle, D. (2013). The robot economy. *Time*, 42–47.

Vujnovic, M., & Kruckeberg, D. (2005). Imperative for an *Arab* model of public relations as a framework for diplomatic, corporate and nongovernmental organization relationships. *Public Relations Review, 31*(4), 338–343.

White, R. (2009). Research on communication for development in Africa: Current debates. *African Communication Research*, 2(2), 203–252.

Who's Who and What's What? (2006). *Amazing grace study guide.* Boston, MA: Walden Media.

Wilcox, D., Ault, P., Agee, W., & Cameron, G. (2000). *Public relations strategies and tactics*(6th ed.). New York, NY: Addison Wesley Longman.

Wilcox, D., & Cameron, G. (2009). *Public relations strategies and tactics* (9th ed.). Boston, MA: Allyn & Bacon.

Wilson, L. (1996). Strategic cooperative communities: A synthesis of strategic, issue management, and relationship-building approaches in public relations. In H. Culbertson & N. Chen (Eds.), *International public relations: A comparative analysis* (pp. 67–80).Mahwah, NJ: Lawrence Erlbaum.

World Wildlife Fund. (2012). *Namibia: Empowering communities to manage their natural resources.* Retrieved from http://www.worldwildlife.org/what/wherewework/namibia.

World Wildlife Fund. (2015, Fall). Carter Roberts talks with Bhutan's prime minister, Tshering Tobgay. *World Wildlife*, 14–15.

List of Contributors

Giselle A. Auger, APR, is an award winning Professor of Public Relations at Rhode Island College. She received her Ph.D. in Mass Communication from the University of Florida and holds an M.A. in International Relations and Strategic Studies from the University of Lancaster in England. Her research focuses on advocacy and nonprofit organizations, transparency, the strategic use of social media, and academic dishonesty. She has more than 20 years' experience in communication industries and her teaching reflects the intersection of practice and academia, making theory and research relevant for her students.

Brigitta R. Brunner, Ph.D., is a Professor in the School of Communication and Journalism at Auburn University. She serves as a Research Fellow with the Imagining America Engaged Undergraduate Research Group. Brunner was inducted into Auburn University's College of Liberal Arts' Academy of Outstanding Teachers in 2015 and was named Educator of the Year by the Public Relations Council of Alabama in April 2013. She was also honored with the Senior Practitioner designation by the Southern Public Relations Federation in 2015. Brunner earned her M.A. at Auburn University, and her Ph.D. at the University of Florida.

Melissa D. Dodd (Ph.D., University of Miami) is Assistant Professor of Advertising-Public Relations at the University of Central Florida's Nicholson School of Communication (Orlando, Florida). She is the author of multiple journal publications and book chapters. Her research has been published in the *Public Relations Journal, Public Relations Review,* and *PRism* refereed scholarly publications. Dodd is co-editor of the forthcoming *Handbook of Public Relations Theory and Methods.* She has presented award-winning research at top-tier academic conferences around the world. Dodd's research interests include social capital, social media, corporate social responsibility, and corporate activism/corporate social advocacy as related to public relations.

Tiffany Derville Gallicano, Ph.D., has practiced public relations for a U.S. Senate campaign, two large public relations agencies, a nonprofit organization, and an educational institution. She recently joined the faculty at University of North Carolina at Charlotte. She has published 18 journal articles about relationship management, social media and pedagogy. She formerly served as an associate professor at the University of Oregon, where she won the School of Journalism and Communication's Jonathan Marshall Award for Innovative Teaching. She serves as the past-head of the Public Relations Division of the Association for Education in Journalism and Mass Communication.

April Gulotta (M.A., Auburn University) is a Lecturer in the School of Communication Studies at James Madison University. She has taught basic speech, presentational speaking, intercultural communication, and diversity and popular culture classes since 2002. Her interest area is popular culture.

Michael Gulotta (M.A., Auburn University) is a Lecturer in the School of Communication Studies at James Madison University. He has taught numerous classes including group communication and presentational speaking classes and has also directed multiple student research projects. His interest area is popular culture, bullying intervention programs, and crisis management in sport.

Linda Hon (Ph.D., University of Maryland) is a Professor and Program Director in the College of Journalism and Communications, University of Florida. Research interests are digital advocacy and the emerging field of public interest communications. Hon was executive associate dean of the College from 2006 to 2012. She is a Flanagan Professor of Journalism and Communications and also held the title of UF Research Foundation Professor. Hon was the recipient of the 2001 "Pathfinder" Award for Best Recent Program of Research in Public Relations given by the Institute for Public Relations. She was the editor of the *Journal of Public Relations Research* from 2000 to 2005.

Jooyun Hwang (Ph.D., University of Florida) is an Assistant Professor at the School of Communications, Elon University. Her research interests include understanding the agenda building and framing process of public relations, corporate crisis communication, and the effects of public relations efforts on publics' attitude and behavioral intentions. Her work has been presented at national and international conferences and published in peer-reviewed journals. She received her Ph.D. from the University of Florida and her M.A. from the University of Missouri-Columbia.

Samsup Jo is Professor at the Department of Public Relations and Advertising, Sookmyung Women's University, South Korea. He earned a Ph.D. from the University of Florida in 2003. His research interests include public relations, specifically public relations function in society, public relations ethics, and organization-public relationship measurement. His articles appeared in the *Journal of Public Relations Research, Public Relations Review, Journalism and Mass Communication Quarterly,* and *Journal of Communication Management.* He is interested in the interactions between organizational sources and news contents. He served as the president of Korean Academic Society of Public Relations from 2014 to 2015.

Amanda Kennedy is an Assistant Professor of Public Relations and Community Advocacy at St. Mary's University in San Antonio, Texas. Kennedy specializes in areas where public relations intersects with feminist, post-structural, and critical theory and ethics, including critical and qualitative methods. Her published and forthcoming research appears in the *Atlantic Journal of Communication, Journal of Media Ethics*, and book chapters about feminist media studies and public relations. Kennedy teaches classes in public relations and communication theory and research methods. She earned her Ph.D. from University of Maryland and M.A. from University of Houston.

Michael L. Kent, Ph.D., is a Professor of Public Relations in the College of Communication and Information, at the University of Tennessee. Kent conducts research on new technology, mediated communication, dialogue, international communication, and web communication. An internally recognized scholar, Kent has published dozens of articles, books, and book chapters. His research has appeared in public relations, management, international, and communication journals including *Public Relations Review, Management Communication Quarterly, The Journal of Public Relations Research, Gazette, Communication Studies, Critical Studies in Media Communication*, and others. Kent Received his Doctorate from Purdue University, and his Master's from the University of Oregon.

Sora Kim (Ph.D., University of Tennessee) is an Associate Professor in the School of Journalism and Communication at the Chinese University of Hong Kong. Her research interests include corporate social responsibility communication, corporate communication, and crisis communication management. Her work has been published at *Journalism & Mass Communication Quarterly, Journal of Public Relations Research, Journal of Advertising, Journal of Business Ethics, Public Relations Review*, and other international communication journals. She was awarded a Page Legacy Scholar Grant from Arthur Page Center and a General Research Fund (GRF) grant from Research Grants Council of HK government.

Christie Kleinmann, APR, is an Associate Professor at Belmont University where she teaches courses in public relations, print/digital design, and sport communication. Kleinmann has presented research at several regional, national, and international research conferences as well as been recognized for her research and mentorship activities. She was named a Page Legacy Scholar and a Page Legacy Educator for her research and teaching initiatives in social responsibility by the Arthur W. Page Center. Research for "The Public Relations Postures of Organizational Civic Responsibility" chapter was funded through a grant by the Arthur W. Page Center at Penn State University.

Dean Kruckeberg, APR, Fellow PRSA, is a Professor in the Department of Communication Studies at the University of North Carolina at Charlotte. He was executive director of the Center for Global Public Relations, a service unit in that department, from 2008 to 2013. He is co-author of *Public Relations and Community: A Reconstructed Theory* and of *This Is PR: The Realities of Public Relations*. Kruckeberg is author and co-author of many book chapters and articles dealing with global PR and international PR ethics. He has given invited lectures about public relations throughout the world.

Kelli Matthews is a Senior Instructor and Area Director of public relations at the University of Oregon. Her 15 years of public relations experience includes managing a boutique consulting firm. In that role, she's been directly responsible for high-level communication, strategic planning, budget management, and leadership for a wide variety of clients. She's also a regularly invited speaker and trainer at events, workshops, and seminars on topics ranging from social media basics to crisis management, media training, and community engagement.

Holly K. Ott (Ph.D., The Pennsylvania State University, 2016) is an Assistant Professor in the School of Journalism and Mass Communications at University of South Carolina. Her research examines corporate social responsibility and sustainability communication. Her work has earned top paper awards at the AEJMC, ICA, PRSA, and ECA annual conferences and has appeared in journals including *Public Relations Journal* and *Journal of Promotion Management*, among others. Ott is actively involved in the AEJMC Public Relations Division where she currently serves as chair of the Graduate Student Liaison Committee and as a member of the Social Events Committee.

Young Eun Park is a Ph.D. student at the Indiana University. She received her MA from the University of Florida. Her research interests are corporate social responsibility (CSR) and the crowdsourcing approach in CSR. She has received the Roschwalb Award in 2015 and the Inez Kaiser Graduate Students of Color Award in 2014 at the Association for Education in Journalism and Mass Communication (AEJMC) Public Relations Division, the Peter Debreceny Corporate Communication Award at the International Public Relations Research Conference (IPRRC) in 2016, and the top student paper at the International Communication Association (ICA) Public Relations Division in 2012.

Erich J. Sommerfeldt is an Assistant Professor in the Department of Communication at the University of Maryland at College Park. Sommerfeldt's research centers on activist group communication, civil society and development communication, social capital, and social network analysis. He is a two-time winner of the Best Article of the Year Award from the Public Relations Division of the National Communication Association.

He has participated in applied civil society research projects in developing nations around the world, including Haiti, Jordan, Ukraine, China, Indonesia, and Pakistan. He earned his Ph.D. in Mass Communication from the University of Oklahoma.

Ashli Q. Stokes (Ph.D., University of Georgia) is an Associate Professor of Communication Studies at the University of North Carolina at Charlotte. Her award-winning research specializes in using rhetorical approaches to analyze public relations controversies, often concerning activism and corporate advocacy. Along with co-authoring a textbook about global public relations with Dr. Alan Freitag, Stokes has published in the *Journal of Public Relations Research, Journal of Communication Management, Public Relations Review, the Southern Communication Journal, Studies in Communication Sciences*, and the *Encyclopedia of Public Relations* among others. Before returning to academia, Stokes worked in agency and corporate public relations in Atlanta, GA.

Maureen Taylor, Ph.D., is the Director of the School of Advertising and Public Relations at the University of Tennessee. Taylor's research has focused on nation building and civil society, dialogue, the use of websites, and new technologies. Her research has taken her to post-conflict nations across the world. In 2010, Taylor was honored with the Institute for Public Relations' Pathfinder Award for her "original program of scholarly research that has made a significant contribution to the body of knowledge and practice of public relations." Taylor is a member of the Arthur S. Page Society and serves as an associate editor of *Public Relations Review*.

Donn J. Tilson, Associate Professor of Public Relations at the University of Miami's School of Communication, holds a Ph.D. in Public Relations from the University of Stirling, Scotland, the first in Europe to graduate with a doctorate in the field. A member of the U.S. Public Relations Society of America's College of Fellows and past chair of the Society's Professional Interest International Section, he has published and lectured internationally as a European University Public Relations Confederation Visiting Scholar. His book, *The Promotion of Devotion: Saints, Celebrities and Shrines* (2011, Common Ground), is a pioneering work on communication, religion, and culture.

Natalie T. J. Tindall (Ph.D., University of Maryland, 2007) is an Associate Professor in the Department of Communication at Lamar University. Her research focuses on diversity in organizations, specifically the public relations function, and the situational theory of publics and intersectionality.

Jan Uhrick (M.A., University of Houston, 2016) conducts research focused on corporate social responsibility and crisis communication. In her thesis, she proposed that the use of corporate social responsibility could potentially reduce monetary and reputational damage during a crisis. She has conducted and presented research with Dr. Jennifer Vardeman-Winter and Dr. Hojoon Choi.

Jennifer Vardeman-Winter (Ph.D., University of Maryland, 2008) is an Associate Professor in the Jack J. Valenti School of Communication, the director of graduate studies, and an affiliate faculty member in the Women's, Gender, and Sexuality Studies program at the University of Houston. Dr. Vardeman-Winter teaches courses in public relations theory and management; critical/cultural public relations; issues and crisis management; and entrepreneurial communication in a practicum setting. Her studies are concentrated in how gender, race, and class affect public relations campaigns, particularly in public health/health care public relations.

Marina Vujnovic, Ph.D., Associate Professor, Public Relations/Journalism Department of Communication, Monmouth University, New Jersey. Her research interests focus on international communication and global flow of information; journalism studies, public relations, and explorations of the historical, political-economic, and cultural impact of media on class, race, gender, and ethnicity. She is an author of the *Forging the Bubikopf Nation: Journalism, Gender and Modernity in Interwar Yugoslavia,* co-author of *Participatory Journalism: Guarding Open Gates at Online Newspapers,* and co-editor of *Globalizing Cultures: Theories, Paradigms, Actions.*

Richard D. Waters (Ph.D, University of Florida, 2007) is an Associate Professor in the School of Management at the University of San Francisco. He is the author of more than 75 peer-reviewed journal articles and book chapters that focus on relationship management within the nonprofit sector, fundraising, and nonprofit communication. He serves on the editorial boards of nine academic journals, including *Public Relations Review* and *Journal of Public Relations Research*. He is the past chair of the Association/Nonprofit Professional Interest Section at Public Relations Society of America, and he continues to consult with Fortune 500 and Philanthropy 400 organizations.

Chang Wan Woo (Ph. D., The University of Alabama) is an Assistant Professor in the School of Communication Studies at James Madison University. He has published his studies in the area of public relations and sport communication. He has taught numerous classes including sport public relations, public relations management, and public relations campaign since 2009. He is currently serving as a coordinator of sport communication minor program and as a faculty adviser of JMU Chapter of PRSSA.

Sifan Xu is a Ph.D. student in the Department of Communication at the University of Maryland. His research interests include activist public relations, relationship management, and the role of social identities in public relations activities. He holds a Bachelor of Arts degree in Communication from the University of International Relations in Beijing, China.

Xiaochen (Angela) Zhang (Ph.D., University of Florida) is an Assistant Professor in public relations at the A.Q. Miller School of Journalism and Mass Communications at Kansas State University. Her research interests involve corporate crisis communication and strategic communication on social media. Angela has presented her research at professional conferences such as AEJMC and ICA and has published in peer-reviewed journals such as the *International Journal of Strategic Communication*. Professionally, Angela has worked in both Corporate Social Responsibility and Corporate Communications departments in BASF (China) Co. Ltd.

Index

For Product Safety Concerns and Information please contact our EU
representative GPSR@taylorandfrancis.com
Taylor & Francis Verlag GmbH, Kaufingerstraße 24, 80331 München, Germany

www.ingramcontent.com/pod-product-compliance
Ingram Content Group UK Ltd.
Pitfield, Milton Keynes, MK11 3LW, UK
UKHW020939180425
457613UK00019B/474